Extraordinary Comebacks

201 Inspiring Stories of Courage,

Triumph and Success

JOHN A. SARKETT

SOURCEBOOKS, INC.®
NAPERVILLE, ILLINOIS

This publication is designed to provide accurate and authoritative information
in regard to the subject matter covered. It is sold with the understanding that
the publisher is not engaged in rendering legal, accounting, or other professional service. If legal advice or other expert assistance is required, the servic-
es of a competent professional person should be sought.—*From a Declaration
of Principles Jointly Adopted by a Committee of the American Bar Association and a
Committee of Publishers and Associations*

All brand names and product names used in this book are trademarks, registered trademarks, or trade names of their respective holders. Sourcebooks,
Inc., is not associated with any product or vendor in this book.

Published by Sourcebooks, Inc.
P.O. Box 4410, Naperville, Illinois 60567-4410
(630) 961-3900
Fax: (630) 961-2168
www.sourcebooks.com

Printed and bound in the United States of America.
VP 10 9 8 7 6 5 4 3 2 1

This book is for everyone who is making,
or is about to make,
a comeback.

"Fall seven times, stand up eight."
—Japanese proverb

"When the morning's freshness has been replaced by
the weariness of midday, when the leg muscles give
under the strain, the climb seems endless, and suddenly
nothing will go quite as you wish—it is then that you
must not hesitate."
—Dag Hammarskjöld

"Where there is no hope, one must invent hope."
—Albert Camus

CONTENTS

Athletics

Business

Film, Television, and Show Business

Justice

Literature

Media

Military

Music, Classical

Music, Pop

Physical and Emotional Challenges

Politics and Public Service

Poverty

Science

Spirituality

ACKNOWLEDGMENTS

First, to the two hundred and one amazing individuals chronicled here: without them, there would be no book.

Next, to former national magazine editor, spouse, and partner, Bonnie, for her incredibly painstaking editing and proofreading. Her skills vastly enhanced this volume.

To Sourcebooks' editors Peter Lynch, Erin Nevius, Carrie Obry, and Rachel Jay, whose comments, insights, and suggestions always made the book better.

To the superb and tireless reference librarians at the Winnetka, Illinois, public library who helped me track down the arcane and esoteric facts that help make these stories come alive: Jill Brasseur, Juli Janovicz, Ray Kearney, Carol Keenan, Jane Levine, Mark Swenson, and Dorothy Szczepaniak.

To publishing expert and attorney Daniel Steven, who kept us on the right track.

To my friend, actor, and screenwriter Tim Kazurinsky, for positive encouragement early on, when the book you hold in your hand was merely an idea; and to my other friends and colleagues, for their timely and thoughtful advice: Rob Balon, Bob Bernstein, Guy Bouchet, John T. Davis, Emmanuel Dowdall, Rod Gibbs, Steve Graham, Ernst W. "Bill" Hammons, Glen Hamrick, Mike Horton, Shaun Hussey, Len Kasper, Joe Kerr, Ekkehard Kubler, Lloyd Morgan, Bob Mucci, Pat Mullen, Dr. K.J. Philip, Bill Plain, Steve Polydoris, Martin Ross, Tim Schmidt, Nick Schoewe, Baird Smart, Maury Wolff, and Dennis Yohe. I appreciate your friendship.

To my children, Sharika, who broke a major logjam along the way, and to Franklin, and Raika, who provided that same kind of positive encouragement all the way to the finish line.

And for Sourcebooks' founder and president, Dominique Raccah, for providing *Extraordinary Comebacks* with a comeback opportunity of its very own.

Sincere thanks to all. —*JS*

INTRODUCTION

I HAD A SETBACK A FEW YEARS AGO. I NEEDED TO make a comeback. The great bull market of the late 1990s broke in 2000, collapsed in 2001, and took a lot of my (and a lot of other people's) hard-won profits with it. Some health problems brought me down, too, commonplace ailments but disturbing enough, high cholesterol, high blood pressure. Around that time I found myself in a large bookstore and wandered over to the section with self-help, inspirational, and motivational psychology titles. I knew what I wanted: a compilation of simple stories, human stories, of people who had made a comeback against the odds. There was no such compilation, even on Amazon. That surprised me. So I would have to find my own. I started looking for stories about individuals who had made a comeback from some kind of adversity, adding them, one-by-one, to a small and informal collection that I had cut and torn from magazines and newspapers over the years. That compilation became this book.

If you made your way to this page, chances are pretty good that you are looking to make a comeback, too, or you know someone who is. I believe this book will help. We all know from experience that life has an uncanny way of knocking us down. The great question: how do we get back up?

There's good news—people *do* get back up. The human spirit is more resilient than hardened steel. It can take the blow, bend, reshape, re-form, come back, transcend. What is human spirit? We know where ideas come from—gray matter—and we have thousands of them each day. But human spirit? No scientist has ever found it, yet we are certain that it exists. It is a "God thing," a faith thing. Spirit can endure, hope, imagine, fight back, overcome. This book tells the stories of more than two hundred individuals who refused to let formidable obstacles stop them. They found a way. No matter what.

You will, too.

When I tell people about this set of stories, they ask me, "What do they have in common? What is the secret to making a comeback?" Two things: First, the people in this book have never quit, not for good. Some might have given in to the sentiment expressed in the blues line, "I'm not going to quit you, but I've got to put you down for a while." But they always picked it back up, whatever "it" was. Georgia O'Keeffe quit painting—for a while. Quincy Jones had to quit playing the trumpet, but became a top music producer. After being fired from Apple, Steve Jobs took a sabbatical, then started a new computer company. Col. Sanders retired at sixty-five from his restaurant business—but, unhappy with his meager pension, came back to found Kentucky Fried Chicken. The list goes on and on and on, proving that nothing can stop you, if you yourself don't stop.

Second, they have worked, very hard. When Food Network star Paula Deen was starting her restaurant business, she worked a day job, a night job, and barbequed all night for her sandwich business. Emmanuel Yeboah pedaled his bike across his native Ghana—370 miles—*with one leg*. Ultramarathoner Dean Karnazes competed in a 226-mile race, running for seventy-five hours straight. Every story is unique, but each individual was making some sort of comeback.

F. Scott Fitzgerald once said, "There are no second acts in American life." But these stories prove that statement is not true. A better, truer statement about setback is, "This too shall pass." A setback can pass into a comeback. If you make it happen.

To be human is to be knocked down, and every single one of us is knocked down at one time or another.

Some early on, some midway, some late. Small ways, big ways. The thing is to get up, to come back. Work. Have patience. As you'll see, many comebacks take years.

So here are 201 Extraordinary Comebacks for you. Motivational speakers are great, and we need them, but these real stories are more eloquent and motivating still. Start reading—anywhere you like. Somewhere in this book you will find at least one story, quote, or image that speaks directly to you, and you'll likely find more than one. It will stick in your mind. Stuck there, it will build your hope, and hope—a real biochemical in your brain— is powerful stuff. It will make you believe. It will give you ideas. Then, it will provide fuel, energy. The memory of your favorite comeback will drive you on when you are feeling too tired, low, or depressed to continue.

It is possible. You can make a comeback. You can make the darkness illuminate the light, as one of our subjects put it. That's why I left the 202nd story empty. It's for you to write with your own life. And it starts right now. I wish you great success and a great comeback.

—*John A. Sarkett*

Chicago, Illinois (the city destroyed in the fire of 1871, only to come back greater than ever in the years that followed…)

4

ADVENTURE

1. HILLARY, SIR EDMUND

DURING A LONG STRUGGLE, THE MOMENT RIGHT before a triumphant breakthrough is often a very dark one—sometimes even pitch black. So it was for Edmund Hillary the night before he would attempt to climb Mount Everest—something no one had ever done.

The physical challenge alone was overwhelming that last night. Camped at an elevation of 25,800 feet (the peak of Everest is at 29,028 feet), his tent was pounded by a wind that an aide said sounded like the roar of one thousand tigers. He breathed with the help of an oxygen tank. His air mattress deflated, and his hip froze where it came in contact with the ice. He couldn't sleep even though he was exhausted. All of this took place in absolute darkness.

Maybe worse than the physical discomfort was the psychological war, the inner demons to vanquish in the face of such a trial. Hillary later wrote that that night he was lonely and afraid. He doubted himself, tormenting himself with the question, What is the sense in trying to climb Everest? It was surely one of the worst nights of his life.

But his worst night was to be followed by his greatest day: May 29, 1953, which marks the first conquering of Everest. This was, for Hillary, a quite literal comeback. A year earlier, in 1952, he tried to climb the 29,028-foot giant mountain and failed, like the fifteen men who had tried before him. But stirred with "second effort," he came back to the mountain and made it to the summit. Many would follow, but Hillary and his loyal native guide, Tenzing Norgay, would be forever first. Hillary famously said that, in making the climb, it wasn't the mountain that he conquered, but himself. And so it is with every comeback.

Hillary formed a bond with the friends he made in the Himalayas and returned in later years to help build infrastructure: mountain airfields, schools, hospitals, clinics. He helped rebuild ancient Buddhist monasteries. Profoundly humanitarian, he deemed these efforts far more worthwhile than the conquering of Everest, with which his name will be forever linked.

2. PEARY, ADMIRAL ROBERT EDWIN

"I shall find a way or make one."

SOMETIMES SECOND EFFORT IS JUST not enough. As recently as 1886 it was thought that the North Pole was located in Greenland, but while exploring there, Admiral (and surveyor) Robert Peary deduced that it was actually farther away. Driven by a fascination with the polar regions dating from his student days, and a desire for fame he confided in a letter to his mother ("I must have it"), he was committed to be the first to find the exact location of the North Pole, the first to stand on the top of the world. His desires were very strong indeed. Braving unimaginable hardship, Peary tried and failed *seven* times to reach the North Pole, breaking a leg and losing toes to frostbite. But some 756 other men had *died* trying—at least he was still alive.

Friends and colleagues urged him to forget his dream and give up, but he also had his partisans and stalwarts, none more helpful than his wife, Josephine. Had Peary been locked away in a Turkish prison, she would have found a way to get him out. As it was, in 1895, he was in straits almost as bad: marooned in northern Greenland without a ship to carry him home. Peary could have traveled over land south to civilization, but then he would have had to take a ship to Denmark and then back to the United States.

Josephine couldn't bear to be without him that long. Instead, she started what writer Napoleon Hill would have called a "mastermind group." She contacted a number of wealthy individuals, like Morris K. Jesup, millionaire founder of the YMCA, and raised $12,000 to hire a ship to fetch her husband. Peary made it home tired, defeated, and talking of quitting. But after resuming his job at the Brooklyn Navy Yard and having time to regain his spirit, strength, and stamina, and after he spent some time on the lecture circuit, soon enough his vision took over again and he was raising funds for another journey.

His fund-raising took a huge leap forward with the incorporation of his "mastermind group" as the Peary Arctic Club in 1904. The group included some of the most accomplished, wealthiest Americans, including President Teddy Roosevelt and many corporate luminaries. The club raised funds for a state-of-the-art vessel to carry Peary to the North Pole. It was the first icebreaker ever constructed; the 614-ton powerhouse featured steel-sheathed, thirty-inch wood hulls, oversized propellers, and engines powered by multiple boilers. It cost some $100,000, a staggering sum at the time. It was completed in 1905 and named *Roosevelt*, after the president and club member.

Thus fortified, Peary set out for the North Pole a seventh and then finally an *eighth* time. Accompanied by his explorer partner African-American Matthew

8

Henson, four Eskimos, and a team of part-wolf sled dogs, he finally reached his goal on April 6, 1909—his life's work achieved, his lifelong goal met. (However, others claim another explorer, Frederick Cook, beat Peary to it, and a controversy ensues to this day.)

First or second, Peary was a casebook of determination. At Arlington National Cemetery, his grave site is topped by a huge globe with his personal credo that may be freshly adopted by any comeback seeker who needs more than just *second* effort: *Inveniam viam aut facium*, "I shall find a way or make one."

3. WEIHENMAYER, ERIK

AFTER TWO YEARS OF SEARCHING FOR ANSWERS AND going from doctor to doctor, the Weihenmayer family finally got a diagnosis: their three-year-old son, Erik, had retinoscheses, an extremely rare eye disease, especially for someone so young. His parents' hearts dropped as the doctors briefed them: Weihenmayer's retinas were detached in the center of his pupils, which prevented him from seeing straight ahead. He did have limited peripheral vision, but by his teens, he would be blind. For little Erik, almost as terrifying as the diagnosis was the desperation and fear he sensed in his parents.

Weihenmayer did lose his sight, but not his courage. He attended school and eventually earned a bachelor's degree from Boston College, graduating with a 3.1 GPA, a double major, and wrestling team honors with a 315-pound bench press. He accepted a job as a teacher at the Phoenix Country Day School.

He also became an accomplished mountain climber—very accomplished. On May 25, 2001, thirty-two-year-old Weihenmayer became the first blind climber to conquer Mount Everest. Then, at thirty-four, Weihenmayer became one of fewer than one hundred individuals to climb all of the Seven Summits, the highest peaks on each of the seven continents. He notched this breathtaking achievement when he scaled Australia's Mount Kosciusko on September 5, 2002.

Weihenmayer has said that, for him, the process of training and achieving is the highest reward, moments of bliss that connect him with who he really is. Making it to the top of a great mountain, he says, is just a representation that on that day you brought an uncontrollable situation under control. The mountain represents for him a small piece of a dream made tangible and irrefutable proof that our lives have meaning.

ARTS

4. ANDREWS, DAME JULIE

EVERYONE'S FAVORITE MUSICAL ACTRESS, Julie Andrews—who starred in *Mary Poppins* and *The Sound of Music*—suffered an unimaginable loss in 1997. Surgery on vocal cord nodules went terribly wrong and she lost her trademark, her beautiful singing voice.

Some might have withdrawn in grief and self-pity, but not Andrews. She turned instead to acting and enchanted fans as Queen Clarisse Renaldi in *The Princess Diaries* movies (2001 and 2004). In the second installment she even made a comeback to singing through the limited technique of sing-speaking.

Spoken or sung, hers is still a voice that can captivate millions. In 2004, she lent her voice to the role of the queen in the wildly popular cartoon movie *Shrek 2*, which became one of the highest-grossing films of all time.

Andrews also turned her attention to children's literature, collaborating with her daughter, Emma Walton Hamilton. Their projects include the *Dumpy the Dumptruck* series and the *Julie Andrews Collection*.

The objective of these books, she says, is to nurture children as they face the road ahead, helping them to see the beauty, even the miracles, that surround them in the face of the world's myriad ills. That is how she handled her own setback and engineered her own comeback with the grace and aplomb of her character Mary Poppins. It is said that art imitates life, but sometimes life can imitate art.

5. O'KEEFFE, GEORGIA

IF YOU EVER HAD TO TAKE A JOB YOU HATED JUST TO make ends meet, you might feel alone, but you surely are not—even some of the world's greatest artists have had to do the same. Georgia O'Keeffe worked as a commercial artist in Chicago and New York and hated every minute of it. She drew lace and embroidery for newspaper and magazine advertisements and was paid by the piece. By each day's end, she was too exhausted to take up her brushes and paints for her own art. She couldn't even stand the smell of the paint or turpentine because it aroused strong artistic ambitions that she couldn't, at that time, fulfill.

So even though she decided to become an artist at age twelve and attended art schools in Chicago and New York, O'Keeffe quit painting altogether from the age of twenty-one to the age of twenty-seven. Then, at twenty-eight, she came back to her art. She started with classes at the Teachers College of New York's Columbia University, studying with Arthur Dow. Synthesizing an Eastern and Western sensibility, Dow concentrated on abstract concepts of line, light, and color. For O'Keeffe, this approach was life-changing. His teaching validated her own ideas about art, which weren't like anything she had ever been taught or had painted. O'Keeffe immersed herself in her new approach and went on to become one of the most famous painters of the twentieth century. She said that she didn't consider herself particularly gifted, but that she did have a lot of nerve and the capacity for a lot of very hard work.

6. MOSES, ANNA MARY ROBERTSON "GRANDMA"

ANNA MARY ROBERTSON, BEST KNOWN AS Grandma Moses, loved to embroider, but as she aged, she developed arthritis, which made embroidery too painful. Her sister suggested painting instead, so Robertson, seventy-five, took up something new. She began to paint the things she knew, farm and country scenes.

The results were utterly original and surprisingly good for a late-starting amateur. Her earliest works were shown and sold at a nearby drugstore and general store in Hoosick Falls, New York. One fateful day, New York engineer and art collector Louis Caldor happened by and purchased the whole lot on display.

Caldor was so taken with Robertson's art that he went another step and began promoting her works to collectors and galleries. Largely through Caldor's efforts, Robertson's work became famous. Her paintings were hung at the Museum of Modern Art in New York in 1939, and she held her first solo exhibition in New York a year later. She was eighty years young.

Even greater acclaim followed. She had many one-woman shows across Europe and North America. In her nineties, her paintings attracted attention all over the world. Her simple scenes of everyday life—people socializing, harvesting, participating in markets and fairs, and engaging in outdoor activities like ice-skating—still captivate wide audiences.

Her most notable works include *Catching the Thanksgiving Turkey* (1943) and *Over the River to Grandma's House* (1944), fitting for the one who was to become known around the world simply as Grandma Moses.

She wrote a lively autobiography at age ninety-two, *My Life's History*. Grandma Moses lived to 101, no doubt propelled to that milestone by her important work.

From the time arthritis forced her to stop embroidering to when she completed her first artworks, only three years had passed. She said if she hadn't taken up painting, she would have raised chickens. (Her fans are glad she chose the former.) The plainspoken original said simply that life is what we make it.

7. PICASSO, PABLO

"Every child is an artist; the problem is how to remain an artist after growing up."

WHEN SOMEONE COMMITS SUICIDE, IT NOT ONLY brings that life to a conclusion but forever alters the lives around that person. In 1901, Pablo Picasso's friend Carles Casagemas took his own life. This plunged Picasso into his renowned three-year Blue Period. His mind was consumed with thoughts of grief, loss, suffering, hunger, and want, and his art expressed it.

That he kept painting even while mourning the loss of his friend is a testament to his inner strength and creativity. *The Soup* (1902), *Crouching Woman* (1902), *Blind*

Man's Meal (1903), *The Tragedy* (1903), and *The Frugal Repast* (1904) were some of his Blue Period masterpieces.

But, as the saying goes, "this too shall pass." Picasso moved to Montmartre in Paris, and his earnings slowly started to improve. Not long after, he made new, important friends: Henri Matisse, André Derain, and Georges Braque. He turned from his Blue Period scenes of suffering to more optimistic scenes of street performers, harlequins, and beautiful girls.

Picasso's work between 1904 and 1906, which now favored red and pink tones, is referred to as his Rose Period. Some famous paintings from this period include *Boy Leading a Horse* (1905), *Woman with Loaves* (1906), and *Portrait of Gertrude Stein* (1906).

New friends, better earnings, a change of scenery— it would take three full years, but after the despair of blue came the joy of pink and red. Picasso once said that every child is an artist; the problem is how to remain one after growing up. By looking out at his world with fresh eyes each day and changing with the times instead of struggling against them, he was able to regain a youthful optimism and new productivity.

8. ROCKWELL, NORMAN

"KITSCH," "SENTIMENTAL," "VACUOUS": THAT'S what the art establishment had to say about the works of Norman Rockwell in the late twentieth century. He was the artist who art critics loved to hate, and a very easy target at that—his work was just too simple, too homespun, too realistic for their tastes. Rockwell wasn't immune from the bashings: his journals show he doubted his own calling, and his medical records indicate that he was treated for depression. But still he kept painting, even in his senior years, with as much focus and energy as ever.

But were his works really worthless or just underappreciated? In an amazing turnaround, by 2000, twenty-two years after his death, the art world that had scorned him now considered Rockwell in vogue. More than three hundred of the painter's *Saturday Evening Post* covers and seventy of his oil paintings went on exhibit in 2000 and 2001, in a two-year, six-city showing. The New York venue for the show was none other than the avant-garde Guggenheim Museum, ironically the very temple of high modern art whose curators wouldn't have dreamed of hanging a Rockwell just a few years earlier.

Both the *New York Times* and the *Washington Post* waxed eloquent on the art, and PBS prepared a documentary on Rockwell's life. *Sunday Morning* on the CBS network covered the exhibit, as did National Public Radio and many other outlets.

As a result of all this activity, *Art in America* magazine featured Rockwell (April 2001), which gave a new and positive outlook on his art. The magazine cited cultural icons Andy Warhol and novelist John Updike as fans, further adding to the bevy of new admirers. Even though Rockwell had long since passed on in 1978, the talent and feeling he poured into his work was ultimately lauded by the same art world that scorned him while he was alive.

ATHLETICS

9. 2002 OHIO STATE BUCKEYES

THE OUTCOME OF EACH OF OHIO STATE'S LAST FOUR football games (against Purdue, Illinois, Michigan, and Miami) had been decided in the last moments—they had to keep coming back to win. Each time the overachieving 2002 Buckeyes simply *refused* to lose. Because of that spirit, their last victory was called by some the greatest college football game ever.

- November 9, 2002, Ohio State at Purdue. With 1:36 to go in the fourth quarter, Ohio State was down 6–3. On a fourth down with one yard to go, quarterback Craig Krenzel threw a thirty-seven-yard touchdown pass to Michael Jenkins. The Buckeyes had risked it all—the unbeaten string, the Big Ten title, the chance to compete for the national championship—on a pass! They took the lead, 10–6. What would legendary Buckeye coach

Woody Hayes (famous for the "three yards and a cloud of dust" run offense) have said?

- November 16, 2002, Ohio State at University of Illinois. The game goes to overtime before the Buckeyes defeat Illinois 23–16.
- November 23, 2002, University of Michigan at Ohio State. An ancient and storied rivalry and always the biggest game of the year for both schools. Buckeye Will Allen intercepts a potential game-winning Michigan pass just short of the Ohio State end zone with 0:00 showing on the clock. Ohio State 14, Michigan 9.
- January 3, 2003, Fiesta Bowl National Championship, Ohio State Buckeyes versus University of Miami Hurricanes. This win takes *two* overtimes to wrest the national championship from the confident Hurricanes in what some call the greatest college football game ever: Ohio State 31, Miami 24. Few expected it; the Buckeyes were 11.5 point underdogs.

What had made the difference in the remarkable 2002 Buckeyes? Credit second-year coach Jim Tressel and his old-school values. Sporting a traditional tie and Ohio State sweater vest on the sidelines, he re-instilled the passion, pride, and tradition of Ohio State football. After each game, he had Buckeye team members stand in front of the band to sing "Carmen Ohio," the school's alma mater. Many kneeled for a post-game prayer. Players were also expected to do well in class, to take responsibility, and to act maturely. Along the way to their national championship, during four consecutive game-end comebacks, nobody believed in the over-achieving Buckeyes—except the Buckeyes and their fans. In the end, that was all that mattered.

The formula kept working: Tressel's undefeated Buckeyes held their No. 1 ranking through the 2006 regular season, with major wins over Texas and Michigan.

10. 2004 BOSTON RED SOX

THEY HAD COME SO FAR THROUGHOUT THE LONG, 162-game baseball season in their quest to win their first World Series since 1918: 98 wins and 64 losses, but things had turned very dark. The Boston Red Sox were down 3–0 to their archrival New York Yankees in the best-of-seven American League Championship series, just one loss from elimination. But as they say, things are darkest before the dawn, and so it would be for Boston. Incredibly, against all odds, the Red Sox rallied to win the next *four* games in a row and win the American League pennant. To put it in perspective, just five NHL hockey teams had come from down 3–0 to win a championship, just three NBA basketball teams, but *no playoff team in baseball had ever done this*.

Then, even *more* improbably, under a full moon and a lunar eclipse the Red Sox swept the next four games against the St. Louis Cardinals and won the World Series. They "reversed the curse" of trading Babe Ruth to the Yankees, January 3, 1920. With this spectacular World Series win, the Red Sox realized the dreams of generations of their fans and had come back from almost certain defeat. Some said it was the greatest comeback in baseball history.

11. AGASSI, ANDRE

AFTER BECOMING THE NO. 1 TENNIS PLAYER IN the world in 1995, Andre Agassi injured his wrist. He slipped to No. 141 by 1997, but with a renewed dedication to training, especially weightlifting, he started the long climb back up the rankings. He appeared in "challenger" tennis events (akin to the minor leagues). This was a very, very long way for the former world No. 1 to fall, but Agassi took it in stride, carrying his own bags, working, sweating, competing, just like hundreds of younger tennis hopefuls. He was not "too big" to have to earn his way back.

And earn his way back he did. By 1999, he was the

old Agassi again and won the French Open championship. Agassi became only the fifth player in tennis history to win *all four* Grand Slam events (Australian Open, French Open, Wimbledon, U.S. Open). He next reached the finals of Wimbledon, and then won his second U.S. Open in a thrilling five-set win over Todd Martin. The win brought him back to a No. 1 ranking and a total of five major titles. He added a sixth just a few months later at the Australian Open.

It took seventeen months for Agassi to make one of the greatest comebacks in tennis history, which set the stage for more momentous tennis in the years to follow, to his retirement in 2006. Because of his humility, his willingness to train harder than ever before, and his love of the game, you might say his greatest comeback had a still longer arc: from a brash, callow youth to whom image was "everything" to a mature, soft-spoken, charity-minded senior statesman of sport. His secret? He has said each day he strives to get *one day better*, no more and no less.

12. ALI, MUHAMMAD

DURING THE FOURTH ROUND OF HIS FIRST BIG FIGHT versus Sonny Liston, February 25, 1964, Muhammad Ali became blinded by ordinary liniment from his opponent. But he suspected foul play and wanted to quit, screaming to his corner, "I can't see. Cut off the gloves!" But manager Angelo Dundee refused to let him, and instructed Ali to "yardstick" Liston with his jab. Ali went back out and fought the fifth round with his right eye closed. Ali wiped his eyes as Liston charged, and whenever he got within range, he reached out and stuck his glove on his head for as long as he could. Ali's arms were longer than Liston's; he knew he had to keep Liston at arm's length, unable to land a knockout punch.

In the sixth round, Ali went on the attack. For the seventh, Liston failed to answer the bell. Ali was the champion. Had he quit, he never would have set the stage to come back twice more and reclaim his heavyweight title lost to Frazier in 1971 by defeating Foreman in 1974 and then Leon Spinks in 1978, making him the first to be a three-time champion.

For many, even more remarkable has been Ali's private yet public bout with Parkinson's disease. Though it has slowed his body and speech, he has refused to allow it to make him a recluse or quench his spirit.

The moral is clear: never quit. And stock your corner with friends who won't let you.

13. ARMSTRONG, LANCE

"I've never been addicted to being on the podium and getting the applause. For me, the rush was the work that went into it and the outcome. That was enough for me."

LANCE ARMSTRONG WAS VERY NEARLY ON TOP OF the world in the autumn of 1996. He was the No. 7 ranked cyclist in the world. He signed a $600,000 contract with France's Team Cofidis. There was only one problem—a soreness in his groin that wouldn't go away. Finally, he saw a doctor. Diagnosis: testicular cancer.

Armstrong had surgery to remove a testicle the very next day, but the situation drastically worsened. Tumors spread to his abdomen, lungs, and lymph nodes. So Armstrong started an aggressive chemotherapy regimen, with the odds in his favor: He was told he had a 65 percent to 85 percent chance to beat the cancer and live. But when doctors found tumors on his brain, the odds of his survival fell to 2 percent. To keep Armstrong positive, the doctors didn't share this number with him. After brain surgery and more chemotherapy, Armstrong beat the 98 percent odds against him. He was declared cancer-free in February 1997.

Now would begin another battle—winning back his place in cycling. Throughout his struggle with cancer,

Armstrong had always said he would compete again, but no one in the racing world believed him. Team Cofidis canceled his contract, but Armstrong replaced it with a $200,000 deal from the U.S. Postal Service team. Back in competitive shape in 1998, Armstrong took fourth place at the World Road Race Championship and won several other big races.

In the summer of 1999, amazingly, he achieved his dream: Armstrong won the 2,274-mile Tour de France by more than seven minutes under his closest rival. Averaging a record-breaking twenty-five miles per hour, he became only the second American to win the Tour de France (the first was Greg LeMond in 1986, 1989, and 1990.) Even more amazing, Armstrong won again in 2000, 2001, 2002, 2003, 2004, and 2005—seven consecutive victories in all. It was arguably the greatest comeback in sports history.

14. AZINGER, PAUL

PAUL AZINGER WON ELEVEN PGA EVENTS FROM 1987 to 1993, but never the really big ones. In addition to the nickname "Zinger," he was tagged the "best player to have never won a major," but got that monkey off his back with his PGA championship win on August 15, 1993. The only thing that brought him down was a nagging pain in his right shoulder, but most players have some aches and pains, right? Still, best to get it looked at. Then came the news: the pain wasn't tendinitis; it was something much worse: lymphoma.

He spent most of the 1994 season in chemotherapy, and it worked, vanquishing the cancer. Thankfully, he could turn his attention to business—but he would have to make a comeback, he would have to rebuild his career. Azinger, by this time, already knew a good deal about comebacks. He was only a mediocre golfer in high school; after winning his tour card in Q-school (pro golf's training and qualification school), he lost it with earnings of only $10,655 in 1982. Failing Q-school a second time, Azinger started playing the minitours and did not end up earning his card for good until 1985.

So back to work. His spouse provided the requisite recharge, or more aptly, kick in the pants. He was complaining about his game to his wife one day. She told him straight-out to stop whining because he wasn't practicing like he used to. Until he did, she didn't want to hear it.

So he began putting in the requisite work, *the amount it takes to win and not just compete*. In 1995, he finished in the back of the pack in most tournaments. But he persisted. The next year was the breakthrough: he took eighth place at the Las Vegas Invitational in 1996. He made a full comeback by winning the Sony Open in 2000. It had been seven long years since his last major tourney win.

His tourney prize record speaks most eloquently of his comeback.

1993 (PGA win)	$1,097,981
1994 (Chemotherapy)	$13,422
1995 (Comeback begins)	$182,595
1996	$232,041
1997	$262,045
1998	$568,233
1999	$562,053
2000	$1,597,139
2001	$1,142,502
2002	$769,924
2003	$222,643
2004	$601,438
2005	$317,739
2006	$702,090

In November 2006, Azinger was named 2008 Ryder Cup captain, to be held at the Valhalla Golf Club, Louisville, Kentucky, Sept. 16–21, 2008. The Ryder Cup pits America vs. Europe in a team competition. Azinger said he was "awestruck" by the honor.

15. BEANE, BILLY

ONCE UPON A TIME, BILLY BEANE WAS THE TOP prospect in major league baseball. Regarded as more gifted than 95 percent of professional players at the time, he signed at sixteen in 1978. He had the "hose" (arm), "wheels" (speed), and body strength to do it all, not to mention the "good face"—the look of a baseball god. He was, as one scout remarked, "a player you could dream on."

The San Diego native was a first-round pick by the New York Mets in the 1980 MLB draft. It was all downhill from there. He proceeded to play with the Mets, the Minnesota Twins, the Detroit Tigers, and the Oakland A's—repeatedly traded as he just wasn't all that good. He generated just a .219 batting average in a 148-game career. What a comedown for the "future Mickey Mantle."

A reflective sort, Beane came to realize he didn't really enjoy playing baseball, was never comfortable with the pressure, and had signed on and played for the money only. He quit baseball at twenty-seven to become a scout—a reverse prestige move that was unheard of.

Off the diamond and in the office now, Beane's new mentor was Oakland A's general manager Sandy Alderson. Unlike his new charge, the boss was not a baseball player prior to managing, but an attorney and marine officer. Something of an iconoclast, Alderson believed in statistics, systems, and science rather than the conventional "eyeball" wisdom of most baseball managers, scouts, and front office types. And soon enough, so did Beane.

When Alderson quit his post, Beane became the A's general manager at thirty-five. He was aided by several notable statisticians such as Bill James, who published the *Baseball Abstract* series, annual volumes of hitherto-overlooked statistics, facts, and analysis on baseball. Paul DePodesta, who was then Beane's assistant in the A's organization, was another statistical devotee. There were even some consulting companies retained along the way, one specializing in arcane baseball analysis, the Society for American Baseball Research (Sabre).

This was all most unorthodox. To most powers that be in baseball, the sport is art, indefinable. To Billy Beane and his various bean counters, it's science. Collectively they became the equivalent of card counters, the "Einsteins of baseball," armed with new evidence and able to see the national pastime in new and startling ways. Here are just a few tenets of their way of analyzing the sport:

1. The single most important thing in the game is to not make an out.
2. Bunts and "hit and run" plays are highly overrated, as are "manufacturing runs."
3. Patience matters: patience to walk, for example.

On-base percentage is more important than batting average.

4. "Taking" the first pitch puts the odds of a successful at-bat in the hands of the batter.

5. Batters can create walks by deciding which pitches to swing at.

6. Pitchers who know how to strike out batters can often be more valuable than 100 mph hurlers. The market, however, values the latter more highly. Beane traded these individuals whenever it was to his advantage.

All of the above were proven statistically, and only statistically. The naked eye cannot discern these facts. Does it work?

Beane's amazing win-loss record as general manager of the Oakland A's went like this:

1998:	74 wins, 88 losses
1999:	87 wins, 76 losses
2000:	91 wins, 70 losses
2001:	102 wins, 60 losses
2002:	103 wins, 59 losses
2003:	99 wins, 66 losses

Beane had come back to baseball as a general manager and achieved the baseball greatness that had eluded him as a player.

[Reprinted with permission, *Stocks and Commodities* magazine, original feature by the author.]

16. BRADDOCK, JAMES "JIMMY" J.

WHEN FIGHTER JIMMY BRADDOCK LOST HIS SHOT AT the light heavyweight title to incumbent Tommy Loughran on July 18, 1929, at Yankee Stadium, it was only a small portent of the bad things to come. Less than two months later, the stock market crashed, the banks failed, and the Great Depression replaced the Roaring Twenties. Braddock, like millions of other people, lost everything. He was now literally fighting to put food on the table for his hungry young family, but he lost sixteen of the next twenty-two fights. He also broke his hand during this time. From time to time, he was able to get day labor on the docks, but there were more workers than jobs and the intermittent assignments weren't enough to pay the bills. Braddock was finally forced to go on government relief to avoid starvation—a humiliating episode for the proud man.

In 1934, however, when a fighter cancelled out at the last minute for his bout with John "Corn" Griffin, Braddock was given the chance to sub in. Expected to last to round two or three, Braddock knocked Griffin out in the third round and shocked everyone. Fighting against the odds again (as always), Braddock went on to defeat John Henry Lewis in ten rounds, then Art Lasky in fifteen rounds. This made the slim Irishman the top heavyweight contender and got him a title shot versus Max Baer as a 10:1 underdog. Braddock was risking his life for this fight; Baer had killed Frankie Campbell in the ring in 1930, which wasn't lost on promoters.

By now Braddock represented the comeback America itself was trying to make from the dire Great Depression. A newspaper reporter tagged him "Cinderella Man." On June 13, 1935, with the whole nation tuned in and cheering him on, absorbing unbelievable punishment and dishing out the same, Braddock won a fifteen-round decision over the champ Baer. Incredibly, the dock worker and welfare recipient was now heavyweight champion of the world.

He held the title for two years, relinquishing it to Joe Louis, the Brown Bomber, in 1937. A year later, he defeated Tommy Farr in ten rounds and went into retirement with this last win under his belt.

Braddock enlisted in the U.S. Army during World War II and served in Saipan. When he returned, he worked as a marine equipment surplus supplier, operating generators and welding equipment—on the same docks where he sought day work in the Depression and helped build the Verrazano Bridge. He passed on in his sleep at age sixty-nine.

The story of how he came back from defeat and deprivation to inspire an entire nation was made into the film *Cinderella Man* in 2005, starring Russell Crowe. It received three Academy Award nominations. As a serious comeback student, consider the film a must-see.

17. CAPRIATI, JENNIFER

JENNIFER CAPRIATI WAS HAILED AS THE FUTURE OF American women's tennis in 1990 at the tender age of fourteen, and she made a down payment on that heady praise as an Olympic champion at sixteen. But then she got in trouble with the police for shoplifting and drug possession at seventeen and again at eighteen. She fell off the tennis radar, needing the time to straighten out her life.

But you don't stay a teen forever, and afterward, the real compensatory work began: the grueling climb back to the top of the ratings, from a very lowly No. 267. She would reclaim her former glory at age twenty-five in an unforgettable match. Playing in Melbourne's oppressive summer heat in January 2002, in the Australian Open finals, Capriati was losing 6–4, 4–0, in her best of three set championship versus Martina Hingis.

A comeback at this point was virtually impossible— for everyone but Capriati. Something compelled her to fight on, and rallying, she broke down the up-until-then magnificent Hingis to win the match 4–6, 6–4, 6–2, one of the greatest comebacks in tennis history. To make the victory even sweeter, it propelled her to the No. 1 ranking in the world. Three months earlier she had told reporters it was never too late to realize your talent, or your dream. Her words were prophetic.

18. CONNORS, JIMMY

AT AGE THIRTY-EIGHT, JIMMY CONNORS APPEARED TO be through with tennis. A wrist injury required surgery. He played only three matches and lost them all. By the end of 1990, his ranking had fallen from No. 14 to No. 936.

The next year he worked his way back up to No. 174. The former champion got a wild card into the U.S. Open in 1991. In the first round he took on Patrick McEnroe, younger brother of nemesis John. Connors trailed two sets and 3–0 in the third set—just twelve points from elimination. But he fought back, winning the third and fourth sets. At 1:35 a.m., after four hours, eighteen minutes of play, Connors won the fifth set 6–4.

Fired up from the huge win, Connors then defeated Michiel Schapers and No. 10 seed Karel Novacek in straight sets. On September 2, Connors turned thirty-nine. Playing Aaron Krickstein, he lost two of the first three sets before tying the match 2–2. Krickstein pushed ahead 5–2 in the fifth—just four points from the win. But the crowd was with the old champion. He came fighting back, tied the set, and won the match in a tiebreaker. The stadium went ballistic.

The buzz was on for the next match; some fans paid scalpers as much as $500 to see the Connors–Paul Haarhuis quarterfinal showdown. They weren't disappointed. Down one set and one break (winning your opponent's service game), Connors rallied to win the final three sets. Sports fans everywhere were in ecstasy. Connors seemed to be defying his mortality, even reversing the aging process, and everyone wanted in on it.

Incredibly, at age thirty-nine, he was in the final four—the semifinals—with all the attendant passion, insanity, and exhilaration. The ancient warrior took on a young and powerful Jim Courier, master of the bone-crushing inside-out forehand. Courier won in straight sets, and the comeback dream stopped just short of the championship match.

The record books will tell you that Stefan Edberg ultimately won the 1991 U.S. Open. But it was Connors who won the imagination of the public through the power of his unlikely point-by-point, match-by-match comebacks and his sheer will to win. Network broadcasters use fist-pumping highlights from that last epic win in the opening graphics of the annual U.S. Open. The match is a classic.

Connors added to his comeback credentials in 2006, this time as mentor, by signing on as coach of 2003 U.S. Open champion Andy Roddick, whose career had fallen on hard times. The Connors magic worked. Roddick made it back to the U.S. Open finals for the first time in three years (2006), and to the Australian Open semifinals (2007).

19. CRAWFORD, ROGER

ROGER CRAWFORD WAS BORN WITH NO LEFT HAND, a right hand with only one finger, a right foot with only three toes, and a left leg that was so deformed it was amputated when he was five. His parents were told he would never walk.

Not only did Crawford learn to walk, but he became captain of his high school tennis team, won four letters, and posted a 44–6 record. For this remarkable effort, he was named Northern California Athlete of the Year.

Roger won a tennis scholarship to Loyola Marymount University and became the first and only severely handicapped NCAA Division I athlete to win a varsity letter, posting a 22–11 record. Crawford tells the story in his book *Playing from the Heart* (1998). His story was also told on *Larry King Live*, *Good Morning America*, CBS's *Inside Edition*, CNBC, *Real People*, *Hour of Power*, *USA Today*, and *Tennis* magazine. NBC earned an Emmy for its television movie on Crawford, *In a New Light*.

Now a motivational speaker, Crawford has a long list of corporate clients. He tells them that he would rather have one leg and a positive attitude than two legs and a negative attitude.

20. CUNNINGHAM, GLENN

"By the grace of God, I learned to run again."

NEARLY BURNED TO DEATH IN A SCHOOL FIRE AT AGE SEVEN in 1916, doctors wanted to amputate little Glenn Cunningham's legs to save his life. His mother said no. Glenn survived, but with the possibility that he would never walk again. Rehab followed, and with it incredible pain for nearly a year to get to the point where he could stand on his own, and finally, walk.

Eventually, normal life resumed, and Cunningham even joined his Elkhart (Kansas) high school track team. As a senior, he set a high school world record in the mile with a time of 4:24.7. He went on to finish fourth at the 1932 Los Angeles Olympics in the 1,500 m; broke the world record for the mile with a time of 4:06.8 at Princeton, New Jersey; and won the silver medal in the 1,500 m at the 1936 Berlin Olympics. He received the Sullivan Award in 1933—the award for the country's number one amateur athlete. In 1938, Cunningham ran his fastest mile in 4:04.4. At that time, of the thirty-one fastest miles ever run, Cunningham had run twelve of them! The small boy who almost died in a fire, and who some thought would never walk, became the "Kansas Ironman."

21. FLUTIE, DOUG

On paper, how could young Doug Flutie be much of a player? He was surely too small (5 feet 9 inches, 175 pounds). Detractors said he had only an "average arm." But you play football in the field, not on the statistics page; when he was on the field, all Doug Flutie could do—was win.

Respect? Elusive in the pro ranks at times, but as an undergrad, as quarterback for Boston College, his size wasn't held against him, and he got respect and more: on November 22, 1984, Flutie played in one of college football's greatest games vs University of Miami. Down 45–41 and forty-eight yards from the end zone, with no time remaining, Flutie scrambled to his right. He dodged a sack, then let the ball fly more than sixty-three yards in the air (not bad for an "average arm.") The ball came straight down over the mass of players untouched—directly into his receiver's arms. Flutie had produced a miraculous 47–45 win! Boston College would finish the season 10–2 and go on to earn its first bowl win since 1941. Flutie earned the Heisman Trophy in 1984—the award for college football's greatest player each year.

Destined to be greatest in the pros, too? The pro scouts and executives didn't think so; they looked at his size, his stats—not his heart. Despite being a Heisman winner, he was drafted an unbelievably low 285th overall by the Los Angeles Rams and promptly traded. So he began his pro career in the upstart U.S. Football League (USFL) with the New Jersey Generals. Not able to compete against the venerable NFL, the USFL would fold after just one year, and in 1986, Flutie was called to the Chicago Bears. Though he had the respect of Coach Mike Ditka, who called Flutie "a winner," the McMahon–led Super Bowl champs did not share the coach's enthusiasm.

The next season he was traded to New England, where he was the hometown boy and a local hero. He stayed for three years. Then, in 1990, he went to the Canadian Football League, where he toiled for eight long years, capturing the Most Valuable Player award an unprecedented six times. He led the league in passing yardage five times and helped his team to capture the Grey Cup three times.

Canada was great, but still, his dream was to make it back home in the NFL. Flutie came back to the NFL in 1998 and led the Buffalo Bills to a play-off spot. He earned himself a Pro Bowl selection and was named NFL Comeback Player of the Year by the Associated Press and *Pro Football Weekly*. In 2001, he moved to the San Diego Chargers to serve as backup and mentor (and sometimes, controversially, replacement) to rising star and "quarterback of the future," Purdue star Drew Brees.

Back in 2003, when the Chargers were 1–7 under a young and struggling Drew Bees, Flutie stepped in for him. At forty-one, he became the oldest player, and the first over forty, to score two rushing touchdowns in one game. He was the oldest player ever to be named AFC Offensive Player of the Week, an honor he earned four times. Not only was he still coming back to play every week—*twenty years* after his Heisman season and long after most of his former teammates and critics had retired—*he was setting records*.

One last comeback brought about by Flutie—a forgotten play in football: Flutie drop-kicked a point after touchdown on January 1, 2005, versus the Miami Dolphins. It was the first time a dropkick had been seen in an NFL game since 1941.

Flutie finally retired May 15, 2006, at forty-three, but turned his attention to a new kind of winning— from the broadcast booth, using his low-key charm and expert commentary to win the respect and admiration of a new generation of fans, some of whom weren't even born when he won the Heisman Trophy.

22. FOREMAN, GEORGE

IN 1968, GEORGE FOREMAN WON THE OLYMPIC heavyweight boxing gold medal at nineteen. He won his first pro heavyweight championship in 1973, knocking out Joe Frazier in the second round. He then signed for $5 million to fight Muhammad Ali in Zaire, Africa, in 1974. In the fight, famously billed as the Rumble in the Jungle, Ali employed the rope-a-dope technique, encouraging Foreman to punch himself to exhaustion. Then Ali knocked him out in the eighth round. It was one of the greatest upsets in boxing history—and a long time before Foreman forgave himself for the loss.

After losing a twelve-round decision to Jimmy Young in 1977, Foreman became a born-again Christian. He was ordained as a minister and retired from boxing. He bought radio time to preach, established his own church, counseled prisoners, and launched the George Foreman Youth and Community Center.

Then, Foreman decided to make a comeback to boxing. In 1987, at the age of thirty-six, ten years out of the ring, he returned sporting a new smiling, rotund fighting persona. Foreman won twenty-four straight comeback fights. He earned a shot at his old title in 1991, fighting Evander Holyfield at the age of forty. He lost the twelve-round bout by decision but gained a wealth of respect from the boxing industry for his remarkable comeback. He stayed with it for another five, long years.

In 1994, at forty-five, Foreman *did* recapture the heavyweight title, and in a dramatic fashion. He defeated then-reigning heavyweight champion, Michael Moorer, twenty-six, with a tenth-round knockout. Foreman became the oldest heavyweight boxing champion in history. His subsequent self-mocking commercials for grills and mufflers made him even more famous, popular—and wealthy.

Foreman has said that old age is a decision you make, not something that happens to you. He decided no one would make that decision for him.

23. HAMILTON, SCOTT

ICE-SKATER SCOTT HAMILTON COULDN'T EVEN STAND up straight, the pain in his stomach was so excruciating. He had been putting off seeing a doctor, but he couldn't take it any longer and went to the Cleveland Clinic. The 1997 diagnosis: testicular cancer. When the doctors delivered the bad news, Hamilton made a joke of it. He used humor to deflect the blows to his body, mind, and spirit. It was a defense mechanism, and it was working.

He underwent twelve weeks of successful

chemotherapy treatments (getting through it, again, by joking with the IV technicians), followed by an equally successful surgery. After just six weeks of recuperation, he was back on the ice rehearsing for his twelfth season of *Stars on Ice*, the production he helped found in 1986.

Hamilton believes the only disability in life is a bad attitude.

24. HARTEL, LIS

LIS HARTEL CONTRACTED POLIO WHEN SHE WAS TWENTY-three and pregnant in 1944. She set about the hard work of reactivating her muscles; after three years of rehabilitation, she was largely successful but nevertheless still paralyzed below the knees. However, she was determined to return to her first love, horseback riding, and compete in the Scandinavian championships. She had to be helped on and off her mount, but amazingly, finished second in women's dressage. In 1952, representing her native Denmark at the Helsinki Olympics, Hartel won a silver medal. Four years later she won a second silver medal at the 1956 Olympics (equestrian events were held in Stockholm). She stayed active in the sport as a trainer and coach. Hartel proved that what one can achieve can sometimes be more a function of mind than of muscle.

25. HAWK, TONY

TONY HAWK STARTED SKATEBOARDING AT SIX AND TURNED professional at fourteen. He had traveled around the world by eighteen, not once, but twice. He had a skateboard named after him. Royalties, exhibition fees, and prize money brought him more than $100,000 a year in income. While still in high school, he bought his first house. He won nearly every competitive skating event for the next ten years. Life was good.

But by the time Hawk was twenty-seven, interest in skateboarding dropped like a skateboarder having a bad fall. Restricted to a $5-a-day allowance for food and having trouble paying the mortgage and utilities, the high life was receding fast in the rearview mirror. Hawk was thinking about packing it in.

Then ESPN called and asked him to skate in something new: the X (as in extreme) Games. So he did. He won, as usual. But even bigger, the sport itself got a much needed vitamin B12 shot in the arm.

About this time, he began working on a move many thought impossible: the 900, i.e., 900 degrees, two and a half rotations in the air. It had been nine years in and out of Hawk's imagination, he said, but until then was too daunting. He had tried it from time to time but had gotten only bruises, scrapes, and lumps for his efforts.

Indeed, during the 1999 X Games Hawk tried and

failed the 900 eleven times. But on the *twelfth* try, he made it, creating a sensation in the skating world. (It took Hillary two tries to conquer Everest; Peary eight times for the North Pole; Hawk, twelve times to make the 900.)

Once a self-described outsider, Hawk's endorsements now make him millions: video games, toys, clothes, even bagels. When Hawk put his imprimatur on Bagel Bites, sales increased 20 percent. Video game maker Activision generates $6 million a year in royalties for Hawk from the game *Tony Hawk Pro Skater*. Not content to merely endorse, Hawk created Tony Hawk's Boom Boom Huck Jam, an extreme sports and rock-and-roll spectacle that plays in arenas around the country.

Hawk stuck with his sport when it was flagging, and with the 900 when it seemed impossible. He kept himself in position to make a comeback personally and for his sport, and reaped rewards that were beyond his, or anyone else's, imagination.

26. HOGAN, BEN

ON FEBRUARY 2, 1949, 150 MILES EAST OF EL PASO, a Greyhound bus pulled out to pass a truck and smashed head-on into a Cadillac driven by golf great Ben Hogan.

The engine was shoved into the driver's seat, the steering wheel all the way into the backseat.

Hogan's injuries: smashed ribs, a broken ankle, a broken collarbone, and a double fracture of the pelvis. A blood clot formed in his legs and, fearing it would move to his heart and kill him, emergency doctors tied off the veins in his legs. They told him he would never walk again, let alone play golf. Hogan didn't accept that verdict. After all, it had taken him two tries to make the tour, and once he did, it had taken several years to earn significant money. So he knew something about sticking with it. He had overcome obstacles before. He would do it again.

Just sixteen months after the accident, at the 1950 U.S. Open at the Merion (Philadelphia) Golf Club, Hogan mounted one of sports' most remarkable comebacks. In those days, thirty-six holes were played in a single day (versus eighteen today). This was exhausting enough for a healthy player, let alone one recovering from serious injuries. His legs were taped from ankle to thigh; he wore a diver's rubber suit under his clothes to make it easier for his body parts to move together.

Fighting the summer heat and the hills of the course, Hogan struggled to steady his legs beneath him on every shot. He couldn't bend over to pick the ball out of the cup after a successful putt; his caddy did it for him. The pain was so bad he considered withdrawing—but he did not.

After four rounds, he played himself into a three-way tie for the lead at 287. In the play-off, he shot a sixty-nine to defeat Lloyd Mangrum and George Fazio and win the championship. Repeat U.S. Open wins followed in 1951 and 1953.

A widely published picture of Hogan hitting a 1-iron to the eighteenth green to win the 1950 championship is considered by many the most famous in golf history. His comeback story was made into a movie, *Follow the Sun*, in 1951, starring Glenn Ford. Hogan served as technical adviser.

When not in a tourney, Hogan practiced prodigiously, and when he was in one, his concentration was like a laser. When golfer Tommy Bolt was asked to compare the young Jack Nicklaus to the veteran Hogan, he said that he knew Nicklaus watched Hogan practice but he never heard of Hogan watching Nicklaus practice. Something of a tough guy and loner, the Ty Cobb of golf, if you will, Hogan said there are three ways to defeat an opponent: you outwork them, you outthink them, and then you intimidate them.

On a softer note, he also said that as you walk down the fairway of life you have to stop to smell the roses, because you only get to play one round.

27. HOLTZ, LOU

LOU HOLTZ COACHED NOTRE DAME FOOTBALL FROM 1986 to 1996, winning the national championship in 1988. He led the Fighting Irish to nine consecutive New Year's Day bowl games and compiled a career record of 100–30–2. But despite this overwhelming success, he was fired. He suffered an emotional breakdown at the press conference; he thought his career was over. The next two years were a low point, made much worse because his wife was suffering from throat cancer. He did some work as a CBS football analyst, but that far from filled his plate.

Then, a turn. He was recruited to coach again, this time for South Carolina. After some soul searching, and with the encouragement of his wife, he signed on. (Small world department: in 1967, long before his Notre Dame success, he had also been fired as an assistant coach from South Carolina.) At that time, after reading *The Magic of Thinking Big*, by David Schwartz, he made a list of 107 things he wanted to accomplish in life. Big things. It became a part of Lou Holtz lore, and he became famous for it.

Holtz applied this notion of "thinking big" when he walked back into South Carolina as head coach in 1999. He had to—the program was in ruins. He had just five offensive linemen on the roster. By the end of the season he had used sixteen, cleverly substituting walk-ons and stray defensive linemen. He also used six quarterbacks that year. The results showed it: 0–11.

But the next year, 2000, after much hard work, his team went 8–4 and won an Outback Bowl victory. The turnaround was the best in Southeastern Conference history and fourth-best in Division I-A history. It turned out his coaching wasn't behind him, as he feared when he was cut loose from Notre Dame. Holtz said the greatest thing in the world was to be around people who genuinely care about what you're doing, to experience their enthusiasm and positivism.

28. IRVAN, ERNIE

THINKING HIS BEST FRIEND WAS DEAD, THE CREW chief ran over to the wall at turn two, leaned over, looked, and promptly threw up. Race driver Ernie Irvan had just crashed into the wall at 190 mph during Winston Cup practice at Michigan Speedway. Emergency workers who extracted him from the shredded car also thought he was dead. He wasn't—but he had critical brain and chest injuries.

An emergency tracheotomy was performed on the spot. Taken in a helicopter to the emergency room, doctors there gave him a less than 10 percent chance of survival. He was unconscious for two days. When he came to, doctors told him he would never drive again, let alone race.

Yet he *did* recover and decided he *had* to race again. Late in 1995, Irvan got clearance to come back and ran again at North Wilkesboro. He led thirty-one laps and finished sixth. Thousands of spectators were stirred to tears. He won two races in 1996. In 1997, Irvan won the Miller 400 at Michigan Speedway, on the very same track where he was nearly killed three years earlier.

In 1999, Irvan again wrecked on the same track, this time during practice for a Busch Series race. Having made his comeback, this time he retired for good, choosing not to tempt fate any further.

29. JANSEN, DAN

AFTER LEARNING OF THE DEATH OF HIS TWENTY-seven-year-old sister, Jane, from leukemia, speed skater Dan Jansen, twenty-three, was devastated—and he was at the 1988 Olympic Games in Calgary. Still, he had a job to do, and he took to the ice within hours with the entire world pulling for him. But less than ten seconds into the race, he fell rounding a turn, slid off the track, and hit the wall. Three days later in the 1,000 m event, Jansen fell again and failed to finish. At Jane's funeral, days later, Reverend John Yockey said: "Dan, we thank you for showing us how to get up again. You have gotten up again with dignity, with graciousness." This would not be his last fall or last setback, however.

Jansen had earlier dedicated his skating to his sister, and in the intervening years, he would work harder than ever to achieve his potential and win the gold medal. But in the 1992 Albertville Olympics (the last Winter Games to be staged in the same year as the Summer Games), Jansen placed fourth in the 500 m and did not attempt the 1,000 m. Unbelievably, at the 1994 Olympic Games in Lillehammer, in the event he was expected to win, the 500 m, Jansen fell yet again. Three major falls—in front of the entire world.

How much bad luck could one athlete endure? He had exactly one race remaining in his career: the 1,000 m. In this race, he overcame it all and set a world-record time of 1:12.43 as he captured his long sought-after Olympic gold medal.

As a motivational speaker, he uses his story of ups and downs to motivate others. He advises having fun along the way to offset the tedium of work that goes into achieving one's goals. Jansen's falls and triumphant comeback were featured in a television movie in 1996, *A Brother's Promise, The Dan Jansen Story*, and more recently in television spots in which he comforts a delivery man who falls on the snow and ice by saying: "I know how that feels."

30. JENNER, BRUCE

SON OF AN ARBORIST, BRUCE JENNER KNEW THE SOUND of a tree limb snapping. Now he heard his own knee snap and it made him sick. Jenner hopped off the gridiron with a dreadful feeling in the pit of his stomach that something was very wrong. As a new Graceland (Iowa) College football player, Jenner had torn the medial collateral ligament in his knee trying to block a punt just three weeks into the 1969 season. He thought sports were over for him. But the knee was repairable, and he had surgery on January 2, 1969, in Danbury, Connecticut. As he was losing consciousness from the anesthetic, he looked up at the surgeon and said, "Doc, do a good job, 'cause I need this knee."

He needn't have worried—the surgery was a success. The cast came off seven weeks later and rehabilitation followed. His knee was so tight it was like a ball of cement, but with the supervision and encouragement of his track coach, he exercised it, painfully, to regain motion. Within sixteen months he was back at Graceland—playing basketball!

He also began his decathlon training in earnest and

found his true calling. Eight years later, after endless hours of training, he won the decathlon at the 1976 Montreal Olympics, becoming, quite simply, the greatest all-around athlete in the world. Jenner said that he always felt his greatest asset was not his physical ability but his *mental ability*. He advises others to abolish their fears and raise their commitment level to the point of no return, and then the champion within will emerge.

31. JOHNSON, EARVIN "MAGIC"

AT THE HEIGHT OF HIS POPULARITY, BASKETBALL legend Magic Johnson, thirty-two, shocked the world when he announced he was HIV-positive in 1991. At the time, there were no powerful pharmaceutical cocktails and AIDS seemed a sure death sentence.

But Johnson fought back, taking medications, working out, and keeping a positive attitude. He made a triumphant reappearance at the 1992 All-Star Game, earning the game's Most Valuable Player Award and leading the West to a 153–113 victory. Johnson went on to play for the 1992 U.S. Olympic Dream Team.

Then he sat out for four and a half seasons. But basketball wasn't out of his system and he made yet another comeback late in the 1995–96 campaign, playing the final thirty-two games of the regular season for the Lakers as a 255-pound power forward and sometime guard. After the Lakers were ousted by Houston in the first round of the 1996 play-offs, Johnson retired once again.

Johnson turned his attention to his own Johnson Development Corp., working to bring economic development to troubled urban areas by opening Magic Johnson Theaters, Starbucks coffeehouses, and T.G.I. Friday's restaurants. And basketball? Still in love with the game some fifteen years after his HIV diagnosis, Johnson was still playing pickup games against guys half his age, as well as playing in the higher-profile NBA All-Star Game Player Skills Challenge (2006).

32. JORDAN, MICHAEL

PRO ATHLETES ARE GODS. SURELY THEY'RE NOT LIKE you and me: they're as big as Yao, as powerful as Shaq, as quick as Payton. They have skills like Tiger, reflexes like Jeter. And pure talent—truckloads of talent—like Michael Jordan. One thing's for sure: they have never, ever suffered the indignity, the unforgettable, lifelong humiliation of getting cut from a team.

Except that guy with all the talent. Michael Jordan. He did. He got cut.

Jordan remembers it well. After varsity tryouts for his high school team, the cut list was posted. Jordan, a tenth grader, went with his friend to see it. His friend made it; he didn't. Numb all day, he raced home from school, went to his room, and cried uncontrollably. When his mom got home from work, he shared the news with her. They cried together.

For most, the basketball dream would end there—but not for Jordan. He played junior varsity, but there was more humiliation to come. At season's end he asked the coach if he could ride with the varsity team to the district tournament just to watch. The coach said no, but Jordan persisted and got him to relent.

When he got to the tournament, the coach had him carry the players' uniforms inside. Jordan's parents had come to watch the tournament, and when they saw him coming in with the uniforms, they thought he was being called up, given a chance to play—but he wasn't. It was precisely this kind of humiliation that pushed Jordan to become better.

The casual observer may think that he was supremely, supernaturally gifted, but the truth is, he outworked all the rest. That was Jordan's gift. Shooting, dribbling, weights, cardio, flexibility—you name it, he did it. He had special exercises devised for his hands. He was always the first one to the stadium before the game, the first one on the court to take shots. *Because* he got cut. He learned what disappointment felt like and resolved to never have that feeling again.

Putting it all in perspective, Jordan said that he missed more than nine thousand shots in his career, lost some three hundred games. Some twenty-six times he was entrusted to take the game-winning shot—and missed. And once he got cut from the team entirely. He failed over and over again, he says, and paradoxically, that is why he succeeded.

33. KARNAZES, DEAN

EARLY ONE MORNING, A PRIEST KNOCKED ON DEAN Karnazes's door. It was his unenviable task to tell Karnazes that his sister, Pary, had been killed in a car accident. She had lost control of the convertible she was driving, it rolled over, and she was thrown out and killed. It was the eve of her eighteenth birthday. Dean said the blow to his family went beyond shock, beyond sadness. The void was bottomless and unbearable.

Eventually, Karnazes went on with his life. He was valedictorian of his college class, followed it with an MBA, and worked his way up the corporate ladder. But the hole in his heart was not healing. At his thirtieth birthday party, drunk and contemplating marital infidelity, Karnazes abruptly walked out, went home, put on a pair of sneakers, and ran thirty miles. A spiritual awakening happened. He says he was transformed from a drunken yuppie fool into an athlete.

He followed this feat with ever greater, ever more unlikely challenges:

- a 50-mile qualifying run
- the Western States Hundred-Mile Endurance Run
- a 135-mile race across Death Valley to Mount Whitney
- a 26.2-mile marathon at the South Pole
- two 200-mile races
- a 226-mile race (seventy-five hours of running)

Sometimes finishing seemed impossible. Sometimes he risked his life. But the sheer willpower to never quit ultimately proved more potent than the challenge. Karnazes tells his amazing story in *Ultra Marathon Man: Confessions of an All-Night Runner.* (This book is a must-read! Even if you are not an athlete it will expand your consciousness as to what is possible when you decide to not quit.)

Karnazes says he runs to give something back to the world because it is the one thing he does best. He runs to honor his sister and unite his family. He runs to savor the trip. He runs to inspire others to reject what he calls "the easy path."

34. Knight, Bobby

"Most people have the will to win, but few have the will to prepare to win."

IN SEPTEMBER 2000, INDIANA BASKETBALL COACHING legend Bob Knight suffered the indignity that is only supposed to be accorded nonlegends. He got fired—despite amassing a 763–289 career record and making Indiana a perennial basketball powerhouse. The catalyzing incident came on campus when the famously volatile Knight touched the arm of a student who rudely accosted him with a "Hey, Knight!" But it wasn't time to retire. Knight was just 117 victories behind former North Carolina coach Dean Smith, who led the NCAA Division I all-time coaching victories list.

Then the comeback: the next season, Texas Tech hired Knight on a five-year contract. The new partnership was a good fit. What the team lacked, he had: an immaculate NCAA rules record and the ability to fill their two-year-old, $68 million United Spirit Arena. (Tech's high-profile women's program consistently outdrew the overlooked men's team.) The Red Raiders men's team was coming off of a 9–19 record, with only four players returning who averaged more than a minute of play per game.

"The General" rolled up his sleeves and went to

work. His teaching prowess took hold—the team went to 23–9 his first year (2001–2), posting the largest record improvement (fourteen games) in the country. They won an NCAA tourney berth, their first in five years. The Knight-Tech juggernaut would motor on the next three years with overall records of 22–11, 23–11, and 22–11.

The 2005–2006 season was subpar at 15–18, but few were betting against Knight going forward, especially as he chased a record that would put him atop all college basketball coaches. He passed North Carolina coach Dean Smith as the most successful Division I coach in history by notching his 880th win on January 1, 2007. It took forty-one years, and nothing, not even a firing at his beloved Indiana, nor the excesses of temperament over the years, nor his detractors—and they were legion—could stop him.

35. LEMIEUX, MARIO

WHEN STRUCK BY THE HAMMER BLOW OF FATE, some people go numb, some laugh, some cry. When Mario Lemieux was diagnosed with cancer, he cried so hard on the way home he could hardly drive. That January day in 1993 was the toughest day of his life. Like Lou Gehrig, the hockey great was struck by a life-threatening disease at the peak of his playing power.

But Lemieux—the first pick in the 1984 draft, the 1985 NHL Most Valuable Player, and the Stanley Cup champion—would mount a series of comebacks that would earn him the nickname Super Mario:

- 1993: In January, doctors remove a 1×2 cm lump on his neck. A biopsy revealed he has a nodular lymphocytic form of Hodgkin's disease, a treatable type of cancer. He began radiation treatment with a goal to return before season's end. He hit the ice the day of his last treatment, March 2, and scored a goal. He lead the team to a seventeen-game winning streak, and in the remaining twenty games, he scored fifty-six more goals.
- 1994–95: He is sidelined by injuries, including herniated back muscle.
- 1995: Another comeback year: he scored 161 goals in seventy games
- 1997: Lemieux retired, due to the negative combination of his back injury and the tight checking style that began to dominate the game. Inducted into the Hall of Fame, his number, 66, was retired by the Penguins.
- 2000: Having spent the better part of the 1990s in financial trouble, the Penguins still owed Lemieux the salary he (and other top players) had deferred

to keep the team going. He decided to capitalize the debt into ownership, gathered other investors, bought the team, and returned to the Penguins as a player. Part of his motivation was so his youngest son could see him play. He returned to the ice on December 27 and did not miss a single beat: he scored a goal that night and added two assists.

- 2002: Lemieux was named to the all-star team and named captain of Canada's gold-medal winning Olympic team.

After hip surgery in January 2004, he retired from hockey on January 24, 2006—thirteen years after his cancer diagnosis. "Le Magnifique" had recorded one of the most dramatic series of comebacks in sports history. His grace, skill, and beauty on the ice would only be exceeded by his courage.

36. Marciano, Rocky

Rocky Marciano loved baseball more than anything, and he was a standout sandlot player in high school and for his local American Legion post. With high hopes, he tried out for the Chicago Cubs in 1947 but didn't make the team. He went back home, disappointed and hurt, but he decided to turn his powerful focus to boxing.

He trained for five long years and fought his way up through the ranks, finally getting a chance at the heavyweight title, every fighter's dream. On September 23, 1952, Marciano challenged "Jersey Joe" Walcott for the world heavyweight championship. The fight started badly for Marciano and got worse. He was knocked down in the first round; after seven rounds, he was behind on points. But there was no quit in Marciano. He kept fighting, against the odds, against a very tough opponent, maybe a superior opponent.

Then came the fateful thirteenth round: with a powerful right cross, his so-called Susie Q, Marciano knocked out Walcott. The fight was over and Marciano was heavyweight champion of the world. He defended that title six times, winning five titles by knockouts. He won forty-nine straight fights—forty-three by knockouts.

With his tremendous knockout punch, he was always in contention for the win no matter how a fight was playing out. His other weapon: work. He realized the fight game was his last chance to better himself, and so he really worked at it. Marciano was a failed catcher, yes, but he became a boxing immortal.

37. MORRIS, JIM

TO FULFILL A PROMISE HE HAD MADE TO HIS HIGH school baseball team, coach Jim Morris attended a Tampa Bay Devil Rays open tryout. He was thirty-five years old and hadn't thrown a professional pitch in twelve years—four surgeries had stopped his career before he'd made it out of the minor leagues.

Yet through some mystery, some miracle, Morris registered 98 mph, 99 mph, and 100 mph pitches on the radar gun. The pros were interested and he signed with the Devil Rays. He was sent to the St. Petersburg spring-training facility to get in shape (the deal: no bonus, no salary, expenses, and a per diem), then to the AA team in Orlando with a raise to $1,500 a month. Morris agonized over being away from home, an adult with responsibilities chasing a child's dream. He agonized over money. His salary didn't cover his living expenses, and wife Lorri's check didn't cover their debts or their new $500-a-month phone tab. Creditors pestered her mercilessly.

Then it came: *the* call, "You're going to the big leagues." It was September 17, 1999. He was to fly to Texas and join the Devil Rays to play against the Texas Rangers. Within a few hours, he was in the lobby of an Arlington, Texas, hotel standing among the likes of Wade Boggs, Fred McGriff, and José Canseco. Having only a few hours sleep, and this being his first day on the job, Morris knew he wouldn't be called on to pitch—of course, he was. In the eighth inning, the Rays down 6–1, Morris came into the game to face Royce Clayton, the Ranger's shortstop. It took just four pitches for the rookie to sit the big star down. Clayton was caught looking at strike three on a 98 mph fastball.

The media went berserk with their new hero. Morris went from absolute obscurity to the "it" player of baseball overnight: newspapers, magazines, television, radio, publishers, and Hollywood all wanted his story. No matter what happened next, Morris's comeback was complete—and with a literal storybook ending. When the season concluded, the Devil Rays sent Morris to the Arizona fall league (top prospects only). His fastball clipped 100 mph, and his ERA was 0.00.

The next season, after facing Paul O'Neill in Yankee Stadium, Morris's career would come to an end—almost as mysteriously as it began. He could only muster 85 mph fastballs and walked in the winning run on four straight pitches. It was back to the surgeon's table and back home to Lorri and the kids—with plenty of repair work to do there, too.

Still, Morris had made a comeback that any rational person would have thought impossible. He became the oldest major league rookie since Minny Mendoza debuted with the Minnesota Twins in 1970 at thirty-six, with a difference of only four months. He was also the oldest rookie pitcher since Diomedes Olivo signed with the Pittsburgh Pirates in 1960 at forty-one, a difference of eight months. His story was told in the book *The Rookie* (2002) and a film starring Dennis Quaid.

Morris can't explain why his pitching prowess came and went so suddenly, but he advises to never close a door on your dreams. You just never know.

38. MUNOZ, RIC

AFTER MARATHONER RIC MUNOZ LEARNED HE WAS HIV-positive, he decided to fight back in the best way he knew how—by running. He has logged 129 marathons and counting. Munoz was featured in a Nike "Just Do It" commercial in 1995, which *Entertainment Weekly* recognized as one of the "50 Greatest Television Commercials of All Time." There was no sound other than the footsteps and heavy breathing of the runner as he moved closer and closer to the camera. Then, the graphics read: "80 miles a week. 10 marathons a year. HIV-positive."

More than ten years later, Munoz was still running some thirty miles per week, building up his distances to ultramarathon level (his personal record for fifty miles was 7:17).

Munoz says that if you've got a challenge you can let it either enervate you or inspire you to go beyond it. He chose the latter.

39. NAMATH, JOE

"You learn you can do your best even when it's hard, even when you're tired and maybe hurting a little bit. It feels good to show some courage."

THE SMILE WAS SO EASY, SO WINNING, THAT MOST casual fans never knew how much pain he was in. Few forget the outrageous "guarantee," however. In Super Bowl III in 1969, the upstart AFL New York Jets were pitted against the venerable, old-school NFL Baltimore Colts. The Jets were nineteen-point underdogs. Fears were expressed for the very life of brash Jets quarterback "Broadway Joe" Namath, whose banged-up knees hurt when he walked, let alone ran. Nevertheless, he told attendees at a Super Bowl awards dinner during the week preceding the game, "The Jets will win on Sunday, I *guarantee* you."

Joe Namath had learned to play hurt and went out and made good on his notorious guarantee, completing seventeen of twenty-eight passes for 206 yards.

The fired-up Jets made big defensive plays that stunned the Colts and the sports world, winning Super Bowl III with a score of 16–7. Namath showed how to overcome the pain—with patience, humor, and always a smile.

40. OWENS, JESSE

ROUGHHOUSING WITH HIS ROOMMATES, OHIO State track star Jesse Owens slipped on some water, fell, and bruised his tailbone. Two weeks later, at the 1935 Big Ten Championships, he was still so sore he couldn't even bend over to touch his knees. Should he withdraw? It was the only reasonable thing to do. But after discussing it with his coach, Owens decided to try to compete. After all, he was already there.

As the sophomore got ready for his first race, the pain miraculously disappeared. He tied the world record for the hundred-yard dash with a time of 9.4 seconds. He set a world record in the long jump at 26 feet 8.25 inches (it stood for twenty-five years). Then he set a world record with 22.6 seconds in the 220-yard low hurdles.

It was called the greatest afternoon in track and field history. But Jesse Owens would go one better at the 1936 Berlin Olympics, where he would win four gold medals (10.1 seconds in the 100 m, 26.5-foot long jump, 20.7 seconds in the 200 m, and 39.8 seconds in the 4 × 100 m relay). This would be the perfect and permanent comeback vis-à-vis Nazi claims of racial superiority.

Owens has said that the battles that count aren't the ones for gold medals; they're the ones that are inside of us—invisible and inevitable.

41. PAIGE, LEROY ROBERT "SATCHEL"

"You win a few; you lose a few. Some get rained out. But you got to dress for all of them."

BASEBALL HAS A LONG HISTORY OF COLORFUL characters: Babe Ruth, Dizzy Dean, Ty Cobb. And then there's Satchel Paige. After a long and storied career in the Negro Leagues—pitching 2,500 games and winning 2,000, or so the legend goes—Paige won a contract with the Cleveland Indians for the 1948–49 season. He was forty-two. He also played for St. Louis (1951–53) and Kansas City (1965).

In 1965, at fifty-nine, he came back to take the mound for the last time, throwing three shutout innings for the Kansas City Athletics. In 1968, Paige suited up as an Atlanta Brave for the requisite 158 days he needed to earn his pension. He was sixty-two during this last comeback, and the sport was paying the legend his due.

Paige Quotes:

- "How old would you be if you didn't know how old you are?"
- "Work like you don't need the money. Love like you've never been hurt. Dance like nobody's watching."

42. PIERSALL, JIMMY

ZANY, BRASH, COCKY, HIGH-STRUNG, AND A LOVER OF the practical joke, Jimmy Piersall was slated for big things with the Boston Red Sox back in 1952. But signs of instability were there, too. On May 24, 1952, he got into a pregame fight with both New York's Billy Martin and teammate Maury McDermott. He sat out the game. Shortly after, years of depression, worry, and anxiety imploded on him. Piersall had a mental breakdown. Shock treatment followed. Piersall remembered nothing about 1952 other than the birth of his daughter in March. The story is told in his book Fear Strikes Out (1955; a film starring Anthony Perkins came out in 1957).

Nevertheless, he came back from that harrowing episode to play the next fourteen years, hitting .272 and 104 home runs. But Piersall remained, well, Jimmy

Piersall. He cleaned off home plate with a squirt gun and led cheers for himself in the outfield. When he hit his hundredth home run, he ran the bases—backward. Piersall's stunts were often anathema to his managers and team executives, but the fans? They loved him.

Piersall retired in 1967 but stayed in baseball, most notably as the Chicago White Sox's radio broadcaster (1977–1981). His barbed comments—aimed at players, the manager, even the team owner's wife—made him a persona non grata in the front office, and eventually got him fired. However, the irrepressible Piersall still popped up on Chicago radio as a sports talk host well into his seventies.

43. RUDOLPH, WILMA

BORN WITH POLIO, WILMA RUDOLPH spent much of her first five years in bed, and from ages five to eleven she wore a leg brace. She had a secret weapon, however, and a powerful one at that: a loving family, including twenty-two siblings from two marriages. Her siblings took turns massaging her crippled leg every day. Her mom, Blanche, a domestic worker, drove her ninety miles round-trip each week to a Nashville hospital for therapy.

Then, one Sunday when she was eleven, she removed the brace and walked down the aisle of her church—she could walk. Her great passion would now be basketball, and she played at every opportunity. In high school, Rudolph scored forty-nine points in one game, a state record. Her athleticism caught the attention of Tennessee State track coach Ed Temple. He recruited her to attend his daily college workouts while she was still in high school. A sociology professor at Tennessee State, Temple's coaching was unpaid. He drove the team to meets in his own car. An unmarked and unsurfaced dirt oval, he lined the school track at his own expense. He did it for the love of the sport and to help young people.

His coaching paid off. At the Rome Olympics in 1960, Rudolph became the fastest woman in the world. She won three gold medals in one Olympics, the first American woman to do so. She won the 100 m dash, the 200 m dash, and ran the anchor leg of the 400 m relay team. She wrote an autobiography, *Wilma*, which NBC used as the basis of a film about her life.

Rudolph died much too young, succumbing to brain cancer at age fifty-four in 1994. She advised other young athletes to be themselves and to have confidence. The triumph can't be had without the struggle, she said.

44. RUETTIGER, RUDY

AFTER GRADUATING FROM HIGH SCHOOL, RUDY
worked at a power plant, then joined the navy, and then
went back to the power plant. But all the while he had a
powerful dream: more than anything, he wanted to attend
Notre Dame and play varsity football. When an industrial
accident killed his best friend, he realized how short life
was, how fragile, how abruptly it could end. Ruettiger was
galvanized into action. At twenty-three, he got into Holy
Cross Junior College in South Bend and worked to qualify
for admittance to Notre Dame. He devoted himself to his
studies and worked as a groundskeeper at Notre Dame's
Knute Rockne Stadium.

Rudy soon discovered he suffered from a mild case of
dyslexia and learned to compensate for it. His grades
improved. After several rejections, he was finally accepted by Notre Dame. He tried out for football and won a
spot on the scout team. (The varsity uses the scout team
to practice against; they replicate the opponent's plays).
His goal, however, was not just to practice—he wanted
to play for the Fighting Irish in a real game.

Over the next two years, Ruettiger won the respect of
his teammates and coaches with his overachieving zeal
and hard-hitting play. As a result, during the last moments
of his last home game, he was sent into the game, where
he sacked the Georgia Tech quarterback. The fans went

wild. When the game ended, Ruettiger's victorious team-mates carried him off the field on their shoulders.

45. SELES, MONICA

ON APRIL 30, 1993, WORLD NO. 1 TENNIS STAR MONICA Seles, nineteen, was stabbed in the shoulder by deranged spectator Gunther Parch. She spent only two days in the hospital, but the psychological wounds lasted much longer. She had nightmares, mental anguish, depression—all aggravated when the German courts found Parch not guilty in October of that year. Her sponsor, Fila, sued Monica during her convalescence, saying it had lost income due to her time away from the game.

It would take two years of physical and psychological therapy, but Seles came back. She won the 1995 Canadian Open and then the 1996 Australian Open, her fourth Down Under win. Her father and coach, Karoly, contracted cancer and died in 1998, and in a great show of mental resiliency Seles rallied from the loss a few weeks later by winning her way to the French Open final. She competed for the U.S. Fed Cup (the national team female equivalent of the men's Davis Cup) in 1996 and 2000 and won a bronze medal at the 2000 Olympics. She continued competing into the new millennium, sometimes beset by injuries.

Looking back on the tragic stabbing, she told one interviewer she didn't believe in holding onto anger, saying if you're going to be mad, it won't make it better—use the energy to try to solve problems instead.

46. SMYERS, KAREN

CHAMPION TRIATHLETE KAREN SMYERS STARTED 1997 with a couple of early victories, then a freak accident occurred—a piece of glass from a storm window sliced through her hamstring. She was laid up for the season. Not one to miss an opportunity, she and husband Michael executed plan B and Smyers gave birth to a baby girl, Jenna, by C-section in May 1998.

Undaunted by the operation, three months later she was well on her way to a comeback for the end of the 1998 season. Then tragedy struck again: while training for the Ironman, Smyers was hit by an eighteen-wheel truck. She suffered six broken ribs, a lung contusion, and a third-degree shoulder separation. After hospitalization and therapy, she recovered.

But in 1999 came another setback, this one bigger: she was diagnosed with thyroid cancer. She needed surgery, but wanted desperately to compete in her second

Ironman competition just one month away. Since she had a slow-growing type of cancer, her doctor acquiesced to her request for postponement. Smyers competed—and placed second—*with thyroid cancer.*

Then she entered the Ixtapa (Mexico) International Triathlon. During the bicycle phase, a fellow competitor fell directly in her path and she flew over her handlebars, hit the ground, and broke her collarbone. This extremely painful fracture limited her ability to train for months.

So in December 1999, Karen finally had her thyroid surgery. Her thyroid gland and all of the swollen lymph nodes on the left side were removed in a six-hour operation. Fortunately, her tumor proved a papillary cancer, which tends to be more easily contained than other forms of the disease.

Nevertheless, after the operation, the surgeon told Smyers that there was abnormal tissue in her neck and he couldn't be sure that the entire tumor had been removed. A radioiodine scan was needed and required her to quit taking her thyroid hormone, which led her to suffer from body-weakening effects of hypothyroidism. Doctors were concerned about fatigue and cramping from training, but Smyers went ahead and trained without adverse effect. Spoken like a true Ironman, she said: "Exercise actually helped me."

Unfortunately, the new scan showed five or six more lymph nodes that appeared to contain thyroid cancer.

Smyers would need a second operation. As usual, she was thinking of her career. Her collarbone fracture had healed and she was now able to train without pain. Moreover, the Olympic trials were just three weeks off, and she desperately wanted to make the team. Even though she couldn't train properly and was suffering from her illness, Smyers managed to place a heroic seventh in the U.S. Olympic Trials—but she needed to be fourth or better to make the team. It was a disappointment, but one that she would soon enough overcome.

Smyers came back to win the U.S. Triathlon Championship in August 2001 and take second place in the famous Hawaii Ironman Triathlon. Coming back from a cut hamstring, a truck accident, and cancer qualifies Smyers as one of the toughest athletes and competitors in the world.

47. STAUBACH, ROGER

STAUBACH EARNED THE NICKNAME "CAPTAIN Comeback" for leading the Dallas Cowboys to seventeen come-from-behind victories in the last two minutes of the game. Dallas teammate Billy Joe Dupree said admiringly that Staubach never knew when the game was over—a great trait for anyone considering a comeback.

How did he do it? Staubach's main virtue was patience. After winning the Heisman Trophy at the Naval Academy, he honored his commitment to his country and then returned to the game he loved as a twenty-seven-year-old rookie. He was one of the very best pro quarterbacks in the 1970s.

The Cowboys' late, great head coach Tom Landry once said that Staubach might be the best combination of passer, athlete, and leader ever to play in the NFL. Many others rank Staubach alongside Johnny Unitas and Joe Montana as the best quarterbacks in the history of the game.

Staubach Quote:

- "Confidence doesn't come out of nowhere. It's a result of something . . . hours and days and weeks and years of constant work and dedication."

48. TAKACS, KAROLY

IN 1938, HUNGARIAN ARMY SERGEANT KAROLY Takacs was a member of his national pistol shooting team and was looking forward to competing in the 1940 Olympic Games. Then, while on maneuvers, a hand grenade exploded and took Takacs's right hand, his shooting hand.

Severely depressed, he nevertheless began training

again with a pistol, this time using his *left* hand. The Olympics were cancelled in 1940 and 1944 due to the war. But a full ten years later, at the 1948 London Olympic Games, Captain Takacs competed for and won his gold medal for pistol shooting with his left hand.

How? Humility had something to do with it. Before the competition, the favorite in the event asked Takacs why he was in London. "To learn something," he modestly replied. After Takacs won, the same individual, on the medal podium, advised him that he had "learned enough."

49. WARNER, KURT

As a child, Kurt Warner played flag football instead of tackle because his family couldn't afford the equipment. He was switched from his favorite position (receiver to quarterback) in high school. He was an All-State (Iowa) quarterback in high school, but no major school offered him a scholarship.

At the University of Northern Iowa, he sat on the bench three of his four college years, and threw plenty of interceptions when the chance to play did come. He was not drafted by the NFL. The Green Bay Packers offered a tryout and cut him. He wound up stocking shelves at the Hy-Vee supermarket in Cedar Falls, Iowa, for $5.50 an hour.

Still, he dreamed of making a comeback to the NFL. He landed a spot in the arena league with the Des Moines Barnstormers. Warner would later credit arena football—the fast and furious "indoor war," as he called it, played with eight men on just fifty yards—with sharpening his field of vision and the quickness of his release. At the time, however, he was miserable, throwing more than his share of interceptions.

In Warner's last two seasons, he won the arena championship both years, which caught some attention in the NFL. After a tryout for the St. Louis Rams, the team assigned him to its European team, the Amsterdam Admirals. He was promoted to the St. Louis Rams bench, a "good bench," as he put it. From there, he filled in for the injured Trent Green and led the league in passing and the team to a 23–16 Super Bowl triumph over the Tennessee Titans (2000). He was named NFL Most Valuable Player and accorded a $47 million contract. He once told an interviewer that you just never know what a player is all about until he gets in there and gets a chance to play.

50. WEDEMEYER, CHARLIE

MICHIGAN STATE FOOTBALL PLAYER CHARLIE WEDEMEYER made college all-star honors, playing in both the East-West Shrine Classic and the Hula Bowl. After college, he became a high school coach and teacher in Los Gatos, California. He and wife Lucy had a daughter, Carri, and a son, Kale. Life was good.

However, in 1977, at age thirty, he was diagnosed with ALS—Lou Gehrig's disease. The disease kills the nerve cells that control muscles, and there is no known cause or cure. Doctors gave him one to three years to live. But Charlie simply refused to go. As the illness progressed, he could no longer walk, talk, or even breathe without his respirator. He could not carry on the fight alone—he called on God, and found the strength to go on in a new personal relationship with God.

Powered by his new faith, he continued coaching. In 1985, his Los Gatos High School football team won the Central Coast Section Championship, attracting national media attention. How could he do it? Wife Lucy read his lips and conveyed his instructions and plays to the assistant coaches and players.

An active Christian and public speaker with a message of hope and encouragement, Charlie believes God has a plan for his life and everyone else's. The Wedemeyers have traveled to speak in venues as far as

England, Italy, Switzerland, France, and Holland. Charlie met with astrophysicist Stephen Hawking, a fellow ALS survivor (they had tea and crumpets). Similarly, Charlie and Lucy host numerous individuals in their home who travel from all over the world to observe the Wedemeyers' overcoming ways.

Charlie's story was featured in an Emmy-winning PBS documentary, *One More Season*, and a CBS movie, *Quiet Victory—The Charlie Wedemeyer Story* (1988). His own book is *Charlie's Victory*. Charlie says he lives to give others hope. What purpose could be greater?

51. WILLIAMS, TED

"A man has to have goals—for a day, for a lifetime—and that was mine, to have people say, 'There goes Ted Williams, the greatest hitter who ever lived.'"

ONE OF BASEBALL'S GREATEST, TED WILLIAMS PUT UP these lifetime statistics: .344 batting average, 521 home runs, 6 batting titles, 2 Triple Crowns (best batting average, most home runs, RBIs in a season), and 2 Most Valuable Player awards.

One amazing stat usually gets left out, however: he missed nearly *five* full seasons during his prime years to serve in the military. Most experts believe he would have been the first to pass Babe Ruth in home runs but for World War II and the Korean War. In 1942, his final season before enlisting as a Marine Corps fighter pilot, Williams won the Triple Crown. He led the American League in batting (.356), home runs (36), and RBIs (137). Three years of military service followed.

When he returned to Boston for the 1946 season, fans and sportswriters alike wondered how the layoff would affect him. Not much: he batted .342 with 38 homers and 123 RBIs, finishing as runner-up in all three Triple Crown categories.

Williams volunteered again for military duty in the Korean War—he could have stayed home as a World War II vet—and missed most of the 1952 and 1953 seasons. Upon his return in 1954, he batted .345 with 29 homers and 89 RBIs in just 117 games. His incredible eye and exquisite timing seemed immune to layoff, military service, aging, you name it. He won a batting title at age thirty-nine, outhitting a young slugger by the name of Mickey Mantle .388 to .365.

At forty-two, in his final at bat in his home field of Fenway Park, he homered. After two astonishing comebacks and an ending like that, there would be no further comeback, not even to doff his hat to the screaming crowd.

Williams Quotes:
- "God gets you to the plate, but once you're there you're on your own."
- "There's only one way to become a hitter. Go up to the plate and get mad. Get mad at yourself and mad at the pitcher."

52. WOODS, TIGER

CAN YOU MAKE A COMEBACK FROM EXCELLENCE? Tiger Woods did in 1997. He exploded onto the pro golf tour that year; in his first seven months, he won four of fifteen tournaments, earned $1.8 million in prize money, and won some $60 million in endorsement contracts from Nike and Titleist. At the 1997 Masters, his three-hundred-yard drives, spot-on iron shots, and cold-blooded putting dominated the field. He won by twelve strokes. But Woods told friends: "My swing really sucks." He believed he could get better, much better.

He called his coach, Butch Harmon, and said he wanted to tear down and rebuild his swing. Harmon said it could be done, but Woods would have to increase his weightlifting to get stronger, it would take months, and his tournament record would plummet. He outlined a monumentally difficult program of hitting hundreds of balls, watching videotape of the swing, and then repeating the process—over and over and over.

Tactically, he had to restrict his violent hip turn, slow his torso rotation, weaken his grip, turn the back of his hand square to the target, and bow his left grip a nanosecond longer. Sounds simple enough, but the changes were dramatic and risky. Other pros changed their swing—Seve Ballesteros, Chip Beck, Ian Baker-Finch—and their games suffered for it.

Woods decided to take the risk and went to work. He made progress, but it was slow. Just as expected, his rampant winning record on the tour slowed, too. In the nineteen months between July 1997 and February 1999, he won exactly one event.

He was often angry, often frustrated, at the shots that landed in the rough, the press, the fans, and the sponsors. But each time he lost, he said he was a "better golfer" than when he won four tourneys in seven months in early 1997. It's not always about winning, he said.

In May 1999, at a practice session near his home in Orlando, the new swing started to come together. He was able to hit with more power and accuracy with a greater variety of clubs, not every time, but with more and more consistency. After a full two years, Woods knew he had turned the corner.

His next tournament was the 1999 Byron Nelson. He shot an "in-the-zone" sixty-one in the first round and tied for seventh by tourney's end. He was thrilled because his swing felt so good. In the next fourteen events, he won ten, including six in a row! To compare, Jack Nicklaus never won more than three events in a row, and never more than seven tour events in one year.

In the ensuing years, Woods put up similar numbers. He had more than come back; he had attained the new level of performance he had targeted. He was willing to take the risks, work hard, and—something exceedingly difficult for a hypercompetitive athlete—*lose* before he could come back and win consistently.

BUSINESS

53. Amos, Wally "Famous"

"You don't know where the road will lead you, but I can say now that there are no tough times, there are only opportunities to grow."

How bad did it get for this famous but failing cookie entrepreneur? One day while promoting his cookies at an event in Utah, Wally Amos got the news that his repossessed home had been sold at auction. His second company, Wally Amos Presents Chip & Cookie, was failing, just as his first, Famous Amos, had.

It wasn't always this bad. Amos had a long history as a winner. He began his career as a successful William Morris talent agent. He was the first to book Simon & Garfunkel in 1964 and later booked The Supremes on their first tour. In 1968 he struck out on his own as a personal manager. After seven years of ups and downs,

Amos felt as though he still hadn't realized his dreams. He consoled himself by baking rich chocolate-chip cookies and giving them away to his friends. "It was therapy," he says. "I was able to forget about all the bad stuff going on around me."

His friends insisted that the cookies were so good he had to sell them. Wally's Famous Amos cookies spawned not just a new company but a brand-new gourmet cookie industry. Though Amos made the covers of *Time* and *People* in 1977, the company's management team failed and Amos eventually lost control of the company, and even his name! His Uncle Noname debuted in 1993; it eventually morphed into Uncle Wally's, today a $30 million muffin business. Amos is still involved with Uncle Wally's as a shareholder and spokesperson.

The Keebler Company acquired the Famous Amos brand in 1999 and rehired Famous Amos himself to promote it. Amos also gained back the use of his name.

Is he bitter? Not at all. "I thank God for all those experiences, good and bad," he said in a telephone interview from the site of his new venture, a retail cookie store named Chip & Cookie, in Kailua, Hawaii. "You don't know where the road will lead you, but I can say now that there are no tough times, there are only opportunities to grow.'"

Amos says he discovered that you should not get too emotional no matter what's going on around you. Keep feelings of both elation and devastation at bay, or at least well under control, he advises, because life is a continuum, sometimes up, sometimes down, and sometimes sideways. If you get down, he believes the best way to cheer yourself up is to try to cheer somebody else up.

54. ASH, MARY KAY

AFTER HAVING TO TRAIN A MAN WHO WAS PROMOTED to become her supervisor at twice her pay, Mary Kay Ash, forty-five, quit her job—she simply could not accept that God meant for a woman's brain to bring in only fifty cents on the dollar. Ash started to write a book on sales for women. She began with an outline of all the good things she had learned from the companies she had worked for, and she made a list of problems she had faced and how to overcome them. She got to thinking that instead of putting all this hard-won know-how into a book, what if someone put it all into a real company. Wouldn't that be great?

Great, indeed. Deciding that there was no one more qualified for the job, Ash founded the Mary Kay cosmetics company in 1963 with $5,000 in savings and her No. 1 asset: creativity. She was determined to give women the ultimate opportunity to promote themselves: no ceilings, glass or otherwise, and no bosses. For her first product she reformulated a skin cream from a leather tannery. The products weren't new, but the way she treated her sales force would be.

Mary Kay sold nearly $200,000 worth of products in the first year. The concept caught on and the company grew exponentially; just five years after its founding, the company went public. Eventually, the Mary Kay sales force would number more than 800,000 people covering thirty-seven markets on five continents. *Fortune* magazine would cite the company as one of "The 100 Best Companies to Work for in America" and one of the ten best companies for women.

Believing in the power of setting goals, Ash famously awarded pink Cadillacs to her top producers. She believed a mediocre idea (another skin cream) that generates enthusiasm will go farther than a great idea that inspires no one, and it surely did. A master psychologist, she also believed in sandwiching every slice of criticism between two thick layers of praise.

55. CARNEGIE, DALE

AS A YOUNG MAN, DALE CARNEGIE ATTEMPTED TO support himself as a motortruck salesperson and despised it, calling himself one of the unhappiest young men in New York. He said he didn't know what made motortrucks run, and furthermore, he didn't want to know. He hated not only trucks but sales itself, his living quarters on West Fifty-sixth Street, the restaurants he ate in, his whole life. He had spent four years studying teaching at State Teachers College, in Warrensburg, Missouri, and in his heart, he wanted to become a public speaker, a writer, a teacher.

So he did something about it. He solicited prestigious Columbia University, then New York University, with offers to teach, but, no surprise, the venerable institutions turned him down. He did find an open door, however: the humble New York City YMCA. The YMCA let him teach adult night classes in 1912. He later credited these unprepossessing origins with his success, saying that he had to be very practical and elicit concrete results from his students, and fast, if he wanted to eat. From his experiences in these classes, Carnegie would ultimately write and publish *How to Win Friends and Influence People* (1930). The book enjoyed immediate success and remains an all-time bestseller. Many volumes followed. Today, Dale Carnegie programs in self-improvement and performance flourish in some eighty nations around the world.

56. CLARK, JIM

JIM CLARK KNOWS WHAT IT'S LIKE TO BE BOTH THE LOW man and the high man on the totem pole. He learned that something so seemingly small as a single decision can catalyze traversing the distance from bottom to top.

Clark's story goes like this: his father abandoned the family, and Clark grew up in poverty. He dropped out of high school just before his senior year to join the navy. Accused of cheating on a placement exam (he didn't), he was shipped out to sea. Onboard, he was bullied, humiliated, and told he was stupid. After the nine-month voyage, he came back into port and took another test, this time, math aptitude. He scored off the charts. An instructor advised Clark to take night classes in math at Tulane University. Eight years later, Clark had a bachelor's degree, a master's degree in physics, and a PhD in computer science.

What pushed him on? Clark says he was motivated by revenge for the injustices he suffered at the hands of officers and bullies. He wanted to make something of himself and prove them wrong. Still, the years following were unsettled. He was married more than once, became a father, and moved around the country frequently. He was fired from the New York Institute of Technology in 1978 for insubordination. He wife left him, saying she wanted a more settled life. He was thirty-eight, and it was the last straw.

For the next year and a half, Clark was deeply depressed. He spent six months in counseling, and then stopped abruptly when he realized it wasn't helping. After telling himself he could go as low as he wished, and realizing he didn't want to go any lower, he made the decision to change, to go from failure to success. He gave himself permission to succeed, to make a comeback.

Clark's next post was at Stanford, and something was different about him—he was attracting the best graduate students to his projects. Clark invented a new chip that transformed the world of computer graphics from two dimensions to three, which revolutionized the art and science of car and aircraft design, virtual-reality games, and Hollywood animation. The chip became the center-piece of Clark's new company, Silicon Graphics Inc. (SGI), which attracted the crème de la crème of engineers. The computers the company produced were expensive, $70,000 and up, but there was a market for them and Silicon Graphics did well. The trouble was that the venture capitalists who had invested in the company made most of the profits, and Clark and his engineers made much less by comparison. Clark eventually lost control of the company, something he took personally.

Taking his rage and turning it into something positive, Clark went on to found a new company and make his real fortune (nearly $2 billion), many times his take from Silicon Graphics. He partnered with Marc

Andreessen, the University of Illinois computer guru who had written the Mosaic program—the original Internet browser. Until then, Clark had been focusing on an idea called the telecomputer. Clark told Andreessen that he felt this concept was ahead of its time and too expensive to build. Andreessen casually said that with twenty-five million people using "the Internet," they were guaranteed a market if they built a better browser. In that moment the company Netscape was born in the minds of its founders.

Andreessen gathered his programming buddies, and they went to work creating the new browser. Shares in the new company were sold to an eager investment community. This time Clark made Wall Street work *for* him, not against him. The high school dropout and naval grunt had become a leader of the Internet revolution, and one of the *Forbes* 400 Richest Americans.

Postscript: Clark's revenge on the venture capitalists who wronged him at Silicon Graphics precluded them from investing in Netscape. One such was Glenn Mueller, who bought a large share in Silicon Graphics early on for a song. Clark harbored resentments at what he perceived as an injustice to him and his engineers. Nevertheless, Mueller, realizing Clark was on to something big, called Clark repeatedly to ask for the opportunity to invest in the new Netscape before the public offering. Clark turned him down each time. On April 4,

1994, the day Netscape was incorporated and went from $12 per share to $48 (and later to $140), Mueller killed himself with a shot to the head.

57. COOK, MARK D.

BEFORE HE BECAME A STOCK MARKET WIZARD, MARK D. Cook went spectacularly bankrupt. He lost $800,000 in one trade, in one day: $500,000 of his own hard-earned cash, and $300,000 from relatives. Staggered by the loss, he stopped trading for two years and spent five years working two jobs to pay it back. In the third year he resumed trading but only broke even. Same for the next year.

But Cook persisted and finally made a profit in the fifth year after the debacle. How? He discovered a new trading signal, the cumulative tick indicator. It led to consistent triple-digit profitability. Several other new approaches followed, and Cook realized his dream of making consistent, serious money from the markets. He had gone from being nearly $1 million in the hole to becoming one of the top traders in the financial industry. Though the common perception is that there is easy money to be made in the markets, Cook offers no easy path for those wishing to follow in his footsteps: when asked, he tells inquirers it takes three to five years of twelve-hour days, and losing, not making, money to learn to become successful in the financial markets. Not what most want to hear, he says.

58. DAVIS, CLIVE

CLIVE DAVIS EVENTUALLY BECAME THE ÉMINENCE grise and grand old man of the record industry, but he walked across some hot coals to get there. In 1973, he was fired from the top post at CBS Records. He was charged with using corporate funds to pay for an apartment renovation and his son's bar mitzvah. These accusations ultimately proved false, but still, the damage was done—his reputation was tarnished and no one would hire him. Since Davis could get work nowhere else, in 1974 he founded Arista Records, which soon began producing platinum records with acts like the Grateful Dead, Barry Manilow, Aretha Franklin, Kenny G, Whitney Houston, and Santana. Many years of success followed. Along the way, BMG acquired Arista.

Despite producing hits with uncanny regularity and outsize sales (Santana's 1999 comeback album sold twenty-five million copies), when his contract was up in 2000, BMG decided to replace the sixty-eight-year-old Davis. He was apparently "too old."

Retirement? Not for Davis. He started another new

record company, J Records (after his middle initial) in the same year. The parting with BMG wasn't entirely acrimonious—the corporate parent invested $150 million in the new company and got half ownership. In his trademark way, Davis ferreted out new stars such as Alicia Keys (whose debut album sold ten million copies). Besides discovering talented young singers, Davis had the ability to take something old and make it new, like Rod Stewart's romantic ballads album, a successful comeback effort by the aging rocker. He went on to sign forty other artists.

Soon, BMG realized that losing Davis was a huge mistake. To get him back to run its flagging RCA label, it paid another $100 million to buy out J Records in 2002. Davis became head of RCA in 2003 and chairman and chief executive officer of BMG North America in 2004—which put him back in charge of Arista, his baby.

Now extremely rich, Davis still maintained a more or less round-the-clock schedule at the office and concert hall. Many of his troops were less than half his age. But Clive says age doesn't really matter because they all share a passion for music. It was that very passion that sustained him through all the years in the up-and-down business of pop music.

59. DEEN, PAULA

SOME FAMILIES GENERATE MORE OPPOSITION TO ONE another than support. When Paula Deen hatched a plan to start a sandwich-delivery business, she telephoned her grandmother to share the idea and maybe get some much-needed support. She described her plan in great detail and got nothing back but silence. Finally, her grandmother asked if she had lost her mind.

Deen laughs about it now on her Food Network television show, but it had to hurt. She was already hurting plenty, looking for a way to support herself after a divorce from her spouse of twenty-seven years. She had $200, a name for her business—The Bag Lady—and a dream. That was it. It would be enough to get her started and, as the old saying goes, a good start can be half the trip.

Why a sandwich business, of all things? Deen had some cooking talent, her grandmother's recipes, and the willingness to work very hard. So she began on June 19, 1989, a second birthday of sorts, she says. She launched the grills at midnight and smoked pork butt all night. She was in her kitchen before 5 a.m. to prepare the sandwiches. When they were all ready, her sons, Jamie and Bobby, packed the meals on ice and delivered them all over Savannah, Georgia.

Deen took on another job managing a restaurant in a Best Western in addition to this daunting routine. She worked sixteen-hour days, seven days a week, for five years, gaining experience that would prove invaluable, while saving her money to open her own restaurant.

She opened The Lady & Sons on January 8, 1996, and kept working just as hard, if not harder. Good things kept happening. For example, Deen compiled a cookbook to sell in her restaurant. She saved $20,000 and used it to print five thousand copies. Just days after they were delivered, a rainstorm drove a tourist inside. This accidental tourist had a great lunch, and was motivated to buy a cookbook. A publishing professional, she knew she was onto something. Her company bought the book rights and rolled it out to a national audience. Then television shopping network QVC invited her on as a guest, and she sold more than seventy thousand books in that single visit. Deen was getting famous.

Another one-on-one encounter yielded outstanding results: when the *USA Today* food editor ate at Deen's restaurant, he was transported—it was his most memorable meal of 1999, he wrote.

Today, with her own show on the Food Network, Deen is a certified food star. Her website shows a picture of her with former President Carter (autographed "with love to Paula"), under the tab "here we are." Here we are, indeed—and all because she refused to settle for a miserable, loveless life and was willing to work very hard. That, and one other important thing: she didn't let her grandmother's remonstrance dissuade her from her dream.

60. Dychtwald, Ken

In his 1977 book *Bodymind*, self-help impresario Ken Dychtwald said that seniors could control their health with yoga. He was thirty-seven. But at age fifty, his own cholesterol level hit 440.

In his 1989 bestseller *Age Wave*, Dychtwald warned baby boomers that they were not investing wisely for retirement. Shortly after, he lost $20 million in a failed business venture.

Dychtwald then decided to take his *own* advice and pay attention to what matters most—health and family. With exercise and medication, he lost weight and dropped his cholesterol level to 130. He took more vacations to create better balance in his life: river rafting through the Grand Canyon with his ten-year-old son and exploring New York with his thirteen-year-old daughter. He renewed marriage vows with his wife, Maddy. With his own life in order now, Dychtwald writes about national issues that need attention, such as Social Security in his 1999 book *Age Power*. He brings the same thoughtful approach to the need to stay active after retirement in his 2005 book *The Power Years: A User's Guide to the Rest of Your Life*.

61. GARDNER, CHRIS

AS AN ADULT, CHRIS GARDNER SEEMED TO BE ON the terra firma after a childhood of horrors. He had seen his mother spend time in prison, been abused by his stepfather, and was raped by a gang leader (who he later paid back by hitting him in the head with a cinder block).

After a stint in the Navy, he was working as a medical supply salesmen, earning a $30,000 salary and supporting his girlfriend and son. Things were looking up. Life, as they say, was good.

Then he made an encounter with the owner of a red Ferrari in a parking lot that turned his life upside down. Gardner was dazzled by the car, the man, the lifestyle. Striking up a conversation, he learned he was a stockbroker, earning $80,000 a month. Gardner had little concept of what a stockbroker was or did, but the rewards were enough: he resolved to become one himself.

Not long after, a loud argument with his girlfriend brought the police to his door. They checked his record and found $1,200 of outstanding parking tickets. He didn't have the $1,200 to settle the matter, so he spent ten days in the slammer. When he got out, his girlfriend and son were gone.

But his dream—he still had that. So he got himself a job as a stockbroker trainee, even though it paid a pittance. He found a place to live in a boarding house.

His girlfriend and son turned up there some months later. She didn't want the baby anymore. The boarding house wouldn't permit children, so the new father-son team were soon homeless. Some nights they stayed in cheap motels, some nights under his desk at work, some nights in Bay Area Rapid Transit (BART) washrooms. It was a crushing responsibility in every way, and a humiliating lifestyle, but Gardener wouldn't relent. When he was a child, being abused himself, he had promised himself he would do a better job as a father, if given the chance.

Eventually Gardner and son found a place to live in a hotel for the homeless operated by Glide Memorial United Methodist Church. Day care took a huge chunk of his earnings, but Gardner stuck with his son, and his promise, and mastered his job.

He mastered the financial trade so well, in fact, that in 1987, he opened his own investment brokerage firm in Chicago. The formerly homeless man was now wealthy, with three homes, plus numerous artifacts of success: a desk made from a DC-10 tail wing, African art, Muhammad Ali-autographed boxing gloves, and much more.

He tells his story in *The Pursuit of Happyness*; Will Smith starred in the film version (2006).

His fame and fortune brought him into contact with world leaders like Nelson Mandela. When Gardner met him in Africa, the icon said: "Welcome home, son." Those words closed and healed a gaping hole in his heart that had been there since he was an abused little child.

"It's the journey," he told ABC News in advance of the movie debut. "As Maya Angelou said, 'I wouldn't take nothing for my journey now.'"

62. GATES, BILL

MAKING A PRODUCT IS NOT SO HARD, BUT GETTING paid is another matter—a common plight among entrepreneurs. Some young companies go out of business over accounts receivable alone, but not this one. Microsoft started out quite modestly by making software for hobbyists. In December 1974, Paul Allen, who was working at Honeywell near Boston, showed Bill Gates a *Popular Mechanics* magazine featuring a $397 computer kit that a hobbyist could build. There was a glaring lack for this product, however: software. Gates and Allen contacted the company that made the kit, MITS, and said they had software for the new computer (they didn't).

But after working more or less day and night for eight weeks, they *did* produce a version of BASIC and showed their work to the company. MITS liked what it saw and contracted for more. Gates dropped out of Harvard, and the pair moved to New Mexico to be near their client and start what would become Microsoft.

The young Micro-soft (they later dropped the hyphen) added five clients in the early days, but they all went bankrupt. Things were shaky, but Gates and crew pressed on. Sometimes it takes a change of scenery to right the ship, and so it was with Microsoft—in 1979 the company moved to Seattle to more easily attract programmers.

The next year, in 1980, IBM commissioned Gates to provide an operating system for its first personal computer. Instead of building one from scratch, he purchased a system called QDOS (Quick and Dirty Operating System) for $50,000 from another company. He changed the name to MS-DOS, and licensed it to IBM.

The IBM personal computer was a success. Licensing fees for the operating system flowed to Microsoft and ensured the company's survival. Eventually, Microsoft would surpass IBM, becoming more than twice its size.

Gates showed that if you can find a way to survive the lean times, you put yourself in position for the better times. First survive, and then triumph.

63. IACOCCA, LEE

AFTER THIRTY-TWO SUCCESSFUL YEARS AS PRESIDENT of Ford Motor Company, Lee Iacocca's conflicts with heir and chairman Henry Ford II got him fired. Even though he knew it was coming, his pride was wounded, he was hurting, and he could have used a supportive phone call from one of his former colleagues. But no one contacted him. He said it was the greatest shock of his life—not the firing, the ostracism.

His wife, Mary, opined that his being fired might be for the best; she had no way of knowing how prophetic her optimistic words were to be. Iacocca, then fifty-four, had the good sense to find a new job quickly to redeploy his anger and emotion into productive action. He assumed the presidency of bankrupt Chrysler in 1979.

For the next ten years, through budget cuts, layoffs, hard-sell advertising, and a government loan guarantee, Iacocca rebuilt and pulled Chrysler from the jaws of death—creating one of the greatest comebacks in U.S. corporate history. In 2005, Iacocca came out of retirement to appear in Chrysler advertisements, reprising the slogan: "If you can find a better car, buy it."

64. JOBS, STEVE

W HEN STEVE JOBS GOT KICKED OUT OF APPLE, THE company he founded, he described it as being punched in the stomach, getting the wind knocked out of him, and not being able to breathe.

The firing was not "just business" either—it was personal. He was ousted by the man he had hired to run the company, John Sculley, former president of Pepsi. While recruiting him, Jobs threw down the gauntlet by asking Sculley if he wanted to "sell sugar water" the rest of his life or change the way people live and work. Phrased this way, Sculley could not turn down the challenge; he came to run Apple in 1983.

By 1985, the relationship had gone south. In July of that year, Sculley told security analysts that Jobs would have no role in the operations of the company "now or in the future." It was the coup de grâce.

Bitter, angry, and defeated, Jobs sold more than $20 million of his Apple stock. Still feeling lost and betrayed, he tried to relax, to get his breath back, so to speak. The digital genius spent time bicycling along the beach and toured Paris and Italy.

After some six weeks of this respite from the corporate grind, Jobs felt a little better. He started getting out. He had lunch with Paul Berg, a Nobel laureate in biochemistry at Stanford University. Berg talked about the time-consuming trial-and-error methodology he used to analyze DNA. Jobs suggested computer simulation to speed things up. Berg said that the necessary computers and software were not available. He said it to the right person.

Fueled with this new vision and playing off his strengths and interests, Jobs created NeXT, a computer company that manufactured workstations and developed the NextStep operating system. Its computers were chic, expensive black boxes that stood out against the beige PC world. The new operating system featured "object-oriented programming," allowing developers to more easily write programs. The company launched in 1986 (the same year Jobs bought the graphics division of Lucasfilm for $10 million and named it Pixar), and sold its first PCs for $10,000 in 1988. The company had its partisans (educators and financial engineers loved it), but it was a mixed success. Still, the company was successful enough that Apple bought it for $400 million in 1996; Apple also got Jobs as interim chief executive officer in the deal.

Sculley had gotten the boot in 1993, and on his comeback at the helm of the company he founded, Jobs was vastly more successful. He introduced new products such as the iMac, the iBook, and the blockbuster iPod. These successes cemented his appointment. Apple shares went from $7 in 2003 to $97 in early 2007, defying the bear market in the NASDAQ and tech world.

John Sculley? After leaving Apple, he worked variously in politics, business, and consulting, never achieving the same prominence he enjoyed while at Apple.

Jobs enlarged his already-mythic status in the tech world by leading tech giants Apple and Pixar. Disney announced plans to acquire Pixar in 2006, and Jobs became Disney's largest shareholder (6 percent). His iPod achieved success in consumer electronics that had eluded the popular but niched Macintosh line. He had avenged his painful ouster personally and in the marketplace and achieved one of the most amazing comebacks in business history, not to mention another type of comeback in 2004 from a rare but treatable form of cancer. How did Jobs do it, create products that were, in his words, "insanely great"? He says creativity is really the business of connecting things, of seeing and synthesis. This ability to connect comes from more thinking or more experience. He also said that design wasn't something you put on top of a product but its "fundamental soul."

65. KROC, RAY

EARLY ON, LIFE WAS ALWAYS MORE OR LESS A STRUGGLE for Ray Kroc. He began his career at age twenty selling paper cups. To make ends meet, he also moonlighted as a jazz pianist.

In 1937, at age thirty-five, he met Earl Prince, the inventor of the Multimixer five-spindle milk shake mixer. Kroc invested his life savings for the exclusive marketing rights to the mixer and spent the next seventeen years distributing it across the country, working through a sales representative network. Grinding it out like countless road warriors, Kroc nevertheless found himself $100,000 in debt. Not the way business is supposed to go: you're supposed to make money, not lose it.

But the information he picked up from his sales representative network would prove invaluable. Kroc kept hearing about his customers, Maurice and Richard McDonald, and their use of his mixers.

The more he heard about them, the more curious he became. Why were customers always mentioning the McDonalds? Turns out the brothers were running *eight* high-end $150 mixers in their hamburger and shake drive-in in the quiet desert town of San Bernardino, California. Kroc went there to see it for himself: a small-ish operation on two hundred square feet out in the desert, but with a humming assembly line, producing hamburgers and shakes at high speed, serving thousands. He realized this was a format that could be replicated.

Kroc, now fifty-two, struck a franchise deal. A close business associate, his then wife, and others thought he had gone "soft in the head," as one put it. But Kroc had no time for them. He had a new vision and plunged into the work he had to do to realize it. The first McDonald's franchise restaurant opened in Des Plaines, Illinois, in April 1955. Opening-day sales: $366.12.

Kroc had found his gold mine. Within another ten years, he was a millionaire.

Today, McDonald's Corporation operates in more than 120 nations around the world and is a member of the Dow Jones industrials, with a market capitalization of more than $50 billion. Kroc changed the way people eat and provided employment for millions.

It took Kroc twenty-seven years to go from selling blenders and racking up debt to his first McDonald's million. He surely paid his dues. Always down to earth, Kroc once said that creativity was a highfalutin word for all the work he had to do between now and next Tuesday. He said success requires two things: being in the right place at the right time and doing something about it.

66. KUDLOW, LARRY

In the early 1990s, Larry Kudlow was a prince of Wall Street. He was chief economist at Bear Stearns, earning a seven-figure salary, in demand, and jetting around the world. But, on his own time, he was binging on cocaine and alcohol. When he started missing work (he once failed to appear before a particularly important luncheon with two hundred institutional clients), he and his employer parted ways.

His wife got him booked into the noted rehab center Hazelden in Center City, Minnesota. Kudlow stayed six months. He was told to stay away from television and out of New York for one year. Following orders, he accepted a position in San Diego, but he was still a nervous wreck. He hit another car head-on, flew through the windshield of his used VW, and was in a coma for days. Doctors thought he wouldn't make it.

Attention to things spiritual aided his recovery. Raised as a Jew, Kudlow's last visit to synagogue had been for his bar mitzvah at thirteen (he was now forty-two), but at this time, he turned to Christianity for solace. He says simply that it worked for him from the first time he set foot in mass. A baptism service in the fall of 1997 at St. Thomas More church on New York's Upper East Side made it official.

About the same time, quietly and modestly, his

career was taking a renewed turn upward. After attending a planning meeting for the Republican National Convention and meeting with a warm response—especially from Representative John Kasich—doors began to open for him. He was offered writing assignments and a post at American Skandia as chief economist. He moved from job to job over the next decade, finally landing in his most high-profile slot with a regular program on CNBC, the perfect platform to air his bullish, pro-business views. Friends describe him as more mellow, graceful, and comfortable in his own skin than he's ever been. Kudlow, somewhat more modestly, was quoted as saying his own goal is to maintain his recovery, day by day.

67. RESNICK, JUDY

"Even I could do that."

WHEN JUDY RESNICK'S FATHER PASSED ON IN 1977, the floor dropped out from beneath her. All her life her father had taken care of her; but now she had nowhere to turn. Resnick grew up in a wealthy family—her father owned several bowling alleys in Los Angeles. She married and divorced young, but not to worry: Dad paid the bills.

Until he died, that is. He had left her 5 percent of the game-machine business in one bowling alley, but his partners stopped paying her income from it, leaving Resnick without cash flow. A few months later, another devastation struck: her sister and mother were killed in a plane crash.

Resnick started looking for work. With no experience, not even the ability to type, she was not in great demand, to put it mildly. But she had one asset: an interest in financial markets. Even that was borne of misfortune—her broker had lost the small stake Resnick had entrusted with him. However, she noticed that while she lost money, the broker made money from commissions. She thought, "Even I could do that."

That observation would be the seed for something greater, much greater. She began looking for work at a brokerage house. Merrill Lynch said no. Shearson said no. She met a woman broker at Drexel Burnham Lambert through a friend. After one interview at the Los Angeles office, an office manager said she wasn't sure what Resnick had, but she had something, and she would take a chance on her. Resnick got a trainee position.

Resnick made a list of everyone she knew and unabashedly called them. Then she got lists of people she didn't know and cold-called them. Selling mostly Treasury bonds and municipal bonds, she earned $106,000—her first year!

A star was born. By her third year Resnick was one of the top women brokers in the firm, and in her best year, she earned $750,000. When she handled a small high-yield bond trade for a regional Florida brokerage, she realized she could create a dealer desk and give small institutional investors the benefit of Drexel's expertise.

She suggested the idea to bond king Michael Milken; two weeks later he transferred her from Drexel's retail side to work on the institutional side. In 1988, she sold more than $200 million in high-yield bonds directly to institutions. Not long after, Milken went to prison for violations of securities laws. When Resnick was pushed by firm management to sell bonds of dubious quality (like Eastern Airlines bonds that were trading at seventy-five cents but eventually fell to zero), she quit.

Resnick and Drexel colleague Neil Dabney set up their own firm in Beverly Hills in 1989. Success came quickly; within just four months, they had paid off their bank loans.

The junk bond market tanked just after they set up shop. While the media was screaming, "Sell!" Resnick was advising clients to buy at the bargain prices. When the bonds recouped, the returns were phenomenal: 30 percent to 40 percent by the early 1990s.

Resnick was named Los Angeles Entrepreneur of the Year in 1994. The award was sponsored, in part, by

Merrill Lynch, one of the companies that had originally turned her down for a job. She wrote about her experiences in 1998's *I've Been Rich, I've Been Poor, Rich Is
Better*. The first chapter is titled "I'm on My Own and
So Are You"—something everyone who has made a
comeback knows through and through.

68. SANDERS, COLONEL HARLAND

WHEN INTERSTATE 75 APPEARED AND BYPASSED HIS
Corbin, Kentucky, restaurant, Colonel Sanders knew it was
all over. He auctioned off his equipment, paid his bills, and
retired penniless at sixty-five. He got his first Social
Security check for $105, too small to live on even in 1955!

This was a crushing blow to his ego and his pocket-
book; in times past, the Colonel had been a successful,
celebrated restaurateur.

When his father, who was a coal miner, passed away,
Sanders took up cooking at age six to help his mother
and feed his siblings. It was his mother who taught him
to cook fried chicken. In 1929, at thirty-nine, he opened
a gas station and small restaurant in Corbin. His cooking grew so popular that he decided to open Sanders
Café. In 1935, Governor Ruby Laffoon made Sanders,
forty-five, a Kentucky Colonel because of his cooking

prowess. By 1939, with the invention of the pressure cooker, he had discovered a method for cooking his signature fried chicken even faster, seasoned with his "secret blend of eleven herbs and spices." The same year his establishment was listed in Duncan Hines's *Adventures in Good Eating*.

So the proud man with the history of hardship, hard work, and success went back to work at age sixty-five to franchise his popular fried chicken recipe. He prayed to God for help, assuring him that if things worked out he would get his share. Not a fancy prayer, he recalled, just an honest one.

Sanders drove from restaurant to restaurant, cooking batches of chicken for restaurant owners and their employees. If they liked it, he shook hands on a deal of a nickel payment to him for each chicken the restaurant sold.

It was a tough life for Sanders. Sometimes a prospect would invite Sanders for a meal, and he was glad to get the food. Other times, he'd say good-night to his host, fumble around in his car until the host was gone, and then settle into the backseat for a night's sleep.

By 1957, after the first two years, Sanders had sold just five franchises. With such a tepid response, most people would have quit, but Sanders, in his trademark white suit, pushed on. By 1960, he had sold two hundred franchises, and six hundred by 1963. He served each franchisee personally. At home, he would mix the spices, pack them in cellophane bags, and his wife, Claudia, would ship them to franchisees. In some ways, it was like a home business, but the concept was right, and it was growing.

In 1964, the seventy-four-year-old Colonel sold the company to an investor group for $2 million and a lifetime yearly salary of $40,000. Kentucky Fried Chicken was listed on the New York Stock Exchange on January 16, 1969. Until he passed away at age ninety, Colonel Sanders traveled 250,000 miles a year visiting the KFC empire he founded. He said that hard work and a positive attitude beat all the tonics and vitamins in the world. The Colonel's secret recipe is kept locked in a safe in Louisville, Kentucky, according to company officials. Sanders today remains one of the most recognizable figures in the world.

69. SOROS, GEORGE

As a young man, George Soros failed to find success in many jobs, including dishwasher, house painter, busboy, and lifeguard. He was fired from a mannequin fabricating workshop (he failed to attach the wigs properly) and from a fancy restaurant (he dropped food on a customer). The headwaiter told Soros that, if he worked hard, he might one day end up as his assistant. Soros just did not seem to fit in anywhere. He said that wherever he had worked he felt like a fifth wheel.

He eventually found his way into the financial field, where, even in his chosen field, he was something of a misfit. Soros says he never actually learned to analyze a company in the conventional way. He took an exam for a security analysis certificate and failed each section.

He did find his niche, however: currency trading. He became famous for making $1 billion by betting on the devaluation of the pound sterling in 1992. (He is called the "man who broke the Bank of England.") Soros would go on to amass an estimated $7 billion fortune. Considered a contrarian maverick, he disdained the conventional wisdom of Wall Street, relying instead on his prodigious intuition.

70. TRUMP, DONALD

IN 1990, REAL ESTATE VALUES FELL HARD, AND Donald Trump's $1.7 billion empire plummeted in value. Trump owed much more on his properties than they were worth: his net worth fell to negative $900 million. Bankruptcy was straight ahead, inconceivable for this Wharton School–trained success icon.

Trump made a decision to fight back. First, he needed more time and new financing. He lined up some ninety banks from around the world for new credit lines to forestall the crisis. Timing is everything: Trump believes that if he had waited just another six months, when everyone else was seeking financing, he would have been in the back of the line to see the bankers, not the front, and he would have been wiped out. By seeking assistance early, he averted the crisis and got the time needed to work out his problems. By 1997, the year his book *Art of the Comeback* was published, Trump was reported to be worth nearly $2 billion. Trump cited passion as the key ingredient to achieving success, passion about who you are, who you are trying to become, and where you are going.

71. TURNER, TED

IN MARCH 1963, AFTER A TWO-YEAR BATTLE WITH depression, Ted Turner's father, Ed, had breakfast, went into the bathroom, and shot himself in the head. Ted, twenty-four, was devastated. After a childhood stained by a complex, difficult relationship with his dominating father, Turner was now without the one person he most wanted to impress, the man he still called his best friend.

In the weeks following, Turner was roiled but able to work. He put grief aside, head down, and plowed forward. He was a rising sales star in his dad's Savannah, Georgia, billboard company, and under his management, profitability increased and expansion followed. In 1970, he bought one of Atlanta's independent television stations, Channel 17. It was losing $500,000 a year, but Turner had a vision.

Creating the first "superstation," Turner broadcast the signal to cable operators. In 1976, Turner purchased the Atlanta Braves baseball and the Hawks basketball teams and broadcast their games. He established the Cable News Network (CNN) in 1980, and Headline News followed in 1982. With a bigger audience, he earned higher advertising revenues. By 1985, the Turner Broadcasting System (TBS) reached 80 percent of U.S. homes who subscribed to cable. He sold the company to Time Warner for $7.5 billion in stock in 1995. Turner responded to his father's tragic death and a lifelong desire to win his acceptance by building one of the largest and most successful media companies in the world.

Flashback: As a young man Turner was a passionate sailor, and he skippered a victory in the 1977 America's Cup onboard his yacht *Tenacious*. Leading in the 1979 Fastnet Race, off the shores of Great Britain, he encountered a vicious Force 10 gale that turned the sea into mountains of waves. Of 306 contestants, 69 did not finish the race, 23 ships were abandoned, and worst, 19 sailors perished. The winner: Turner's *Tenacious*. During the storm, he said, his only thoughts were of winning.

FILM, TELEVISION, AND SHOW BUSINESS

72. BALL, LUCILLE

THEIR TWO BUSY SHOW BUSINESS CAREERS LEFT little time for each other, and Lucille Ball's marriage to Desi Arnaz was on the rocks. To save it, Lucy thought they should work together. She proposed pairing up for a television comedy, but CBS network executives gave a flat-out no to the idea—some thought the public was not ready for a Latino in a domestic role (one account has studio execs and sponsors put off by his Cuban accent, as well as his drumming and singing; another account cites, less oblique-ly, racial prejudice), and others thought Lucy too glam-orous to be accepted as a housewife. So Lucy devised her own solution: Arnaz and Ball would go on a nationwide tour with their vaudeville act to prove that audiences liked them. Lucy reasoned that if no one would give them a job together, they could create one themselves. She kept her tel-evision dream alive, too. When their tour proved successful, the couple put together their own television pilot, which they were willing to finance themselves ($19,000 for a kinescope, which CBS eventually paid for). Persuaded by the national tour, the pilot, and Lucy's relentless hounding, the network agreed to give their TV show a try.

I Love Lucy premiered on October 15, 1951. It was an immediate hit, and Ball was vindicated. The show ran for six years and was always in the top three in the Nielsen ratings. Eventually the show won more than two hundred awards, including five Emmys. The program that almost never was became a television classic and now runs endlessly in syndication. Ball said her secret throughout the whole ordeal was to keep busy to ward off discouragement and to make optimism a way of life.

73. BURNS, GEORGE

The 1930s were a golden age for Hollywood, and for comedian George Burns. Burns made fourteen films in the thirties, but then a dry stretch as big as the Sahara followed. He didn't make a single film for thirty-seven years. Hollywood just wasn't calling. However, Burns kept working wherever he could, making appearances on radio and television and in Las Vegas.

Then Burns received an offer to appear in *The Sunshine Boys* (1975). He won an Oscar for his performance at age eighty. Suddenly popular again, he followed his Oscar-winning performance with *Oh, God!* (1977), *Going in Style* (1979), and *Oh, God! You Devil* (1984), among other films. Burns kept working until he was ninety-eight, and a few weeks after turning one hundred, he passed away. But with his great comeback in film and renewed and expanded popularity at such an advanced age, he was able to give an Oscar-worthy performance, if you will, in the real-life business of aging gracefully. His strategy was to keep working, never quit. One of his favorite quips was that he considered retirement at sixty-five ridiculous. When he was sixty-five, he said, he still had pimples.

74. CARNEY, ART

ART CARNEY FIRST ACHIEVED FAME AS NORTON ON Jackie Gleason's *The Honeymooners* (1955–56). After that show's success, however, Carney hit a rough patch. Working on Broadway as Felix Ungar in Neil Simon's *The Odd Couple* (1965), depressed over the end of his marriage, and weighed down with drinking and drugs, he suffered a nervous breakdown and entered a mental health facility just a few days short of his forty-seventh birthday.

When he left the institution the following year, Carney rejoined Jackie Gleason on Gleason's television variety series and stayed on for the next four years. The welcoming gesture from his former acting partner proved to be an emotional life preserver. He returned to Broadway in 1969 in the comedy *Lovers*, which garnered him a Tony nomination.

Five years later came the greatest achievement of his professional life: his performance as an elderly man who sets out on a road trip in *Harry and Tonto*, which won him the 1974 Academy Award for best actor. Carney withstood depression, drinking, and hospitalization to claim the highest prize in his craft, and (largely) maintained the victory in the years following. Numerous film and television projects followed for the next twenty years and his successful recovery spawned yet another comeback. Carney and his first wife, Jean Myers, remarried in 1980.

75. CLARK, DICK

"It's been a long, hard fight. My speech is not perfect, but I'm getting there."

IN LATE 2004, TELEVISION ICON DICK CLARK SUFFERED a stroke and was not able to man his post on his annual *New Year's Rockin' Eve* program to usher in 2005—a post he had filled every year since 1972.

But exactly one year later, after a long, slow, and painful rehabilitation, Clark was back at the helm of his New Year's countdown. Sitting behind a desk with the New York street scene in the background, Clark, seventy-six, was sometimes hoarse and had difficulty speaking, but he said: "I wouldn't have missed this for the world." He told viewers, "Last year I had a stroke. It left me in bad shape. I had to teach myself how to walk and talk again. It's been a long, hard fight. My speech is not perfect, but I'm getting there."

Clark stayed at his desk past 1 a.m. that night as the crowds thinned out. "I've had a wonderful time tonight," he said. "There's nothing like being in Times Square on New Year's Eve and, believe me, this is one night I will never, ever forget."

He was back at his post again one year later to welcome 2007, stronger still, and speaking more clearly than the year before.

76. Disney, Walt

In 1922, Walt Disney was invited to a client's office to sign a contract for a new cartoon but demurred, saying he couldn't come because he didn't have any shoes. He wasn't kidding. His only pair was falling apart, and Disney had left them at the shoemaker for repairs and didn't have the $1.50 to get them back.

Disney was really down on his luck—living out of his cramped office, subsisting on leftovers from two kind Greeks who ran a nearby restaurant. His client, a dentist by the name of Dr. McCrum, picked up the shoes himself, paid the tab, and drove Disney to his office to sign the contract. The picture, *Tommy Tucker's Tooth*, was made, but Disney's struggling little company, Laugh-O-Gram Films, still went bust.

This was just one embarrassing incident in a whole string; Disney had been trying, and failing, to get some traction for his cartooning career for several years. Three years earlier, after just one month with Pesmen-Rubin Commercial Art Studio in Kansas City, Missouri, Disney was laid off because of a lack of business and because he "couldn't draw." So he started his own business, Iwerks-Disney Commercial Artists. Disney won a contract to produce a union newsletter, but after just a month he left to join the Kansas City Slide Company for $40 a week. Iwerks-Disney ended in bankruptcy.

With some remaining Iwerks-Disney assets and $15,000 from local investors, in 1922 Walt Disney incorporated Laugh-O-Gram Films. The company produced the animated and live-action film *Cinderella*, but within weeks, Walt ran out of money and was forced to let his staff go. By July 1923, Laugh-O-Gram was in bankruptcy.

Still he pressed on, leaving Kansas City and moving to Los Angeles to join his brother, Roy. In October 1923, the Disney Brothers Studio signed a contract with a New York film distributor to produce six short films for $1,500 each, with an option for six more. Then came his breakthrough: In 1928, during a five-day train trip from New York to Los Angeles, Disney conceptualized the character Mickey Mouse, who would star in the famous *Steamboat Willie*. And the rest, as they say, is history.

Despite being laid off and told he had no drawing ability, as well as two bankruptcies, Walt Disney followed his passion, stayed with his dream, and ended up revolutionizing the cartoon industry, not to mention creating Disney World and a vast entertainment empire. Children of all ages are grateful for his perseverance.

77. IT'S A WONDERFUL LIFE

"Strange, isn't it? Each man's life touches so many other lives. When he isn't around he leaves an awful hole, doesn't he?"

THE 1946 HOLIDAY MOVIE *IT'S A WONDERFUL LIFE* was a box-office flop. Made for $3.18 million, it took in an estimated $3.3 million in theatrical rentals. Artistically, however, it fared much better. The picture earned five Academy Award nominations: best picture, best actor (Jimmy Stewart), best director (Frank Capra), best sound recording, and best film editing. But the film didn't win any of these, and over the next fifteen years, it was largely forgotten.

So forgotten, in fact, that no one from National Telefilm Associates renewed the copyright. When it expired after twenty-seven years, in 1973, unburdened by royalties and rights fees, television stations gave the film repeated holiday-time airings for the simple fact that it was free. Slowly but surely, *It's a Wonderful Life* became *the* Christmas movie classic. Many fans don't consider the holiday season complete without at least one viewing. The creators agree: it was both director Frank Capra's and star Jimmy Stewart's favorite movie. And that of a few others, too. In 2006, this once-forgotten story was voted the "most inspirational film of all time" by the American Film Institute's jury of 1,500 film artists, critics, and historians.

Another comeback from initial box office mediocrity, *A Christmas Story* (1983), chronicles little Ralphie's quest to acquire a Red Ryder BB gun for Christmas vis-à-vis the leitmotif from all quarters, "You'll shoot your eye out, kid." Shot in Cleveland in a 1940s setting, it gained cult status through marathon showings on TNT starting in 1997 and TBS starting in 2004.

Inspiration, plus repetition, creates success—in its own time.

78. JONES, QUINCY

THE PAIN WAS LIKE A SHOTGUN BLAST TO THE BACK of his head. That's how musician and producer Quincy Jones described his 1974 cerebral aneurysm. He had double vision and a feeling of vertigo, and when he tried to sit up he couldn't. He was rushed to the hospital, where he underwent two operations and was given a one in a hundred chance of survival. Jones *did* survive, in fact, but his trumpet playing did not. He had to give it up, and even though he didn't know it, the stage was being set for much greater success.

After the operation, he recuperated for six months then went back to his "second job," the record business. He launched Qwest Records in 1975 and attracted the likes of Michael Jackson, Donna Summer, James Ingram, and Chaka Khan. The company, and Jones, flourished for the next decade.

But then, in 1986, Jones suffered another setback: this time, he had a nervous breakdown. With the help of his positive attitude and spiritual outlook on life, he recovered from that setback as well. Despite these stumbling blocks, Jones became *the* preeminent pop music producer. He's the winner of eighty-four Grammy nominations, more than anyone else.

79. KLUGMAN, JACK

A HEAVY SMOKER, ACTOR JACK KLUGMAN (MESSY Oscar Madison in television's *The Odd Couple*) was first diagnosed with cancer of the larynx in 1974. Surgery followed, and he was able to resume his acting career easily enough; it was a sobering episode for sure, but not scary enough for him to quit smoking. The cancer returned in 1989, however, and a partial laryngectomy followed. Klugman was left with one vocal cord and a very raspy voice.

His *Odd Couple* partner, Tony Randall, was the first one to make a hospital visit. He encouraged Klugman, saying if and when he was able to come back they could do a stage version of *The Odd Couple* to raise funds for the National Actors Theatre, which Randall founded. At first Klugman thought this an unlikely possibility, but Randall pressed him for a date. Klugman's voice therapist said Klugman could perform in six months. The publicity machine was turned on and, after "working like Rocky," Klugman indeed returned to the stage for this very special performance in 1991. Klugman said that this gesture from his acting partner saved his life because it gave him a goal, a reason to keep moving forward. More than a decade after his stage comeback, Klugman was still working, appearing on television and in his one-man show, admonishing others about the consequences of smoking in public service advertisements, and inspiring millions to fight back against insurmountable odds—and win.

80. KUDROW, LISA

AFTER YEARS AS A STRUGGLING ACTOR, LISA KUDROW auditioned for and won the role of Roz Doyle, the producer of Frasier Crane's radio show on the sitcom *Frasier*. She was thrilled because she knew that the show would be a big hit, big enough, she said, that she would never have to worry about paying the rent again. But the excitement was short-lived—very short-lived. Before filming even started, Kudrow was fired.

The very next year, however, 1994, Kudrow was hired on a new show called *Friends*, which would become one of the most popular shows in TV history. For just the final *Friends* season (2003–4), Kudrow, like all cast members, received $1 million per episode, making approximately $24 million for the season. Not to mention winning spots in a string of other productions along the way (some thirty-five credits after her 1994 break, including a signature role in *Romy and Michele's High School Reunion* (1997). Sometimes life has a way of taking away one opportunity to make room for an even bigger one.

81. PACINO, AL

"Who speaks of triumph? To endure is everything."

AFTER STARRING IN *THE GODFATHER* (1972, AND ITS sequels in 1974 and 1977), *Serpico* (1973), *Dog Day Afternoon* (1975), and *Scarface* (1983), Al Pacino's career stumbled a bit with the Colonial-era drama *Revolution* (1985). The movie wasn't well received, and most actors would have just shrugged it off and turned their attention to the next script. To Pacino, it was an earth-shattering disaster: he didn't make a movie for four years.

Pacino's "sabbatical" was something of a lost period for the actor—friends said he was racked with self-doubt. He told *Newsweek* (June 3, 2002) that during this time he considered selling his house for the money, but "Who wants to do that?" he asked.

After this time spent in the wilderness away from Hollywood, he regained his confidence and bearings and jumped back in the saddle, stronger than ever. Pacino and success met up again, and he began making almost a film per year, including *Sea of Love* (1989), *Scent of a Woman* (1992), *Donnie Brasco* (1997), and *Any Given Sunday* (1999).

Pacino's favorite quote, from *Requiem* by Rainer Maria Rilke, summarizes his experience: "Who speaks of triumph? To endure is everything."

82. REEVE, CHRISTOPHER

HOW QUICKLY CAN ONE'S LIFE CHANGE? THE unsettling answer: in a flash. One moment, Christopher

Reeve was approaching a rail jump in an equestrian event (May 1995); his next conscious moment, he found himself lying in a hospital bed, in traction, with a heavy metal ball suspended behind his head attached to a metal frame secured with screws to his temples. It all happened in just one instant: his horse had balked at the jump, and Reeve was thrown headfirst onto the ground. His hands tangled in the bridle, preventing him from breaking the fall, and his head separated from his spine. Reeve, best known for playing the title role in *Superman* (1978), was now paralyzed.

Just two years later, he would make a comeback by directing the HBO movie *In the Gloaming* (1997) and starring in a remake of *Rear Window* (1998). Reeve became a real-life man of steel and inspiration to those battling any foe, whether paralysis, disease, or other setback. He traveled the world to raise funds for spinal cord disability research on behalf of the American Paralysis Association.

When asked to define a hero, Reeve said that he had originally thought a hero was someone who acted with courage without considering consequences; now, he thought a hero was an ordinary individual who finds the strength to endure in spite of overwhelming obstacles. Before he succumbed to heart failure on October 10, 2004, Reeve left an indelible image of exactly that kind of heroism in the minds of millions.

Tragically, just seventeen months later, Reeve's wife, partner, constant companion, and relentless supporter,

Dana, succumbed to lung cancer. A nonsmoker, she was just forty-four.

83. REYNOLDS, BURT

WORKING ON THE MOVIE *CITY HEAT* IN 1984, BURT Reynolds was hit in the head with a chair, a real metal chair, not the breakaway balsa wood prop that was supposed to be there. It shattered his jaw at the temporomandibular joint. He kept working, but the unrelenting pain was worse than a migraine, making him constantly nauseated. He took as many as fifty painkiller pills a day, including morphine and Halcion, but they had little effect. His weight fell from 190 pounds to 140. The Hollywood buzz was that Reynolds had AIDS. Despite the fact that he was the No. 1 box-office star in the world for five years in a row, and in the top ten for thirteen years, no one would hire him. He didn't work for three years—not that the pain would have let him.

Finally, after going from physician to physician trying to find relief, he came across a Florida dentist who spent ten hours a day rebalancing every tooth in his head. It took weeks, but Reynolds finally found relief.

A full five years after the accident, Reynolds got a part in the comedy *Breaking In* (1989), followed by the CBS sitcom *Evening Shade* (1990–94), a comedown from his film days, but at least a job in the industry. Financially, however, he was about to slide down another slippery slope. A vitriolic divorce from Loni Anderson and some bad investments (he lost $28 million in a restaurant chain) led Reynolds to file for chapter 11 bankruptcy in 1996. He had $10 million in assets and slightly more than that in debts—his onetime $40 million fortune was gone.

To repay his debts, Reynolds swallowed his pride and worked in low-budget, straight-to-video productions (*The Maddening* and *Frankenstein and Me*, both in 1996) and made-for-television movies (HBO's *The Cherokee Kid* and TMC's *The Raven*, both in 1996). He played supporting roles in some higher-profile films, like a televangelist in *Citizen Ruth* and a sleazy senator entranced with stripper Demi Moore in *Striptease* (both in 1996).

Then came *Boogie Nights* in 1997, which showcased his understated comic performance as porn mogul Jack Horner. Reynolds received an Academy Award nomination for best supporting actor for that performance. All at once he was back in demand as a film actor, appearing in *The Hunter's Moon* (1999), *Mystery, Alaska* (1999), and *Pups* (2000). He racked up some 35 film credits in the period 2000-2007—including hits like *The Dukes of Hazzard* (2005) with Jessica Simpson.

Reynolds said in interviews that the same individuals who shunned him when he was injured told him after his Oscar nomination that they had always known his comeback was certain—the "hypocrisy of Hollywood," he said. In his sixties, Reynolds emerged from the drubbing life gave him with his health, craft, and dignity intact. He has said that if you hold on to things long enough, they come back into style: "like me."

84. RIVERS, JOAN

JOAN RIVERS FAILED TO BECOME A DRAMATIC ACTRESS. Told she lacked looks and talent, she switched to comedy, but with the same reaction. Her own mother told her she had no talent for the business and that she was throwing her life away. Still, plucky Rivers auditioned for the *Tonight Show* seven times. After the last attempt, the talent coordinator told her they just didn't think she'd work on television. But she persisted and went on to make a major career in stand-up comedy, and proved her naysayers to be magnificently wrong.

Then, in 1987, her husband Edgar, 62, committed suicide. That same year her talk show was canceled and she became a pariah in her industry. She lost $3 million in a failed jewelry business, became estranged from her daughter, and, not surprisingly, suffered a major bout of depression. She tells the story of overcoming it all in

Bouncing Back: I've Survived Everything—and I Mean Everything—and You Can Too (1997).

Her style of moving through depression is to slap yourself out of despair, get your feet moving, and just get on with it. Wallowing in self-pity helps no one, and besides, there is always someone worse off than you. Among other things, Rivers recommends:

- Give yourself time and permission to grieve your loss in the way you wish. (Cry, go to your house of worship, go shopping, spoil yourself, or all four.)
- Create a healing space for yourself.
- Write a list of everything that is depressing you and then a list of everything you love. It will help you purge the former and focus on the latter.
- Ask friends for help, when appropriate. But don't wear them out. See a therapist if you need one.
- Fill your days. Get busy with a new career or take up a sport. Exercise releases endorphins, which induce feelings of happiness.

Rivers's by-the-bootstraps advice has kick-started many a comeback, including her own. She suggests starting small, saying, "He who limps is still walking." Taking her own advice and beginning with minor television appearances, Rivers worked her way up to starring on Broadway in *Sally Marr . . . and Her Escorts* in 1994. When she was nominated for a Tony, she realized that for the first time in a long time, life was wonderful again.

85. ROBINSON, EDWARD G.

AFTER TWENTY-EIGHT YEARS OF MARRIAGE, MOVIE
actor Edward G. Robinson's wife filed for divorce in 1955.
All divorce is hurtful, but this one was especially so: To pay
for the settlement, the sensitive, art-loving actor was forced
to sell his prized possession, his world-class collection of
nineteenth- and twentieth-century art. One of the largest
in the world, his collection sold for $5.125 million, a huge
sum back in 1955. During this period Robinson was also
deeply troubled by a maladjusted son, who was frequently
in trouble with the law and attempted suicide several times.
His career was flagging, too. His work slowed to a trickle
after he was blacklisted following testimony to the House
Un-American Activities Committee. It was a painful time,
but, like all things, it would pass.

In 1956, Robinson returned to Broadway in the role
of an elderly widower who marries a young bride in
Paddy Chayefsky's *Middle of the Night*. It was prophetic:
Robinson, sixty-three, fell in love with and married Jane
Bodenheimer, thirty-eight, the dress designer for the
show. His work, and his new love, kept the actor going
for another fifteen years.

In this chapter of his life, Robinson took up painting
himself. His new wife hung his own paintings where he
had once proudly displayed masterworks by Monet and
Picasso. In the opinion of a close friend, this gesture

139

turned an erstwhile art gallery into a real home. He was also able to rebuild a second art collection over time, albeit a more modest one.

86. SHATNER, WILLIAM

AT AGE THIRTY-EIGHT, WILLIAM SHATNER, *STAR Trek*'s Captain Kirk, was an international star but unemployed and broke. The original *Star Trek* series had run from 1966 to 1969 and reruns were syndicated, but cast members received fees only for the first five showings of each episode. Shatner had trouble getting television and movie parts because he was so identified with his *Star Trek* character, so he spent the next ten years in touring plays, often living out of a camper that was hooked up to a pickup truck.

Then, in 1979, along came the *Star Trek* motion picture. Shatner, then forty-eight, finally got his payday. The movie was followed by several sequels. A dedicated actor and talented writer, Shatner went on to play *T. J. Hooker* in the 1980s television series, wrote the *TekWar* series, served as a spokesperson for Priceline.com, and played Denny Crane on the TV series *Boston Legal*, for which he won an Emmy in 2005.

Shatner also came back from personal devastation.

His wife, former model Nerine Kidd, drowned in their pool in 1997. Shatner thought it was the end for him emotionally and believed that he would never recover. After grieving for a long time, he came to the realization that it wasn't just him suffering, it was all of humanity, in one way or another. A horse lover, he was acquainted with trainer Elizabeth Martin, who had also lost a spouse, to cancer two years earlier. She sent him a sympathy card written in striking red ink, he contacted her to thank her, and they talked about their losses. They eventually married in 2001. Having come through the fire, each one separately, they say they are grateful for each and every moment together.

87. STALLONE, SYLVESTER

ON MARCH 24, 1975, IN CLEVELAND, OHIO, Muhammad Ali fought a journeyman fighter from New Jersey named Chuck Wepner, "The Bayonne Bleeder." Bleeder or not, this was Wepner's heavyweight championship bout, and his chance to be a "somebody." Even though the 6 ft. 6 in. boxer ranked in the top ten and had fought Foreman, Frazier, and the rest, he was a twenty-to-one underdog. Ali said the fight would be over in three rounds.

On that fateful night, however, Wepner put up the fight of his life, stunning the boxing world. He knocked Ali down in the eighth round, but in the end, Ali's skill won out over Wepner's heart, and Ali won in a TKO in the final seconds of the fifteenth round. The forgettable fighter had put up an unforgettable fight.

A young actor happened to see the fight.

Within three days, with a ballpoint pen and spiral notebook and in a state that he later described as a "frenzy," he wrote the screenplay *Rocky*. The actor was, of course, Sylvester Stallone.

The script was strong and well-written, and studios were eager to buy it for as much as $250,000—a fortune to a struggling actor, but Stallone demanded that a) he must play the title role and b) he must receive a share of the profits. Producers Irwin Winkler and Robert Chartoff accepted the bold terms. *Rocky* went on to become one of the biggest hits of all time, winning its author and lead a Best Actor nomination. Audiences saw it as the quintessential triumph of the underdog story, a mythic comeback legend for modern times.

Rocky was made for just $1 million, a small budget even in 1976. Stallone was paid a salary of all of $23,000 for his acting performance. It was a great investment for all participants. The film took in $225 million worldwide.

But that was just the start. *Rocky* would prove to be a billion dollar idea:

Released	Movie Name	Worldwide Gross
11/21/1976	Rocky	$225,000,000
6/15/1979	Rocky II	$200,182,160
5/28/1982	Rocky III	$125,049,125
11/27/1985	Rocky IV	$300,400,000
11/16/1990	Rocky V	$119,946,358
12/20/2006	Rocky Balboa	-

Totals	$970,577,643

Source: http://www.the-numbers.com/movies/series/Rocky.php

Stallone knew a lot about comebacks from his own life. This was just the biggest to date.

His was not a happy childhood. On July 6, 1946, in the Hell's Kitchen neighborhood of Manhattan, Sylvester Enzio Stallone was born to a chorus girl and an Italian immigrant. During his birth, an accident with the forceps cut a nerve in his face and left parts of his lip, tongue, and chin paralyzed. His speech would always be slurred slightly, and his lower lip would droop; it wasn't an act for *Rocky*, it was real.

Besides the nerve damage, Stallone suffered from rickets. His parents fought each other and fought to keep food on the table for Sylvester and his younger brother, Frank (who also became an actor). Most of Sylvester's first five years were spent in foster homes. As a result, he was starved for attention and affection, and he believes this catalyzed an interest in acting.

When Stallone was eleven, his parents divorced; Sylvester was assigned to his tough dad. By the time he was a teenager, Stallone had attended twelve different schools and racked up several expulsions for behavior problems. His grades were terrible, and his classmates bullied him. He made it bearable by creating fantasies in which he would cast himself as a hero and defender of the underdog.

When he was fifteen, Stallone relocated to Philadelphia to live with his mother and her new husband. While in a school for emotionally disturbed children, he began lifting weights. He added fencing, football, discus, and most significantly, theatre. The time spent in the gym paid dividends. He graduated and got an athletic scholarship to the American College of Switzerland. While there, he also served as a girl's athletic coach.

Theatre was an outlet again. In his spare time, Stallone starred in a school production of Arthur Miller's *Death of a Salesman*. By now he was hooked; he decided to become an actor. Returning to the U.S., he studied drama at the University of Miami. In 1969, he moved to New York.

Like most starving actors, he worked odd jobs. He was a regular at auditions around town, but only occasionally got hired; and when he did, it was off-

Broadway. Consequently, for the cash, he appeared in a pair of soft-core porn films, *Party at Kitty's* and *Stud's*. After he became famous, the latter was retooled as *The Italian Stallion*.

After being turned down for a part in *The Godfather* (1971), Stallone turned to writing. He married actress Sasha Czack in late 1974. They moved to California with the hope of getting the big break that would supercharge their careers, be it writing or acting. Stallone got a taste of that longed-for success when he wrote the screenplay for and costarred in *The Lords of Flatbush* (1974). It was a moderate success, and it led to a few more roles. The big break was still elusive.

Then, Stallone saw the Ali-Wepner fight, created his own acting vehicle from it, and catapulted to the top of the acting pyramid.

Additionally, Stallone penned and starred in three *Rambo* films and *F.I.S.T.* (1979). The Internet Movie Database (imdb.com) lists more than forty major credits after *Rocky*.

Then, at age sixty, Stallone made yet another comeback with *Rocky Balboa*, the sixth and supposedly final in the series. He told the press that part of his motivation was that both he and viewers were not entirely satisfied with *Rocky V*, and that he wanted to end the series right. In a radio interview in advance of the launch, Stallone revealed deeper motivations as well: He wanted to respond positively to the issues raised by his friend

Susan Faludi in *Stiffed: The Betrayal of the Modern Man* (1999), regarding the emasculation and discarding of the male in modern society, especially the older male. (Stallone himself is a case study in the book). Stallone wanted to show that the older male still had utility, still had dignity, pride, worth—that he could make a comeback, and a huge one at that. As he says in the film, it's not about how hard you can hit; it's about how hard you can get hit and keep moving forward.

Or as the advertising slogan for the sixth *Rocky* puts it: "It ain't over till it's over." What could say it better than that? And who could say it better than the cultural icon Rocky himself?

88. STEWART, JIMMY

AS WORLD WAR II LOOMED, JIMMY STEWART (WHO HAD won a Best Actor Academy Award for *The Philadelphia Story* in 1940) decided to join the army. He was turned down for being underweight. The actor embarked on an eating binge, made his weight, and at age thirty-two reported for induction to the air force on March 22, 1941, at Fort McArthur, California. He was initially assigned to serve as a flight instructor, but after repeated requests, Stewart finally got his wish to fly combat. A superb officer and pilot,

Stewart was promoted to squadron commander and major in January 1944. He flew a heavy combat schedule and won the Distinguished Flying Cross twice. Stewart was the leader of a one-thousand-plane raid on Berlin on March 22, 1944. Back at base camp, in England, he went to the movies in his spare time.

After the war, the unassuming hero wasn't sure he wanted to come back to acting, and some wrote him off (the *New York Times* published a feature "The Rise and Fall of Jimmy Stewart"). But Frank Capra finally persuaded him to appear in his picture *It's a Wonderful Life* in 1946. He received another Academy Award nomination for best actor, a successful comeback to his original profession indeed.

Stewart went on to appear in some eighty films, including *Harvey* (1950), *Rear Window* (1954), *Vertigo* (1958), and *Anatomy of a Murder* (1959). He believed in treating the audience not as customers, he said, but as partners. And just as he came back to Hollywood, he returned to his military career in a little-known but significant way. The decorated officer had one last mission before retiring from the air force: in 1966, during his annual two weeks of active reserve duty, Stewart requested a combat assignment and participated in a bombing strike over Vietnam, according to his stepson Michael McLean. Stewart was fifty-eight and still fighting for his country.

89. FLYING WALLENDAS, THE

"Life is being on the wire; everything else is just waiting."

IN 1947, TRAPEZE ARTIST KARL WALLENDA AND HIS family members created the ultimate act in the high-wire world: the seven-person chair pyramid. Four men stood across a thirty-five-foot high-wire, two pairs of them yoked together by shoulder bars. On top of them stood two more men yoked with a shoulder bar. At the highest level was the seventh person: a woman standing on a chair! The pyramid was successfully performed for fourteen years, from 1948 to 1962.

Then, tragedy struck. During a performance at the State Fair Coliseum in Detroit on January 30, 1962, a stumble by the front man brought the pyramid down. Three men hit the ground. Two died that night; the third, Wallenda's son Mario, survived but was paralyzed from the waist down. Wallenda and his brother Herman had fallen from the second level but caught the wire. The woman at the top tumbled down onto Wallenda, who miraculously held on to her until a net was created beneath her. The girl suffered a concussion, and Wallenda came away with a cracked pelvis and a double hernia.

In spite of the devastating loss, the Wallendas performed the very next evening, feeling they owed it to those who lost their lives. To further prove that life goes on and that defeat can be overcome, they performed the pyramid again in 1963 and then after a hiatus again in 1977, recreated primarily by Wallenda's grandchildren for the movie *The Great Wallendas.*

In the years following, Karl Wallenda continued performing with a smaller troupe. He created new challenges for himself, most notably his death-defying "sky walks" between buildings and across stadiums. Some thirty thousand people watched him walk a twelve-hundred-foot trek across the Tallulah Falls Gorge in Georgia, after which the sixty-five-year-old patriarch performed two separate headstands at a height of more than seven hundred feet.

During a sky walk in San Juan, Puerto Rico, in March 1978, seventy-three-year-old Wallenda fell to his death. Several ropes were misconnected along the wire and caused the fall. High-wire performance is truly in the blood of the Wallenda family; even after Wallenda's death, the sixth and seventh generations kept the tradition alive. In 1998, during the Moslem Temple Shrine Circus in Detroit, the site of the Wallendas' greatest tragedy thirty-six years before, the current generation of Wallendas reunited from three separate groups—the Flying Wallendas, the Fabulous Wallendas, and the Great Wallendas—to recreate their most famous achievement, the seven-person chair pyramid.

Then, they upped the ante. For Fox TV's *Guinness Records Primetime*, the Wallendas assembled an eight-person, three-level pyramid on February 20, 2001, and later added two more family members to form the first ten-person pyramid. The Wallendas came back against tragedy and fear and conquered both. They are a living realization of what patriarch Karl Wallenda said: "Life is being on the wire; everything else is just waiting."

In yet another amazing comeback, on September 19, 2006, Mario Wallenda, 64, quadriplegic from the 1962 accident, went back up on the high wire in downtown Chicago, crossing the Chicago River from the Merchandise Mart on his motorized "sky cycle." It was his first such public performance since the 1962 accident. Retired from his job in a contact lens lab, and drawing Social Security, he said he was looking for something to do that made him feel alive and productive again.

JUSTICE

90. Brockovich, Erin

Behind the glamorous, Julia Roberts–portrayed Erin Brockovich of the movies is a real-life woman. As an administrative assistant and researcher, Brockovich organized the facts for a legal case against Pacific Gas and Electric (PG&E) on behalf of the citizens of Hinkley, California. PG&E had polluted the groundwater around Hinkley with chromium-6, and as a result locals suffered miscarriages, cancers, and skin disorders. The case was eventually settled for $250 million; Brockovich received a $2.5 million bonus.

Her life had been a real struggle to that point. Suffering from dyslexia, she had difficulty getting through school. She was divorced twice and ultimately married three times. She raised her children by herself. She suffered from loneliness, fear, depression, and panic attacks. But she also had an inner resilience that pushed her forward in her search for fulfillment. It was that inner strength that powered the investigation of PG&E. Brockovich was born with some of that strength, but part of it came from her father, who sent her a letter when she was young that she carried with her everywhere for more than twenty years.

That letter included some famous lines from President Calvin Coolidge: "Press on. Nothing can take the place of perseverance. Talent will not. Nothing is more common than unsuccessful men with talent. Genius will not. Unrewarded genius is almost a proverb. Education will not. The world is full of educated derelicts. Persistence and determination alone are omnipotent. The slogan, 'press on' has solved, always will solve, the problems of the human race."

In her autobiography, Brockovich advises readers to become their own heroes, to write and realize the screenplays of their own lives. And, of course, to "press on."

91. MANDELA, NELSON

NELSON MANDELA WAS FIGHTING RACIAL DISCRIMINATION during the South African Apartheid, but government officials claimed he was inciting civil unrest. Convicted of treason, the sentence was chilling: life in prison.

Mandela was shipped off to the maximum security Robben Island Prison in 1964. Conditions were harsh, but he endured by controlling those parts of his life that he could. Rising early, the former boxer would exercise. He loved music, so he and other prisoners would organize concerts, especially around Christmastime. He encouraged fellow prisoners, teaching them songs and poems and sharing positive words. In 1975, he even wrote that he believed that, in his lifetime, he would step out into the sunshine and walk with firm feet. It was unlikely, yes, but ultimately prophetic.

As international pressure mounted on his behalf, Mandela became a cause celebre and was eventually released from prison in 1990. It had been twenty-six long years, and the years had taken their toll. His hair was gray, but his posture was straight, and his health was intact, to the surprise of many. He went right back to his calling ("the struggle is my life" were his words), working for a free South African society, trying to create a more equitable dissemination of power. This time laws and institutions changed, and as a result, Mandela was recognized with the Nobel Peace Prize in 1993. He was elected president of South Africa in 1994 and held the post for five years.

Not content with changing the structure of his nation, he even altered the outward appearance: by his own style of dress, Mandela promoted a new fashion style in South

Africa. The new style of dress was called "Madiba smart" (after his clan title) and featured bright, long-sleeve silk shirts worn with dress slacks. On his eightieth birthday in 1998, the ever-youthful and optimistic icon of freedom married his third wife, Graça Machel.

LITERATURE

92. BRODSKY, JOSEPH

BORN IN 1940, JOSEPH BRODSKY WAS HAILED AS THE greatest Russian poet of the post–WWII generation, and that attracted a lot of attention, much of it unwanted. He refused to conform to Soviet communism and was convicted of being a "social parasite." Sentenced to five years of harsh labor in a Soviet prison camp, he served eighteen months and was expelled from Russia in 1972. Less than twenty years later, he would be named poet laureate by the U.S. Library of Congress (1991 to 1992).

According to Brodsky, he was a normal Soviet boy, but literature (specifically, Fyodor Dostoyevsky's *Notes from the Underground*) turned him upside down. He said he came to disbelieve in political movements and put his faith in *personal movement*, the movement of the soul when a man who looks at himself is so ashamed that he tries to make some sort of change within himself, not on the outside. Brodsky turned to poetry to express this, which he said was the only means of ensuring against someone else's, if not his own, banality.

He studied with the Russian poet Anna Akhmatova and, after his exile, moved to the United States, where he made homes in both Brooklyn and Massachusetts. He was, by and large, a frugal, industrious, and solitary figure. His focus paid off. In 1987, he was named Nobel laureate in literature. In 1993, he cofounded the American Poetry & Literacy Project, a nonprofit organization that aims to spread poetry far and wide, like gas stations, or cars, as he said.

On January 28, 1996, in his Brooklyn apartment, Brodsky died of a heart attack. He was just forty-six. The man had been despised in one arena and celebrated in another. The lesson? Perseverance, courage, staying true to one's vision. But Brodsky is also proof that sometimes we have to move physically to begin the process of making a comeback and realizing our dreams.

93. Clancy, Tom

"Nothing is as real as a dream; the world can change around you, but your dream will not. Because the dream is within you, no one can take it away."

Tom Clancy volunteered to serve in Vietnam, but was turned down for poor eyesight. Still, a fascination with all things military stirred inside him. Though he had never been inside a submarine, in 1984 he wrote *The Hunt for Red October*. Clancy's manuscript was rejected by dozens of publishers before he submitted it to the U.S. Naval Institute Press. Displaying an unusual vote of confidence in a first novel, they paid him a $5,000 advance and printed 14,000 copies.

President Ronald Reagan called Clancy's book "the perfect yarn," and sales went through the roof. It was eventually made into a movie starring Sean Connery. *The Hunt for Red October* contains such accurate descriptions of high-tech military hardware that former Navy Secretary John Lehman once joked that, had Clancy been in the navy, he would have had him court-martialed for security violations. Clancy went on to produce a long string of military titles, earning tens of millions of dollars and countless fans.

94. EVANOVICH, JANET

AFTER TEN YEARS OF REJECTION, WOULD-BE WRITER Janet Evanovich burned a boxful of rejection letters, sat on the curb, and cried. Thinking her dream was over, she went to work as a temp. Four months later, an editor called and offered Evanovich $2,000 for a romance manuscript she had long since mailed and forgotten. Evanovich wrote some twelve more for-pay novels and then decided to move into the mystery genre. She created Stephanie Plum, bounty hunter, surrounding her with zany, offbeat characters who spout knowing, humorous lines.

Success followed. The eighth book in the series, *Hard Eight*, made it to No. 1 on the *New York Times* best-seller list for fiction in 2003. *To the Nines* and *Ten Big Ones* followed in short order, and then *Eleven on Top* and *Twelve Sharp*. One reviewer likened her style to a 1930s screwball comedy: fast, funny, and furious.

Evanovich describes herself as a "boring workaholic with no hobbies or special interests." And her legion of readers is glad of it. She denies that Stephanie Plum is autobiographical, but admits she "knows where she lives."

95. KING, STEPHEN

OUT FOR HIS DAILY FOUR-MILE WALK NEAR HIS summer home in Lovell, Maine, on June 19, 1999, superstar author Stephen King was hit by a minivan. Suffering a collapsed lung and several broken bones, he was raced to the hospital at 110 mph over country roads. King nearly died.

Recovery was slow and painful, and the physical therapy was grueling. King doubted his ability to ever write again. But he *did* write again, five weeks after the accident, and King eventually said it offered the best therapy of all, even though it didn't seem that way at the outset. There was no inspiration that first day, only a stubbornness and a determination and a hope that things would get better, he said. That resolve was enough to get King started.

King finished *On Writing*, his tome about the craft of writing, in 2000 and turned to his long-stalled *Dark Tower* series in the following years. He even ended up writing himself, and his near-fatal accident, into the seven-volume series. He later told interviewers that he was using the work as a painkiller because it was more effective than any pharmaceutical the doctors had prescribed.

Though King has permanent physical ailments as a result of the accident, he didn't lose his sense of humor. He eventually purchased the van that caused him so much pain for $1,500 so he could smash it with a sledgehammer.

96. L'Amour, Louis

"I discovered that rejections are not altogether a bad thing. They teach a writer to rely on his own judgment and to say in his heart of hearts, 'To hell with you.'"

Louis L'Amour received some two hundred rejections before his first book, *Hondo*, was published in 1953. After that, he consistently produced three novels a year for the next twenty-five years. He would come to be regarded as the greatest author of western novels, and see more than one hundred titles make it into print—and stay in print. His popularity increased throughout his career, and more than three hundred million copies of his work have sold to date, one hundred million alone since his passing in 1988. L'Amour once said that a wise man fights to win, but he is a twice a fool who has no plan for possible defeat. L'Amour's plan—to persist—turned out to be the best possible plan B.

How many would-be writers have the fortitude to withstand two hundred rejections? Not many, but L'Amour was not unique. Some other ultimately successful authors who met rejection before they met success:

- Norman Mailer (*The Naked and the Dead* was rejected twelve times)
- Jack Canfield and Mark Victor Hansen (their *Chicken Soup for the Soul* was turned down by thirty-three publishers)

- Dr. Seuss (his first book was rejected forty-three times)
- Alex Haley (two hundred rejections before *Roots*)
- F. Scott Fitzgerald papered his bedroom walls with countless rejection letters before he eventually sold a story.

Saul Bellow put it best in a widely published quote on writing: "I discovered that rejections are not altogether a bad thing. They teach a writer to rely on his own judgment and to say in his heart of hearts, 'To hell with you.'"

97. LONDON, JACK

AFTER LEAVING SCHOOL AT AGE THIRTEEN TO WORK as a cannery worker, then as a sailor, an oyster pirate, a fish patroller, and at times subsisting as a hobo, Jack London resolved to further his education. Completing a high school equivalency course in just one year at age seventeen, he enrolled at the University of California at Berkeley and read continuously. He also wrote short stories, but none sold. London dropped out to join the Alaskan Klondike gold rush in 1897, but came back home to Oakland, California, broke.

He thought of getting a job at the post office, but something compelled him to write just *one more* short story. Unlike his others, this one sold—and fast.

Meanwhile, the post office came through with an offer. He had come to the fork in the road. Now London would have to choose: the insecurity of being a writer, or the steady paycheck from the government?

During his last job interview, the rudeness of a postal supervisor catalyzed the decision: he would write. London, now twenty-five, resolved to work hard at it, to "dig," as he put it, and to never miss his early-morning one-thousand-word writing stint. (London was so dedicated he could eventually sense when his one thousand words were up and sometimes stopped like this, right here

in the middle of a sentence.) Employing this method between 1900 and 1916, London completed more than fifty books, including fiction and nonfiction classics like *Call of the Wild* and *Sea Wolf*, hundreds of short stories, numerous articles, and countless letters (he received some ten thousand letters each year).

London once said: "You can't wait for inspiration. You have to go after it with a club."

98. MELVILLE, HERMAN

"So far as I am individually concerned, and independent of my pocket, it is my earnest desire to write those sort of books which are said to 'fail.'"

AFTER BRIEF STINTS AS BANK CLERK, FARM HAND, factory worker, and teacher, teenager Herman Melville decided to study surveying. His goal: win a job with the booming Erie Canal project. There was just one problem—he couldn't get hired. He had no hope of attending college (no funds), and no better job prospects, so at nineteen, he signed on to a ship as a cabin boy and went to sea. Two years later, on a whaler bound for the South Seas, conditions onboard were so bad that he and a companion went AWOL in the Marquesas Islands. They lived for a month with the Typees, reputed cannibals. They were finally rescued by an Australian vessel, but Melville knocked around Tahiti and several other islands before making it back to New England in 1844.

By this time he was flat broke in dollars but quite wealthy in experience, so he took up writing. His brother found a publisher for his first adventure book, *Typee*, and it sold reasonably well. So, too, did his second novel, *Omoo*.

By the late 1840s Melville viewed writing not just as a way to make money, but as art. "So far as I am individually concerned, and independent of my pocket, it is my earnest desire to write those sort of books which are said to 'fail,'" he wrote in 1849. Be careful what you wish for: Two years later, at age thirty-two, he wrote the complex, allegorical *Moby Dick*, which many regard as the Great American Novel. However, back then, among readers and critics it was just very, very long and much too difficult—a "failure." Melville got his wish; his popularity waned.

The rest of Melville's life went downhill, too. One son committed suicide, another was a drifter, and his daughter suffered from crippling arthritis. Melville wound up taking a secure but low-paying job as a customs inspector in New York.

Yet, despite it all, he kept writing. The manuscript of *Billy Budd* was found in his desk when he died in 1891, but was not published until 1924. Nevertheless, it sparked a full-blown revival of interest in his work, catalyzing Lewis Mumford's *Herman Melville* (1929). Now many scholars consider Melville the foremost American author of the nineteenth century—perhaps the foremost American writer, period.

Melville said: "It is better to fail in originality than to succeed in imitation."

99. MILLER, ARTHUR

ARTHUR MILLER WROTE *THE MAN WHO HAD ALL THE Luck* as a novel but couldn't find a publisher, so he retooled it as a Broadway play in 1944. It ran for less than a week; four "sad" performances, as he described them in his autobiography *Timebends*. However, it was this rewriting of his novel that allowed Miller to discover himself as a playwright, and even as a person, he later said.

His next play, *All My Sons*, won the New York Drama Critics Circle Award and a special citation at the very first Tony Awards ceremony in 1947. *Death of a Salesman* followed and secured Miller his place among America's greatest dramatists. Even though *Time* magazine said in its February 21, 1949, issue that "it was no more than an altogether creditable play," *Death of a Salesman* would win the Pulitzer Prize for drama, the Tony for best play, and the Drama Critics Circle Award. It is now considered the preeminent masterwork of American tragedy. Miller said his job as a playwright was to ask questions, and then to face the absence of precise answers "with a certain humility."

100. MILTON, JOHN

"He who reigns within himself and rules passions, desires, and fears is more than a king."

ENGLISH POET JOHN MILTON BECAME BLIND AT AGE forty-four. Nevertheless, in 1667 at the age of sixty, he wrote the classic *Paradise Lost* with the assistance of his secretary Andrew Marvell. In 1671, suffering from gout as well as blindness, he produced *Paradise Regain'd* and *Samson Agonistes*. As a writer, many scholars consider Milton second only to Shakespeare.

How did he do it—even though blind? First, he was extremely well educated. After graduating from Christ's College, Cambridge, in 1632, Milton studied another six years on his own, devouring subjects like theology, philosophy, history, politics, literature, and science in preparation for his chosen career as a poet. Second, he developed his brainpower. Writing while blind forced him to organize vast amounts of material solely in his *mind*, without the benefit of paper and pen.

Third, Milton was very much a creature of habit, and his brick-upon-brick approach to work brought him compound dividends over time. He woke each day at 4 a.m. and listened to an assistant read the Bible to him in original Hebrew. Contemplation followed, and at 7 a.m., he would undertake further reading and correspondence.

The rest of the day would be entirely devoted to writing. After dinner, he would walk in his garden. At 8 p.m. there would be some form of entertainment, either a poetry reading or organ playing or other music. He was in bed by 9 p.m. He followed that routine every day, day after day, and it was the key to his productivity.

Milton Quotes:

- "The mind is its own place, and in itself can make a heaven of hell, a hell of heaven."
- "A good book is the precious lifeblood of a master spirit."
- "Assuredly we bring not innocence into the world, we bring impurity much rather: that which purifies us is trial, and trial is by what is contrary."
- "The superior man acquaints himself with many sayings of antiquity and many deeds of the past, in order to strengthen his character thereby."

101. ROWLING, J. K.

BY CHRISTMAS 1993, J. K. ROWLING WAS IN DIRE straits. She was newly divorced, caring for a young daughter, living on welfare, and staying with her sister and brother-in-law in Edinburgh, Scotland, where she knew almost no one. She intended to teach but needed an education certificate, which would take a year to earn. Beaten down? Yes. Defeated? No. She had an asset *literally* worth billions: her imagination. She had conceptualized the Harry Potter character three years earlier on a train trip and knew that this time in her life would be her sole chance to turn her notes and outlines into a finished manuscript.

So she made what she described as a "huge, superhuman effort." Rowling would take her daughter in a carriage to the park, hoping the fresh air would ultimately tire the baby out, and when she fell asleep, Rowling would pitch camp in a local café and write longhand on a legal pad. Later, she would retype the manuscript on a manual typewriter, and then sneak into the computer lounge at a local college, where she would retype the material, all the time terrified that she would be found out as a nonstudent. Fortified with a $12,000 grant from the Scottish Arts Council, she finished the first volume of what would be the *Harry Potter* series. Rowling has said she felt very low during those lonely days in Edinburgh, and without the challenge of writing, she would have gone mad. What mattered most to her, she said, was that she had produced a book that she could be proud of.

After a year's worth of rejections, Bloomsbury bought *Harry Potter and the Philosopher's Stone* (*Philosopher* became *Sorcerer* for publication in the United States) for some $4,000. It caught the fancy of the public slowly but surely. Rowling kept at it: she was teaching part-time and writing the next installment, *Harry Potter and the Chamber of Secrets*, on her own time. The publisher Scholastic then purchased the U.S. rights. Interest in the book catapulted and the first three volumes took over the top three slots of the *New York Times* best-seller list after achieving similar success in the United Kingdom. The fourth in the series, *Harry Potter and the Goblet of Fire*, became the fastest-selling book in history, with a first printing of 5.3 million copies and advance orders of more than 1.8 million. The film *Harry Potter and the Sorcerer's Stone* took in nearly $1 billion after release in 2001, ranking fourth in all-time, worldwide box-office receipts (other *Potter* installments ranked eighth and tenth and seventeenth).

All-Time Box Office Rank	Title	Worldwide Box Office
4.	*Harry Potter and the Sorcerer's Stone* (2001)	$968,657,891
8.	*Harry Potter and the Goblet of Fire* (2005)	$892,194,397
10.	*Harry Potter and the Chamber of Secrets* (2002)	$866,300,000

17.	*Harry Potter and the*	$789,458,727
	Prisoner of Azkaban	
	(2004)	

By the end of 2006, Rowling's six volumes had sold some ninety million books.

Now ranked among the wealthiest women in the world, Rowling has come a very long way indeed from her very first book, *Rabbit*. She was six and never stopped "scribbling," she said.

102. SEUSS, DR. (THEODOR SEUSS GEISEL)

SOME FORTY-THREE PUBLISHERS REJECTED THE FIRST manuscript from Theodor S. Geisel (better known as Dr. Seuss), *And to Think That I Saw It on Mulberry Street*. He considered burning it, but in 1937 a friend published the book for him. It had moderate success.

Seventeen years later, in May 1954, *Life* magazine published a report that schoolchildren were having trouble learning to read because their books were boring. This inspired Geisel's publisher to commission a book of 250 words (his idea of how many words at one time a first grader could absorb). Nine months later, in 1955, Geisel produced *The Cat in the Hat* with just 220 words. It achieved instant success.

In 1960, publisher Bennett Cerf bet Geisel $50 that he couldn't write an entire book using only fifty words. He did: *Green Eggs and Ham*. (Cerf never paid the $50.) Dr. Seuss would go on to become the most widely loved children's writer, selling more than one hundred million copies of his books.

In 1986, at age eighty-two, Dr. Seuss made yet another comeback after a twenty-six-year publishing hiatus: he produced *You're Only Old Once*, a book for the "obsolete children" of the world.

103. SOLZHENITSYN, ALEKSANDR

A CRITICAL REMARK ABOUT STALIN IN A LETTER TO A friend brought Aleksandr Solzhenitsyn eight years at hard labor in prison. He wrote about his experiences upon release in 1953 and spent the next decade or so teaching high school math and physics and writing in his spare time. His short novel *One Day in the Life of Ivan Denisovich* and the film version that followed created a major stir because they broached the taboo subject of Stalin's forced labor camps.

After 1963, Solzhenitsyn's work was banned in Russia for years. The standoff intensified in 1968 after the publication abroad of *The First Circle* (referring the first circle of Dante's *Inferno*) and *The Cancer Ward*. His winning of the 1970 Nobel Prize in Literature further exacerbated the situation between the writer and his native government. Public statements by Solzhenitsyn, as well as the publication of the first volume of *August 1914* and the first volume of *The Gulag Archipelago*, prompted Soviet authorities to finally exile him to the West in 1974.

After moving first to Zurich, Solzhenitsyn and his family eventually settled in a small Vermont town. Over the next several years he completed the *Gulag Archipelago* (a novel in three parts), *The Oak and the Calf* (memoirs of his last ten years in the Soviet Union), *The Mortal Danger: Misconceptions about Soviet Russia and the Threat to America*, and *Three Plays*.

When the Berlin Wall fell in 1989, so, too, did his nemesis, and Solzhenitsyn faded from public view. One might say simply that his work here was done: suffering through imprisonment, deprivation, and the threat of death, he helped pull down his oppressors using the power of words.

104. TAKAHASHI, SHINKICHI

SHINKICHI TAKAHASHI DROPPED OUT OF HIGH SCHOOL and moved to Tokyo from Shikoku, a small fishing village, in hopes of starting a literary career. Instead, he came down with typhus and landed, penniless, in a charity hospital. When he recovered, he worked as a waiter and newspaper office gofer. He published his first work, *Dadaist Shinkichi's Poetry*, in 1923; he happened to be in jail at the time for "impulsive actions," and the book was handed to him through the bars. He tore it up in frustration—his work was succeeding, but his life was in shambles. He returned to writing, however, with *Gion Festival* (1926) and *Poems of Shinkichi Takahashi* (1928). A few critics commented positively, but his books were off-putting to most.

Still seeking that *something* to give his life meaning, he sought the tutelage of Shizan Ashikaga, Rinzai Zen master of the Shogen Temple. He threw himself into the new Zen training, which involved hours of ascetic mental exercises. It proved too much and, exhausted from the harsh training, he was sent home to his family. Confined to a tiny room for three years, he wrote poems to pass the time.

Takahashi went back to Tokyo again in 1932 for more of Ashikaga's Zen training. He became his full-time disciple in 1935 and studied with him for the next seventeen years, years of both hardship and satori (enlightenment). In 1951, he was given his *inka*, the master's testimony that he had successfully completed the course, just one of seven students so honored over many years. He left the temple and made his living in newspaper journalism. He married in 1951 and lived happily with his wife and their two daughters.

At this time, he also decided upon his life's purpose in coming back to writing, specifically poetry. By 1970, his first collection of poems, *Afterimages*, had appeared in the United States and the United Kingdom to critical acclaim. Takahashi's hallmarks were clarity, power, and a straightforward identification with all he observed. Eventually, he would be recognized as one of the twentieth century's greatest poets.

His friend, translator, and advocate Lucien Stryk, professor of literature at Northern Illinois University, once wrote that we don't fully grasp the wisdom of the saying that troubles are "only in the mind." But when we empty the mind and point it in the proper direction, he says, it becomes "the only light we need."

105. Terkel, Studs

After refusing to testify against left-wing activists to Senator Joseph McCarthy and the House Un-American Activities Committee in 1953, Studs Terkel's television show (*Stud's Place*) was cancelled and he was blacklisted. Terkel eventually landed a job writing a jazz column with the *Chicago Sunday Times* and supplemented his income with acting.

In 1958, he returned to broadcasting via Chicago's FM classical radio station WFMT. More or less a volunteer at the outset, Terkel developed an hour-long radio interview program, the *Studs Terkel Show*. The show ran for some five decades, and Terkel interviewed thousands of remarkable individuals. He parlayed his trademark interviews into a series of best-selling books. His first book, in 1967, was *Division Street: America*. It was followed by a long list of successful titles, including *Working*, the Pulitzer Prize–winning *The Good War*, *Race*, *Coming of Age*, *American Dreams: Lost and Found*, and *Will the Circle Be Unbroken?* Described variously as a historian and a sociologist, Terkel prefers the title "guerrilla journalist with a tape recorder." In love with both the humor and the tragedy of life and consumed with the foibles of the common man, he advises each one of us to make the most of every molecule we've got, as long as we've got a second to go.

106. THURBER, JAMES

As a youngster, James Thurber lost the sight in his left eye in an arrow-shooting accident while playing William Tell. In his mid-forties, he lost the vision in his other eye. However, Thurber decided to use humor as an antidote for life's ills. Assisted by his wife, he wrote short stories and drew cartoons as a staff member of *New Yorker* magazine from 1927 to 1933, and thereafter as a contributor until his death in 1961. He lampooned the frustrations of modern life in his books *The Owl in the Attic and Other Perplexities*, *The Seal in the Bedroom and Other Predicaments*, *Fables for Our Time*, and *The Secret Life of Walter Mitty*. He also wrote children's books, such as *The Thirteen Clocks*.

Thurber's surreal, minimalist *New Yorker* sketches became prototypes of the sophisticated cartoons for which the magazine is famous. He remanufactured tragedy into humor and is regarded by many as the foremost American humorist since Mark Twain. Generator of thousands upon thousands of quips, some hilarious, some piercing, he once said it was better to know some of the questions than all of the answers. He also suggested not looking back in anger, or forward in fear, but around in awareness.

107. TWAIN, MARK

"Always acknowledge a fault. This will throw those in authority off their guard and give you an opportunity to commit more."

SAMUEL CLEMENS, MOST WIDELY KNOWN BY HIS pen name, Mark Twain, started off as a full-time printer and sometime writer for his brother's Hannibal, Missouri, newspaper. When things got slow, and when there was space, he would contribute light verses and satire. That predilection for the printed word would ultimately be his North Star, but it would be a while before he came back to writing. After stints as a printer in New York and Philadelphia, Clemens returned to the Midwest in 1857, now age twenty-one, to work for the Keokuk, Iowa, *Daily Post*. The paper assigned Clemens a series of comic travel letters. He wrote five, and then decided to become a steamboat captain instead. And so Mark Twain had quit writing before he had even become Mark Twain.

Clemens became a pilot's apprentice that year, 1857, and received his pilot's license in 1859 at age twenty-three. He worked at the job for two years, until steamboat traffic was stopped by the Civil War. Part of the captain's lexicon was the term *mark twain*, a boatman's call announcing the river was just two fathoms deep, the minimum for safe navigation.

He volunteered in the Confederate Army; he hated it and lasted only a few months. Clemens came back to writing in 1861, employed by the *Virginia City Territorial Enterprise*. This time, he stuck with it: After writing a humorous travel letter signed by the name of Mark Twain for the paper, he continued to use the pseudonym for nearly fifty years and became America's foremost humorist.

Twain Quotes:

- "All you need in this life is ignorance and confidence, and then success is sure."
- "A person who won't read has no advantage over one who can't read."
- "A person with a new idea is a crank until the idea succeeds."
- "Always acknowledge a fault. This will throw those in authority off their guard and give you an opportunity to commit more."

108. WHITMAN, WALT

WALT WHITMAN PAID TO HAVE BOTH HIS FIRST (1855) and his second (1856) editions of *Leaves of Grass* published—and both sold poorly. Whitman was expecting a much better fate, especially after sending a copy to Ralph Waldo Emerson and receiving these words back in a letter:

"I find it the most extraordinary piece of wit and wisdom that America has yet contributed. . . . I greet you at the beginning of a great career." Whitman had consciously hoped to answer Emerson's earlier (1843) essay *The Poet*, which called for a truly original national poet. A word of encouragement, at the right time, can mean everything, and Emerson's letter had a profound impact on Whitman. He stuck with his poetry, in spite of the neglect by the marketplace, and his persistence was rewarded. His third edition of *Leaves of Grass* was published by a Boston firm, not Whitman himself, in 1880. His genius was being recognized, albeit slowly.

The subsequent 1882 publication of *Leaves of Grass* did even better. It generated enough money for Whitman to buy a "a little shanty of my own," the only home he ever owned, 328 Mickle Street in Camden, New Jersey. Whitman was now sixty-five. In a few more years, he would be recognized as America's foremost poet. It had taken *twenty-seven years longer* than he had hoped or expected, but because he never gave up on his life's work and calling, he was ultimately successful.

Whitman Quotes:

- "And there is no trade or employment but the young man following it may become a hero."
- "Have you heard that it was good to gain the day? I also say it is good to fall, battles are lost in the same spirit in which they are won."
- "Henceforth I ask not good fortune. I myself am

good fortune."

- "How beggarly appear arguments before a defiant deed!"
- "The words of my book nothing, the drift of it everything."

MEDIA

109. Bradshaw, Terry

Is there anyone who better represents hale, hearty, successful American manliness than Terry Bradshaw? He's a winning Super Bowl quarterback (four times!), Hall of Famer, Most Valuable Player, NFL broadcaster, and commercial spokesperson. On top of the world? Surely, but that's just the "outside man" everyone sees on television. There's an "inside man," too, for each one of us, and it's not always what it seems.

Bradshaw suffers from depression and attention-deficit disorder, and he takes medications for both. Bradshaw says he is not on a crusade for drugs or medication and is not looking for sympathy. The drugs simply allow him to function normally and feel good about his health. He also recommends being honest with the people around you. He communicates publicly about the issue because he knows that sports heroes and celebrities have the ability to influence others—and he wants to be a positive influence.

Sometimes part of a making a comeback is as simple, or as difficult, as getting proper medical attention and following through with the medications, treatments, and procedures you need.

110. BROTHERS, DR. JOYCE

LOSING A LOVED ONE IS A SETBACK THAT EVERYONE has to deal with at some time. Psychologist Joyce Brothers lost her husband of thirty-nine years, Milt, in 1989. She was devastated, learning firsthand that psychologists don't necessarily handle grief better than other people do. She went through the traditional stages of grief, becoming angry, despondent, resigned, and finally accepting. Brothers had always thought of herself as half of their whole, and she was afraid that if she lost Milt she would fall apart. But she didn't. She realized she could function alone, and surprisingly well.

She ate the foods she liked. She slept when she wanted to sleep. She had always put others first, but now she learned to put herself first. It was a new attitude. Her work became more meaningful to her; she appreciated more than ever the opportunity to help others. She took more speaking engagements and worked on new projects, like film cameos. She traveled more, often with family members, including an unforgettable trip to visit headhunters in Borneo, who showed her their shrunken heads.

These changes and adventures illustrate how far she had come, overcoming her grief and creating a new life in the process. Brothers made her comeback one moment, one day, at a time. After taking time to work through her loss, she said she looked forward to getting up in the morning because every day was an adventure—something she thought she would never feel again when she was in the depths of her despair.

111. BUCHWALD, ART

SUFFERING FROM CRUSHING DEPRESSION, HUMORIST Art Buchwald was hospitalized in 1963 at thirty-eight and again for manic depression in 1987. Meanwhile, his column was running in 550 newspapers worldwide. Ever the humorist, Buchwald quipped to a university audience that he considered suicide but wouldn't follow through because he feared he wouldn't make it into the *New York Times* obituaries.

With the help of doctors and medications, Buchwald

recovered and used his fame to educate the public about mental health issues, especially the stigmatization of mental illness in the workplace. His appearance on *Larry King Live* in the early 1990s to discuss depression generated a record number of requests for video copies. Depression is just another disease, Buchwald argued. As such, it is treatable, but unless a person has personally experienced it, he or she cannot possibly understand what it is like. He believes we need to be reminded that many of history's most gifted individuals struggled with mental illness, like Winston Churchill, who called his depression "the black dog that follows me everywhere." But for Buchwald, the "dog" had finally stopped following him because he was smart and strong enough to seek treatment.

There was one last great comeback in store for the fabled humorist. Hospitalized in February 2006, doctors told him he would have only several weeks to live unless he underwent kidney dialysis. But Buchwald declined, choosing hospice care instead, and turned to work as his medicine, penning a new book, *Too Soon to Leave* (2006). The medicine worked very well: Despite his doctor's dire warnings, he lived nearly another full year. Full indeed. His last year turned into a glorious farewell tour (his son Joel called it a "victory lap"), where he received visits, honors, interviews, and plaudits from thousands of friends, acquaintances, and admirers. His worry, in jest, about *The New York Times*? Not to worry at all. At his passing, he was featured on page one of their website with a video feature, in addition to three full web pages lauding his life and accomplishments. The publication suggested the last year of his life was the most remarkable out of his eighty-one years. The *Times* said someone once called him a "Will Rogers with chutzpah." And never more so than in death. To have chutzpah—and humor—in the face of one's mortality—what could be a greater statement of one's courage? Or a greater comeback?

112. CARTER, BETSY

IN 1983, BETSY CARTER'S TEETH WERE KNOCKED out in a car accident. Not long after, she had a hysterectomy. Then, her husband of seventeen years announced he was gay. After these devastating events, Carter said she felt she was being blown to pieces, gasping for breath, swimming in air.

An editor by trade (*Newsweek*, *Esquire*, *Harper's Bazaar*), in 1986 she launched a new magazine, *New York Woman*, and hoped for a return to "normal life." But a few months later, her upstate New York weekend house burned down, destroyed by an arsonist. Looking for some solace in therapy, Carter surely didn't find it:

her psychiatrist concluded that in an earlier life she had been an evil person and suggested an exorcism. Then, in short order, her new publication closed down, she was diagnosed with breast cancer, and she needed to undergo a mastectomy and chemotherapy.

Then things smoothed out. She met and married her new spouse, who also works in publishing. She moved forward in the magazine trade, freelance writing for such publications as *New York*, *Good Housekeeping*, and *O, The Oprah Magazine*. She took up writing fiction as well, calling it her Act II. Carter said she felt that fiction allowed her to be in charge and tell people what to do, at least the people that reside in her imagination. Published in 2005, her debut novel, *The Orange Blossom Special*, is a story about the relationships among residents of late-1950s Gainesville, Florida. *Elle* magazine called it a "warm, wise book."

But how do you get to the level of "warm and wise?" Carter's advice on making it through terrible trials includes being easy on yourself and cheerful. That rather simplistic-sounding advice may be the hard part of making a comeback, at least for those of us who are so very, very good at beating up on ourselves. Many of us are far better at that than any of our family, friends, or enemies, because we put so much more time in on the job, sometimes 24/7. Decide now to change this behavior. Decide to be your own best advocate. Decide now to take the same energy that you usually put into putting yourself "down" into building yourself up. When you notice yourself mindlessly pummeling yourself, going over old mistakes, regrets, woulda, coulda, shouldas, STOP! Say "Take Two." Start over. Be positive. Repeat positive images, words, experiences, poems, songs, pictures to your mind's eye. If you won't do it for yourself, who will? If you need someone to give you permission to do this, your humble servant, your author, hereby grants you permission right here and now.

Secondly, Carter suggests sharing bad news with your inner circle as rapidly as possible: don't keep things to yourself, it's too painful. Take advantage of the support that others can give you.

113. Cavuto, Neil

With a $5 million, five-year contract with Fox News, business anchor Neil Cavuto was riding very high. But when he began to see blind spots and his skin felt prickly, he thought he was having a recurrence of the Hodgkin's disease that attacked him in the late 1980s.

The good news was that he wasn't. The bad news: he had multiple sclerosis (1996). For three or four days, he was silent. He didn't want to talk to anyone; he was too angry with the world. Finally, he told his bosses and then his viewing audience.

Cavuto was able to get on top of it. How? He tries to look at the good and bad things and balance them out. For example, he says the disease "sucks, but life doesn't suck." He brings the same kind of upbeat attitude to his financial reporting. It has been a challenge to keep going on the air. When the multiple sclerosis acts up, his shoulders lock up, his head spins, and he has no feeling in his arms or legs.

But, courageously, Cavuto manages to hide this from his viewers. He refuses to reorder his priorities, slack off, or take things easy. His wife, Mary, says that he probably was working harder after the diagnosis than before, refusing to relent. Meanwhile, Cavuto, facing full disability from the disease, says that for now it's full steam ahead.

114. GARDNER, CAROL

"For Christmas I got a dog for my husband . . . good trade, huh?"

AFTER TWENTY-SEVEN YEARS IN A CUSHY MARRIAGE to a college president, Carol Gardner, fifty-two, found herself smack in the middle of a tough divorce. When the wheels of change stopped turning, she had lots of debt, no job, and no income. Her attorney advised her to "get a therapist or a dog." Therapists cost money and a dog gives you unconditional love, so Carol got herself a four-month-old English bulldog and named her Zelda. Zelda provided love and much, much more.

A friend tipped Gardner off to an annual Christmas card contest at a local pet store. First prize was forty pounds of free dog food every month for a year. Years earlier, Gardner had been an advertising executive, so she decided to dust off her skills and go for it. She borrowed a Santa hat, filled her bathtub with bubble bath, and lowered Zelda into the tub. With the red hat on and a beard made from the bubbles, Zelda made a striking canine Santa. Carol snapped the photo and sent it off to the store with the one-liner: "For Christmas I got a dog for my husband . . . good trade, huh?" The spunky quip won.

Encouraged, Gardner used the shot in her own Christmas cards that year, and the response was overwhelming. Soon she was producing a whole series of Zelda cards. The line has expanded to include books, calendars, housewares, jewelry, stationery, and stuffed animals. Zelda does more than just bring smiles, though. Zelda books help learning disabled children learn to read and write by pouring on the humor and warmth. Zelda is also the official "spokesdog" of the

Delta Society Pet Partners, an international program dedicated to the human-animal healing bond.

Gardner says she receives letters and email daily from fans thanking her for adding a smile to their lives, whatever their struggle. So when you're working hard at making your comeback, don't forget to smile, or even better, laugh. And, by the way, Zelda is something else for Gardner: a $50 million business that's still growing. Zelda joined the Hallmark team; her business was acquired in December 2004 for a significant sum.

115. GRAHAM, KATHARINE

AFTER SHE HEARD THE STARTLING SOUND OF A gunshot, Katherine Graham raced to find her husband. She opened the door to a downstairs bathroom and her worst fears were realized: her manic-depressive husband, Philip, had committed suicide.

Some thirty-three days after the funeral, Katharine Graham, then a forty-six-year-old mother of four, took on her late husband's job of running the *Washington Post*, the only "sensible step to take," she later wrote. Her history with the paper went back to her school days: Her father bought the paper as a retirement hobby in 1933. She had worked on her school newspaper, spent summer vacations working at the *Post*, and began her career as a reporter for the *San Francisco News*. She joined her father's paper one year later. Eventually she would marry, settle down to raise children, and support her husband, who was running the paper.

As the new president of the Washington Post Company, Graham wrote that she would put one foot in front of the other, shut her eyes, and step off the edge. In 1965 she hired managing editor Benjamin C. Bradlee, who made journalism history by publishing both the Pentagon Papers in 1971 and the breaking Watergate reports in 1972.

In 1979, Graham appointed her son, Donald, to the post of publisher, which kept the management of the business in the family, a goal she had set during the harrowing days after her husband's suicide. Graham remained active in the business, which included, in addition to the *Post* and *Newsweek*, New Jersey's *Trenton Times*, four television stations, and a 49 percent interest in a paper company. She won a Pulitzer Prize for her best-selling autobiography *Personal History* in 1998, one of the greatest comeback stories in journalism. She wrote that to love what you do and feel that it matters— how could anything be more fun?

116. HUTTON, LAUREN

LAUREN HUTTON WAS NOT MET WITH OPEN ARMS when she moved to New York City at the age of twenty-one. Short, gap-toothed, the spunky girl from the swampy backwoods of Florida—most of the city's top modeling agencies simply didn't want her. But she pressed on and found one that *did*, the Ford Agency, in 1963. Several years later, her big break came. Editor Diana Vreeland put Hutton on the cover of *Vogue*, and she went on to appear there a record twenty-five times. Revlon signed her to the industry's first $1 million modeling contract in 1974, and an acting career followed.

When Hutton turned forty-one, Revlon fired her, but she had some consolation: an $11 million fortune, which she turned over to her boyfriend to manage. He lost it—all. So, out of financial necessity, Hutton launched the Lauren Hutton's Good Stuff cosmetics line for older women. It proved successful, a superb comeback against the vagaries of the modeling business.

But all the ups and downs of her lifetime would pale against what happened next. Hutton went on a celebrity motorcycle ride through the Nevada desert in 2000. As the troupe was about to head out, friends Dennis Hopper and Jeremy Irons noticed Hutton did not have the proper protective gear, so Hopper gave her a reinforced leather jacket and Irons had her replace her helmet.

Their concern was an omen. The troupe took off, and within several hours, the inexperienced Hutton sped ahead of the group at more than 100 mph. Maneuvering around a sharp turn, she hit some soft gravel and flew twenty feet into the air, landing in a ravine. The bike came straight down and exploded. Hopper reached her first and thought she was dead: her ribs had punctured her lungs and she had many broken bones. She was rushed to a hospital and placed on life-support systems.

Hutton's recovery took a year-and-a-half of painful physical therapy, but it didn't damper her love of travel or her zest for life. She later traveled to Zambia, Java, Botswana, Burma, Belize, even dogsledding in Alaska. She says traveling makes her love God and life and puts a smile on her face. Hutton chose to see the world on her own terms and have fun on the journey. And she chose to make several comebacks—against the modeling naysayers, after losing a fortune, even after an accident that almost took her life. Taking graceful aging to a new level, she posed nude for *Big* magazine at age sixty-two.

117. KERR, GRAHAM

IN HIS EARLY DAYS AS TELEVISION'S *GALLOPING Gourmet*, Graham Kerr created dishes overflowing with cream, butter, and egg yolks. Many were deep-fried and laden with fat. Then in 1972, a car accident nearly killed him, leaving him partially paralyzed. During recuperation Kerr began to experiment with a low-fat cooking style for his family. The new food wasn't a hit: it was simply too tasteless, too bland, too big a change from the rich fare they were accustomed to. So he put the idea aside.

When his wife, Treena, suffered a heart attack in 1986, fourteen years later, Graham came back to his low-fat concept. This time around, he developed a way of cooking that combined delicious food with a healthy and creative lifestyle. He put it all together in *Graham Kerr's Gathering Place*, 130 one-hour television programs completed in 2000, released internationally in 2001, on PBS in 2002; it's also available in book form. The theme was healthy and *tasty* food alternatives. Carrot cake, roasted vegetable lasagna, and sweet-and-sour red cabbage casserole with pork tenderloin are just a few of the "new" recipes he prescribed—all delicious, all very healthy.

Kerr says the programs are the culmination of twenty-three years of intensive nutritional research combined with a lifetime of cooking experience. He followed up the series with *Graham Kerr's Simply Splenda Cookbook* (2004).

Kerr is active with the American Diabetes Association, Egg Beaters, and similar groups and companies—a huge and serious change for the once hedonistic *Galloping Gourmet*. Kerr's new mission is to serve those who choose to make healthy, lasting lifestyle changes.

118. KING, LARRY

ARRESTED IN MIAMI ON DECEMBER 20, 1971, ON charges of grand larceny, local radio host Larry King, thirty-seven, was "in debt to sustain an extravagant lifestyle," according to mugshots.com. The actual facts of the case are ambiguous and unproven, but reports allege that King tried to capitalize on his relationship with Richard M. Nixon's attorney general John Mitchell by setting up a series of meetings for financier Louis Wolfson. After accepting payment, King was unable to complete his side of the transaction. When Wolfson was released from prison for securities violations, he went after King to recoup the money. That's when King was arrested.

King was released without bond, and a judge dismissed the charges a couple of months later. But the arrest flattened his career in Miami: King was fired from the AM station WIOD, Channel 4, and the *Sun Reporter*. Off the air for four years, he worked as the public relations director for a Louisiana racetrack and wrote for *Esquire* magazine, including a major feature on New York Jets quarterback Joe Namath, for which he received $25,000.

It took time, but by 1978, things were looking up. King began a national late-night radio show on the Mutual Network. In 1985, he moved to CNN. The move led to book deals, including *Tell It to the King* in 1988 and later *The Best of Larry King Live*. More than forty thousand interviews later, King occupies a one-hour, prime-time slot on CNN, where he interviews the biggest newsmakers of the day. For many, watching King's show is a nightly ritual.

King says that he reminds himself every morning that nothing he will say this day will teach him anything—if he's going to learn, he must do it by listening.

119. LIMBAUGH, RUSH

In his early days in radio, Rush Limbaugh was fired from no less than *seven* jobs. It took a toll on the endlessly ebullient radio personality. After being fired in

McKeesport, Pennsylvania, in 1984, Limbaugh spent seven months doing nothing. Then he was hired by KBFK in Sacramento, California, to replace the often offensive Morton Downey Jr.

Within a year, Limbaugh became the most listened-to host in Sacramento and was syndicated to fifty-six stations. He signed a two-year contract with EFM Media Management and went to New York City in 1988. By 1993, his nationally syndicated three-hour show was the most popular in the country. He capital-ized on his fame with books, *The Way Things Ought to Be* in 1992 and *See, I Told You So* in 1993. Limbaugh's radio show was attracting between twelve and twenty million listeners each day.

The individual who was fired *seven times* became the highest-paid radio personality *ever* after signing an eight-year, $250 million contract with Premiere Radio Networks in 2001. Without a college degree or even a sound resume, Limbaugh proved that persistence can be more powerful than anything else.

In 2003, Limbaugh revealed he was addicted to painkillers and entered rehab. Another comeback fol-lowed: he was back on the radio after only a thirty-eight-day hiatus. His six-hundred-station EIB network promptly distributed a news release indicating that his audience and ratings were intact. None of Limbaugh's famous bluster was lost in the transaction—he suggested to his viewers, tongue-in-cheek, that most likely his return made the sky seem brighter, the water purer.

120. MCGRAW, DR. PHIL

IN THE LATE 1980S, PSYCHOLOGIST PHIL MCGRAW was reprimanded by his licensing board and decided to throw in the towel on his career. Here's what happened: at the behest of a patient's family, Dr. Phil had hired a nineteen-year-old patient to keep closer watch on her. The patient filed sexual abuse charges with the Texas State Board of Examiners and Psychologists, which reprimanded McGraw in 1989 "for hiring the woman too soon after she was a patient," calling it "an inappropriate dual relationship." He was required to take ethics classes. McGraw told *TV Guide* on September 12, 2002, that the charges were false and that he had never so much as patted the woman on the back.

What appeared to be a humiliating setback turned out to be a tremendous springboard. It catalyzed McGraw's desire to leave his field. He sold his counseling practice in 1989 and cofounded Courtroom Sciences Inc. (CSI), which assists lawyer clients by conducting mock trials, behavioral analysis, jury selection counsel, and mediation. A tremendous success, CSI generated some $20 million per year in revenues. For most, that would be a big enough comeback, but fate had even more in store: CSI also put McGraw in touch with a client who would dramatically change his life, Oprah Winfrey.

In 1996, cattle ranchers sued Winfrey, claiming that she defamed the beef industry. She hired CSI to help prepare. It was a difficult time for Winfrey, but McGraw's tough, straight talk was effective. She wanted to just settle the case and put it behind her, but McGraw advised her to fight back, to take the case to trial. The case was dismissed six years later.

In 1998, McGraw began appearing on the *Oprah* show as Dr. Phil, dealing with life strategies and relationships. He became a popular fixture, and in 2002, he launched his own show. A slew of books followed in its wake, on relationships, marriage, family, and weight loss. The failed counselor had more than made a comeback—he transformed himself into a hugely successful businessperson and television icon.

121. MILLS, HEATHER

HEATHER MILLS'S TROUBLED CHILDHOOD READS like nineteenth-century British fiction. Her father beat his wife as well as Mills and her siblings. Her mother abandoned the family when she was nine. Mills began stealing to feed herself and her siblings. When her father was arrested for fraud, Mills left home. She joined a traveling fair and eventually became homeless, living under London's Waterloo Bridge in a cardboard box.

As a young adult, Mills righted her ship, becoming a successful model and then a modeling agency owner. Then tragedy struck: crossing a street in London, she was hit by a police motorbike on August 8, 1993. To save her life, surgeons amputated her mangled left leg. Somehow in the midst of it all, she found the courage to say something good was going to come of this accident.

That something good started in her spirit. Mills refused to be a victim. She learned to ski again. She surfed and went Rollerblading. She began to speak publicly about her accident and recovery. She visited the disabled, launched a crusade to provide artificial limbs to amputees in war-torn countries, and undertook a public affairs battle against land mines.

Then, in 1999, she met former Beatle Paul McCartney at the Pride of Britain award ceremony. As a lover of jazz and classical music, she claimed to be only passingly familiar with Beatles tunes. The pair fell in love, married, and Mills and her causes were catapulted to a new level of public recognition. However, the marriage was not a cakewalk. Mills said the media harassment was the worst ordeal of her life. She endured it, but unfortunately, the marriage itself did not: divorce proceedings began in 2006.

Mills was wounded by life, but remained a caring and outgoing person who was able to rise above any setback through her strength of character and positive outlook. She has said that life can be either something you drift through passively or something you take in both hands and turn around. She chose the latter.

122. ONASSIS, JACQUELINE KENNEDY

WIDOWED TWICE AND AT JUST FORTY-SIX, Jacqueline Kennedy Onassis had to determine how to make yet another comeback and how to spend the rest of her life. She had any number of possibilities: suggestions included a run for Senate, New York City commissioner of cultural affairs, fashion designer, ambassador to France. She declined them all. Her former White House social secretary, Letitia Baldridge, suggested publishing, and it seemed to resonate. Onassis was a voracious reader, fluent in several languages, an expert in the arts, and had personal relationships with many potential authors.

Baldridge went the next step and negotiated a job with Viking Press. It seemed promising—Jackie needed an outlet; Viking needed a star. But when Viking published a British novel fictionalizing an assassination of Edward Kennedy, Onassis felt humiliated and compromised. She resigned from her position but didn't give up on publishing. Six months later, she accepted a post as acquisitions editor at Doubleday. This time around, the experience was more successful. Her colleagues were more congenial and Onassis redoubled her efforts to blend in.

She came to work earlier than her customary 10 a.m. start at Viking, made her own copies, dialed her own phone calls, got her own coffee, and lunched in the cafeteria with everyone else. She carried on the conscious, conscientious campaign to fit in outside the office as well. When the company hosted a Central Park picnic, Onassis was there, in casual attire, sipping beer with her office mates. When a coworker had a Christmas party at her home, Onassis attended, mingled, and sang holiday songs.

She changed her business instincts, too, to think more commercially. In 1979, her first year at Doubleday, she acquired *Call the Darkness Light*, by Nancy L. Zaroulis. The feminist-themed work became a bestseller, and the paperback rights sold for $550,000 to New American Library. Onassis received a raise to $50,000, was promoted to full editor and then senior editor, and went on to acquire many other bestsellers.

Among them:

• *Dancing on My Grave* (1986), ballerina Gelsey

Kirkland's account of her career, drug addiction, anorexia, and suicidal despair.

- *Joseph Campbell and the Power of Myth* (1988) by Bill Moyers.
- *The Last Tsar: The Life and Death of Nicholas II* (1992) by Edward Radzinsky.
- *Healing and the Mind* (1993) by Bill Moyers.

One question remained: Why did Jackie work, when as a living legend and a woman of independent means, she didn't have to? She told *Ms.* magazine editor Gloria Steinem in an interview that she was, in fact, working so that she had access to the real world like other women of the new generation. Onassis's motto might have been that bliss is productivity. She once recounted the story of a taxi driver who said to her incredulously, "Lady, you work and you don't have to?" When she said yes, he turned around and said with a broad smile, "I think that's great!"

123. RAPHAEL, SALLY JESSY

LOOKING FOR WORK IN THE LATE 1960S, SALLY Jessy Raphael moved twenty-five times, sometimes sleeping in her car. She couldn't pay off her credit card bills for twenty-six years, got fired eighteen times, and never made more than $22,000 per year, according to various accounts. But she was stubborn, and she knew what she wanted to do. Raphael eventually turned all the minor setbacks into one very major triumph: a twenty-year run on syndicated television.

Raphael started her media career at young age, reading the junior high school news on WFAS-AM in White Plains, New York. At eighteen, she married and moved to San Juan, Puerto Rico, where she said they let her do everything: reporting, comedy, weather, and hosting the morning show and a cooking show as well. She decided to change her name in Puerto Rico, taking her father's first name, Jessy, and her mother's maiden name, Raphael, motivated by the Puerto Rican tradition of a person using both parents' last names.

Her first marriage ended in the late 1960s. Raphael left Puerto Rico and settled in Miami, but eventually headed north in search of broadcasting work. Times were tough, but while she found work as a rock-and-roll disc jockey and a television puppet show host, she did not find that one secure job she was looking for.

In 1969, Raphael landed a morning television anchor post and afternoon radio program in Miami. She stayed on until 1974 and, in 1976, moved to New York City to cohost a morning radio talk show.

In 1981, Raphael moved to late-night talk radio on NBC *Talknet*. For three hours each night, live from

Rockefeller Center, she took calls and listeners connected to her reassuring manner. She found a national audience, and from there it was just a short leap to television: *Sally Jessy Raphael* launched October 17, 1983; after only six months, it was successful enough for national syndication. The woman with the trademark red glasses would be a television fixture for the next nineteen years, until 2002.

There would be heartbreaking setbacks along the way. In 1992, her adopted son, nineteen, was seriously injured in a car accident and spent three weeks in a coma. Just as he recovered, her daughter Allison died in her sleep after combining alcohol and painkillers for a back injury. Raphael took time off to grieve but came back to her post. Still about her life's work, she presently hosts a weekend radio show, *Sally JR's Open House*, on the Internet.

124. RAY, RACHAEL

AFTER A ROMANCE GONE SOUR, A VIOLENT MUGGING in front of her Queens, New York, apartment in the mid-1990s, and a broken ankle, Rachael Ray, then twenty-seven, gave up on the Big Apple. She had lasted two years, working at the Macy's Marketplace candy counter, then Agata & Valentina specialty foods, and now she was packing it in and going home to Mom. She moved back into her mother's rustic cabin in the woods in Upstate New York and snagged a job at a food shop in Albany as a buyer and cook, preparing hundreds of pounds of food each day. Fatefully, she also created a class to teach people how to prepare a meal in thirty minutes.

Ray took her show on the road, first to grocery stores, then to Schenectady television. She added a cookbook and persuaded a small Manhattan publisher to publish it. She was now a regional celebrity. Three years later, a Food Network executive heard Ray on public radio; the very same week, a *Today* producer saw her book and called to slate her. After driving with her mom for nine hours through a snowstorm, Ray returned to New York and appeared on the NBC morning showcase. She was a smash and the Food Network executives knew it. The very next day, they contracted with her for a reported $360,000.

Since then, Ray has sold 4.5 million books, inked a $6 million book deal with Random House, and, of course, appears on the Food Network daily in not one but *four* shows: *30 Minute Meals*, *Inside Dish*, *$40 a Day*, and *Tasty Travels*. Her eleventh book is *365: No Repeats*. She also publishes a food and lifestyle magazine, *Every Day with Rachael Ray*. She leaped off the cable channel onto network stations with her own daytime syndicated talk show in 2006.

125. WALLACE, MIKE

IN THE MID-1980S, AT THE PEAK OF HIS JOURNALISTIC career, tough, brash, iconic CBS newsperson Mike Wallace was overwhelmed by depression. At first he couldn't sleep; then he couldn't eat. Finally, he couldn't function at all and stayed in bed. Eventually, he attempted suicide—he wrote a farewell note, took an overdose of pills, and fell asleep, but his wife, Mary, found him just in time. He revealed this to *60 Minutes* colleague Morley Safer on a program celebrating his career and retirement on May 21, 2006.

The period of depression was catalyzed when CBS and Wallace were defendants in a $120 million libel suit in 1982 for claims made in the documentary *The Uncounted Enemy: A Vietnam Deception*. The program alleged that General William Westmoreland had intentionally fabricated reports of enemy troop strength during the Vietnam War to mislead the American people. The day-after-day process of repeatedly being called a liar, a cheat, and a fraud in court had crushed Wallace's self-esteem, and he could not cope with the fact that his fate was in the hands of the jury. He was afraid that if he lost the case, his life as he knew it would be over. Like every victim of depression, Wallace had lost perspective.

His regular doctor told him to pull himself together, that going public with his mental woes would be bad for his career. But wife Mary knew something much more serious and life-threatening was taking place. She called a local hospital, seeking psychiatric help for him, and in so doing, likely saved his life. Wallace was treated successfully with drugs and talk therapy.

CBS eventually settled the suit in 1985, and the pressure on Wallace lifted. His psychiatrist recommended that he taper off his medicine, but he quit cold turkey. Not long after, he broke his wrist playing tennis and fell into another deep depression. He was seventy-five. But having fought off the demon of depression once, he knew it could be done again.

So he got back on medication and began psychotherapy. At the behest of his doctor, he started exercising. He also reached out to others, especially friends who suffered depression and overcame it, like columnist Art Buchwald and author William Styron. Most important, he said, he didn't give in. It worked, and his spirits slowly but surely returned to normal. Wallace has said that the twenty years since his suicide attempt turned out to be the happiest of his life.

MILITARY

126. CHURCHILL, WINSTON

"Success is the ability to go from failure to failure without losing your enthusiasm."

WINSTON CHURCHILL'S LIQUID ASSETS WERE invested in U.S. stocks—and wiped out in 1938. The former British Chancellor of the Exchequer (the equivalent of the U.S. Secretary of the Treasury) was sixty-four, out of office, broke, and humiliated. To pay his living expenses, he wrote prolifically: newspaper columns, magazine articles, and books, sometimes in what he called "double shifts." He was earning approximately $1,500 per week for a syndicated newspaper column, but with an aristocratic background and lifestyle, he was spending far more. With no other recourse, he decided to put his beloved eighty-acre estate, Chartwell, up for sale. He took out a full-page advertisement in a leading newspaper; Great Britain gasped.

Foreseeing that Churchill may be the only political leader with the foresight and ability to stand against Hitler's Germany, a friend arranged for an emergency loan from a wealthy industrialist. The crisis was averted and Churchill stayed in his home, toiling diligently at his writing desk to repay his debts. Destiny would come calling soon enough.

Churchill returned to executive office as first lord of the admiralty in 1939 and then prime minister in 1940; Germany attacked British air forces in that very summer. In his first speech in the House of Commons, after the fall of France to the Nazis, he said: "You ask, 'what is our aim?' I can answer in one word: Victory—victory at all costs, victory in spite of all terror; victory, however long and hard the road may be." There were more setbacks ahead, but Churchill was more than equal to them; Western civilization would survive the threat of Nazi domination

Over his long life, Churchill had also overcome childhood bullies, parental neglect, a car accident, depression, and innumerable political and military foes to become one of the handful of very great men of the twentieth century, and one of the greatest comeback stories of all time.

Churchill Quotes:

- "Never give in, never give in, never, never, never, never—in nothing, great or small, large or petty—

never give in except to convictions of honor and good sense."

- "When you're going through hell, keep going."

127. MacArthur, General Douglas

AFTER A LONG AND DISTINGUISHED MILITARY CAREER that included attending West Point, service in World War I and the Philippines, becoming the youngest-ever army chief of staff (at fifty in 1930), and serving as military adviser to the Philippines as major general, General Douglas MacArthur retired. But when negotiations with the Japanese government meant to avoid war failed in 1941, President Roosevelt recalled MacArthur to active duty.

His assignment: defend the Philippines. The Japanese Air Force attacked the U.S. Pacific Fleet at Pearl Harbor on December 7, 1941, the day that would "live in infamy." The next day the Japanese followed with air strikes on the Philippines; they destroyed half of MacArthur's 227-unit air force and then invaded the island nation. MacArthur ordered a general retreat to the Bataan Peninsula. He was then ordered to leave Bataan for Australia in February 1942 to oversee operations, which he did, but with his famous promise: "I shall return!"

How dire was the situation? Much more so than is commonly realized today. Biographer William Manchester wrote that the Japanese quest for world dominion had spread like a cancer. The Allies could simply not believe that an Asian nation was surpassing them on every level, but it was: strategy, tactics, troop strength, efficiency, training, experience—in all, the Japanese were superior.

With the entire Southwest Pacific now in Japanese hands, and with some Allied strategists estimating it would take ten or more years to retake the territory, MacArthur organized an innovative island-hopping counteroffensive that lasted from 1942 to 1945 and ultimately triumphed. He regained more territory with less loss of life than any other commander since ancient times. MacArthur made good on his promise to return to the Philippines three years later, in 1945, when Allied forces retook the island, first Bataan (Feb.), then Manila (March). On August 6, the atomic bomb fell on Hiroshima, on August 9, another on Nagasaki. As supreme commander of the Allied powers, MacArthur presided over the formal Japanese surrender on September 2, 1945.

Calling for the rebuilding of Japan in peaceful, productive endeavors, MacArthur said that if nations couldn't resolve differences without war, Armageddon would result. The problem was spiritual, he said. *Time* correspondent Shelley Mydans called his thinking "Olympian" and said it spanned populations and centuries. The great man of war seemed an even greater philosopher.

Indeed, during the postwar period when MacArthur ruled Japan, many locals revered him as a godlike figure, producing art, poetry, plays, and the like to extol his kindness and intelligence—a remarkable turn of events for the military man who was calmly surveying the enemy bombers overhead just a few years earlier while they fired down on him and his men.

128. McCain, John

"Glory belongs to the act of being constant to something greater than yourself, to a cause, to your principles, to the people on whom you rely and who rely on you in return."

On October 26, 1967, American A-4 Skyraider pilot John McCain, thirty-one, was shot down over Hanoi, Vietnam. He parachuted into Truc Bac Lake, breaking both arms and a leg. An angry mob found and beat him. McCain was imprisoned for the next five and a half years at Hoa Lo Prison, the infamous "Hanoi Hilton." He endured repeated beatings, torture, and solitary confinement for two years. He tried to hang himself twice; both times he was cut down and beaten by the guards. McCain was finally released when the war ended in March 1973.

A military man through and through, McCain wanted to continue on as a naval aviator, even though he had lost much of his strength and flexibility. So he underwent nine months of painful rehabilitation but did indeed return to flying. He retired after twenty-two years in the cockpit in 1981, earning, along the way, the Silver Star, the Bronze Star, the Legion of Merit, the Purple Heart, and the Distinguished Flying Cross.

McCain had gotten his first taste of politics in 1977 when assigned as the navy's liaison to the U.S. Senate. That same year, he moved to Phoenix and joined the Reagan revolution. His political trajectory was like that of the A-4s he had piloted: he was elected to the U.S. House of Representatives in 1982 and to the Senate in 1985. (McCain notably was instrumental in the establishment of diplomatic relations with Hanoi in 1995.) Quickly rising to become a national leader, he campaigned for the presidential nomination in 2000 and 2007. He has the honor of having a naval destroyer, the USS *John S. McCain*, named for him.

McCain Quotes:

- "Glory is not a conceit. It is not a decoration for valor. Glory belongs to the act of being constant to something greater than yourself, to a cause, to your principles, to the people on whom you rely and who rely on you in return."

- "War is wretched beyond description, and only a fool or a fraud could sentimentalize its cruel reality."

MUSIC, CLASSICAL

129. BACH, JOHANN SEBASTIAN

"I was made to work. If you are equally industrious, you will be equally successful."

IT IS UNQUESTIONABLY ONE OF THE GREATEST ironies in the history of art that during his lifetime, J. S. Bach was regarded as, well, no Bach. He composed, he played the organ, he taught competently, but few grasped his genius.

In 1722, Johann Kuhnau, the cantor of St. Thomas's Church in Leipzig, Germany, died. Bach, thirty-seven, applied for the post, but was turned down. The vacant post was offered first to Georg Philipp Telemann from Hamburg, who declined, and then Christoph Graupner of Darmstadt, who also declined. Graupner, however, recommended Bach to the council. Upon receiving this word, a member of the council remarked something to the effect that "since the best musicians were unavailable an average one would have to be selected." This "average musician" is now generally considered the supreme musician and composer who ever lived.

In addition to composition, part of his job was to teach Latin to poor students. But Bach gave up half his salary to delegate this duty so he could compose magnificent church music that neither the ecclesiastical nor the civic authorities particularly wanted. His vision was paramount, and he stayed true to it, whatever the cost. He stayed on in Leipzig for twenty-seven years, composing the great passions of St. John and St. Matthew, some two hundred cantatas, and many other works.

Perhaps Bach was thinking of his legacy when he went to work on *St. Matthew Passion*, because it was this work that would ultimately achieve for him the recognition he deserved. The original sheet music is still in existence, beautiful in design, magnificently bound, with biblical words highlighted in red ink. Some critics regard the work as the supreme cultural achievement of all Western civilization. The radical skeptic Friedrich Nietzsche (1844–1900) said, upon hearing it, "One who has completely forgotten Christianity truly hears it here as gospel."

But for many years after Bach's death, the work was considered too difficult to perform, and so it was unpublished and unheard. In 1829, forty-four years after Bach's death, composer and conductor Felix Mendelssohn, twenty-two, organized a performance of the piece, heavily abridged, in Berlin on Palm Sunday. That performance of *St. Matthew Passion* ignited a resurgence of interest in Bach's work. As the years went on, Bach became many times more celebrated and revered in death than at any time during his sixty-five-year span on this planet. Of the thousand or so works that have come to us from Bach, only eight were published in his lifetime.

Bach Quotes:

- "The aim and final end of all music should be none other than the glory of God and the refreshment of the soul."
- "There's nothing remarkable about it. All one has to do is hit the right keys at the right time and the instrument plays itself."

130. BARTÓK, BÉLA

IN 1943, HUNGARIAN COMPOSER BÉLA BARTÓK'S LIFE hit rock bottom. Vocationally, he was a concert pianist who was not performing and a composer whose works were not being performed. Psychologically, things were equally bad, if not worse: Bartók was an alienated war refugee, tortured by the fate of Europe and especially his homeland, Hungary. Living in New York, he was subsisting on a $3,000-per-year grant from Columbia University to study the folk music of Yugoslavia, but the grant ended January 1, 1943. Depressed, he had stopped writing music for some two years by this time. Within days he found himself in the hospital, suffering from what would be diagnosed as leukemia.

As bleak as things were, Bartók had one remaining asset: his friends. Fellow Hungarians Joseph Szigeti, a violinist, and Fritz Reiner, a conductor, inveighed upon the American Society of Composers and Performers (ASCAP) for funds to cover Bartók's medical bills, even though he was not even an ASCAP member. Then they convinced famed conductor Serge Koussevitzky to provide a commission from his foundation for an orchestral work.

Koussevitzky personally visited the now eighty-seven-pound Bartók at Doctors Hospital in New York in early 1943. Koussevitzky had been charged by the foundation's trustees to deliver a $500 check as the first half of a fee for a composition for full orchestra, the second half to be paid on completion. Bartók said it was impossible, due to his condition, but the conductor insisted that the award was nonreturnable. There was no deadline.

The assignment would catalyze a huge change in Bartók. Being sought after, having a new goal, and having important work to do was miraculous medicine to him. In a mind-body turnabout that would make Deepak Chopra's heart jump, Bartók's health took an upswing, he gained weight, and he was able to leave the hospital. With the help of ASCAP, he was able to spend the last days of summer at the Saranac Lakes in the Adirondacks. There he composed, between August 15 and October 8, the *Concerto for Orchestra*, the longest, most complex, and most celebrated score from the Hungarian whose music was the veritable definition of passion and excitement.

Bartók wrote: "The general mood of the work represents, apart from the jesting second movement, a gradual transition from the sternness of the first movement and the lugubrious death-song of the third, to the life-assertion of the last one." The work was first performed December 1, 1944, by the Boston Symphony, with the composer in attendance. Bartók had literally left his deathbed to write what many cite as the foremost work of twentieth-century orchestral repertory.

131. BARTON, RACHEL

EN ROUTE TO A VIOLIN LESSON, STEPPING OFF HER commuter train on January 16, 1995, the doors clamped shut on the strap of Rachel Barton's case for her 378-year-old Amati violin, and nineteen-year-old Barton was dragged for three hundred feet between the train and the wooden platform. Her leg was mangled. An alert fellow passenger applied a tourniquet and she was rushed to the hospital. To save her life, surgeons amputated the leg. In the following years, some twenty-five surgeries would follow. After painful physical therapy, Barton learned to walk unassisted.

She never thought of quitting her career, only of making a comeback. The violin virtuoso pursued her dream of introducing classical music to millions of new listeners. In 1996, she performed the national anthem at the Democratic National Convention. A fan of hard rock and heavy metal since childhood, she recorded an album of rock songs in early 1998. Her group, Stringendo, arranged songs by artists from Ozzy Osbourne to Led Zeppelin to Nirvana, plus several classical selections. She made the rounds of the rock-radio circuit, doing interviews and pointing out the classical influence in rock music.

In 2002, Barton received a $35 million settlement from the train company but continued to perform, tour, and record, including little-performed works by eighteenth-century African American composers, works for solo Baroque violin, and concertos by Joseph Joachim. Most telling of all: mention of the accident is nowhere to be found on Barton's website. This fiercely independent musician wished to be known only for her music, not for her tragedy or disability. She once told a reporter that everything she is and everything she has experienced goes into her music.

132. BEETHOVEN, LUDWIG VAN

"The barriers are not erected which can say to aspiring talents and industry, 'Thus far and no farther.'"

AT TWENTY-SIX, LUDWIG VAN Beethoven began to suspect he was losing his hearing. By thirty-two, he was sure of it. From this, he extrapolated that he was dying and was overcome by anxiety and despair. Beethoven had suffered many things—an alcoholic father, a long list of unrequited loves—but the enormity and finality of a premature death surpassed them all. Still, he put on a brave front in a famous letter to his brothers known as the Heiligenstadt Testament. After making provision for his worldly possessions, he wrote "with joy I hasten towards death . . . farewell."

Beethoven, however, was wrong. He did not die or stop composing. In 1802, when he wrote his will and prepared to die, he had written only two of his nine symphonies, only 36 of his 138 musical works. The year after, 1803, he wrote his groundbreaking Symphony no.

3 and four years later the immortal Symphony no. 5. Through his work, he overcame his disability.

Beethoven Quotes:

- "Music is a higher revelation than all wisdom and philosophy."
- "Music is the mediator between the spiritual and the sensual life."

133. CARRERAS, JOSÉ, AND THE THREE TENORS

IN HIS AUTOBIOGRAPHY, THE GREAT TENOR JOSÉ Carreras said that when his doctor told him he had leukemia in 1987, he felt like a time bomb had exploded in his head. He was given a one in ten chance of survival—but survive he did. He credits his teams of health-care professionals in Seattle and Barcelona and the support of family, friends, and fans (he received thousands of letters).

Within three years, albeit difficult ones, Carreras was able to resume his career with the Three Tenors. Celebrating his return, the Three Tenors sang together for the first time, for charity, in Rome on July 7, 1990. Carreras donated his proceeds to foundations fighting leukemia. Plácido Domingo, born in Spain but raised in Mexico, aided four Mexican villages devastated by an earthquake. Luciano Pavarotti's share was split among several medical causes, including a marrow transplant center in Pesaro, Italy.

Pavarotti told reporters that his pay was being together with his colleagues. Sales of tickets—ranging from $25 to $335—generated $1 million. With only six thousand seats available at the Rome venue, some one hundred thousand would-be concertgoers were turned away. Tickets to the event were in greater demand than for the World Cup final held in Rome the same night. This was the first telling sign that the Three Tenors were on to something big—very big. The live recording of the concert sold a stunning eleven million copies, the most in classical music history, making big profits for the record company. The tenors, however, got nothing.

They were able to come back with a for-profit idea: more than thirty concerts in world capitals from 1990 to 1999, plus multiple live CDs. One newspaper report had each tenor earning $10 million for just five concerts, but over the years, they put on many more than that. It made thousands of fans around the world ecstatic and the tenors wealthy beyond their wildest imagination.

134. GLENNIE, EVELYN

THE NERVES IN EVELYN GLENNIE'S EARS DETERIORATED at age six; by eleven, she wore hearing aids. She would eventually go completely deaf, but Evelyn would not quit the thing she loved most: music, especially percussion. Instead, she adapted, learning to sense the music by vibration rather than by sound.

Glennie was accepted into the Royal Academy of Music, where she won a set of major prizes, including the Queen's Commendation Prize for all-around excellence. Another award permitted her to undertake postgraduate studies with marimba virtuoso Keiko Abe in Japan.

In 1986, Evelyn made her London debut at Wigmore Hall as a solo percussionist to rave reviews. She would go on to appear with leading orchestras and on radio and television. She has produced numerous CDs and DVDs on her travels and performances.

To enhance her sense of sound wave vibration, she often performs in bare feet, picking up signals from the concert stage. When performing as soloist before a symphony orchestra she also relies on her sight, focusing on the conductor's baton and her fellow players as well. Composers like John McLeod and Richard Rodney Bennett have composed concerti specifically for her.

Ebullient, striking, and energetic, Glennie radiates a confident, charismatic glow whether performing on stage as a soloist or teaching a master class. The casual observer would never suspect she is deaf.

135. Horowitz, Vladimir

A SPOUSE CAN OFTEN BE ONE'S GREATEST CRITIC, for good or for ill, and so it was with piano virtuoso Vladimir Horowitz. His wife, Wanda, knew her music; she was, after all, the daughter of maestro Arturo Toscanini. After a series of 1983 concerts in Japan, Wanda said Horowitz was terrible and that he would never play again.

Horowitz himself thought the reviews so horrible that he would never play again, his biographer, Harold Schonberg, relates. So Horowitz stopped playing concerts, stayed in his apartment, and put on weight. His speech stopped making sense, and he "moved around like a zombie," one friend said. Some thought he had Alzheimer's disease.

Fortunately for the world of classical music, both Wanda and Horowitz were wrong, dead wrong, about being finished. His greatest concerts lie ahead, and in just three years. Horowitz made so many comebacks in his life, perhaps his inner circle should have known another was always possible. Despite sitting atop the mountain of twentieth-century classical pianists for most of his life, despite a fame and adulation that made him the rock star of the classical world, Horowitz was tortured by stage fright and emotional problems all his life. He suffered extreme mood swings from elation to bitter despair.

He had one thing in his favor, however: he never quit the stage or the keyboard—not for good. After the Japan debacle, Horowitz's manager, Peter Gelb, proposed making the documentary *Vladimir Horowitz: The Last Romantic*. This provided the spark and motivation he needed. Horowitz left his antidepressants and lost weight, but most important, he got back to the keyboard. A friend said practicing helped him keep his grip on reality and helped save his life.

His assistant, Mrs. Giuliana Lopes, contributed as well, nursing him back to health, cooking for him, traveling with him, keeping his spirits up. The film was made and debuted at Carnegie Hall on November 15, 1985. It provided the self-confidence he needed to make a return to the concert stage.

The film was also a springboard to the greatest triumph of his life: his homecoming concert at the Great Hall of the Moscow Conservatory on April 20, 1986. It was an international event, recorded and telecast around the world. It was as great a thrill for Horowitz to visit his homeland as it was for the classical world to hear him.

Horowitz never entirely vanquished depression, but it never vanquished him either: we have his recordings to prove it. Five retirements, five comebacks:

1936–38: Retired due to complications from an appendectomy, phlebitis, and depression. He eventually worked his way back through associations with musicians Sergei Rachmaninoff, Rudolph Serkin, and Adolf Busch.

1953–65: Retired from the stage due to nervous collapse brought on by his intense performing schedule and difficulties with colitis. Yet he continued to record, being picked up by Columbia after being fired by RCA. Some reports claim he received electroshock treatment in the early 1960s.

1969–74: Retired again from the stage for unknown reasons, possibly depression, but continued to record. Sought electroshock treatment in the early 1970s.

1983–85: Retired due to unsatisfactory performances caused by antidepressant side effects; he stopped their use in 1984. In 1986, he made his greatest comeback musically and physically with his triumphant return to perform in Moscow, from which a best-selling live CD was made.

1987–89: Horowitz made a final retirement from the concert stage at age eighty-six, but continued to record until his death in 1989.

What made the art of Horowitz so great? He once said it was his willingness to take risks; he wanted to never be afraid to dare.

136. PERLMAN, ITZHAK

ITZHAK PERLMAN CONTRACTED POLIO AT AGE FOUR. Unable to play sports like other children, he focused all his energies on music. He studied at the Tel Aviv Conservatory and then Juilliard. He debuted at Carnegie Hall at age eighteen and is widely regarded today as the foremost violinist of his era. But it hasn't been easy: not the musical part or the physical part.

With all eyes fixed on him he laboriously takes the stage and crosses to his chair step-by-step, yet with a warm, charismatic smile and often a quip or word to elicit the same from the orchestra and audience, as he did at the Ravinia Festival in Chicago on July 12, 2006. He carefully seats himself, laying his crutches at his side. He unlocks his leg braces, moves one foot behind and the other forward, just so. He lifts his violin from the floor, holds it under his chin, and checks the tuning. And when he is fully ready, then and only then does the music—in this case, the Mozart Violin Concerto No. 5—begin.

He has said that sometimes it is the job of the musician, the artist, to find out how much music one can still make *with what one has left*. His body has its limitations, but his spirit—none. In addition to violin, he has added conducting and teaching to his professional endeavors. He has appeared on the great stages of the world, as well as on television, from *Sesame Street* to the *Tonight Show*. Perlman fans are as transfixed by his smile, warmth, and humanity as they are by his virtuosity.

137. RACHMANINOFF, SERGEI

HE SAID HE FELT LIKE A MAN WHO HAD SUFFERED a stroke and lost the use of his head and his hands. That's how the great Sergei Rachmaninoff described his nervous breakdown following the "failure" of his First Symphony in 1897. Composer César Cui famously had written of it: "If there were a conservatory in hell, if one of its talented students were instructed to write a program symphony on the 'Seven Plagues of Egypt,' and if he were to compose a symphony like Mr. Rachmaninoff's, then he would have fulfilled his task brilliantly and would delight the inhabitants of hell."

Words have power, and lots of it: Rachmaninoff was crushed and stopped composing for three years. Eventually, however, he was persuaded to see a psychiatrist-hypnotist who provided the composer with a positive self-talk mantra: "You will begin your concerto. You will work with great facility. The concerto will be excellent." It worked. Changing his style to be somewhat more audience friendly, Rachmaninoff wrote his Piano Concerto no. 2 in 1900. It would be regarded as one of the most passionate, powerful, and dramatic concerti ever written—a comeback concerto.

Ironically, since his death many music historians have called the First Symphony his most original composition, as well as his greatest contribution to symphonic literature. So Rachmaninoff needn't have tortured himself after all—he only needed to have patience and self-confidence and, above all, to keep working.

138. SCHUBERT, FRANZ

BEFORE PASSING AWAY MUCH TOO YOUNG AT THIRTY-ONE in 1828, Franz Schubert had time enough to write nearly one thousand compositions. In terms of sheer annual output, no composer was more prolific. Had Beethoven died at thirty-one, in terms of symphonies alone, we would have only his first. Schubert produced nine.

But it remained for composer and music critic Robert Schumann to rediscover Schubert and help engineer a comeback for his somewhat forgotten music. He visited Schubert's brother, Ferdinand, in 1839 to review the manuscripts on hand (Schubert had died in 1828) and came across a remarkable composition, a complete symphony in C major. Schumann showed it to his friend, composer-conductor Felix Mendelssohn, who gave it a world premiere and subsequent performances. He had to fight for it: his musicians hated its length and complexity. The prestigious Vienna Society of Friends of Music had turned it down back in 1828 with a brief and pointed comment that it was too difficult, too pompous.

Eventually, the work would make its own comeback: Schubert's Symphony no. 9, as it was numbered, would come to be regarded as one of the great treasures of Western civilization and a staple of orchestral repertory.

139. Solti, Sir Georg

"It is with very, very great hardship, and with tears, that one learns the discipline of oneself."

He would grow up to become one of the most dynamic, electrifying conductors on the concert stage, but when Georg Solti was six, he was a typical boy; his passion was soccer, not music. But his mother noticed he sang well and clearly, so she arranged for piano lessons.

His teacher, a German harpist from the Budapest Opera, was very "old school." When young Solti erred or disobeyed, he would hit his fingers. To make matters worse, the lesson was given by an open window, where the youngster could see his friends playing soccer. After six months, Solti talked his mother into letting him quit the lessons and happily returned to soccer.

Then, at eight, he was singing in music class and another student was accompanying on the piano. Solti knew the student was terrible and that he could do much better. It awakened his musical ambition. Swallowing his pride, and with the prompting of destiny, he came back to his mother and said that he would like to take lessons again. Fortunately for music lovers around the world, she agreed.

At ten, Solti entered the Erno Fodor School of music; at twelve, he entered the Franz Liszt Academy,

Hungary's foremost music school. This was a somewhat unusual accomplishment for a child, even a precocious one, and it laid the foundation for the rest of his life. In the years following, Solti would build a career as the foremost conductor in the world. To do so, he had to flee the Nazis and leave home. As he parted from his family at the train station, en route to Switzerland, his father began crying, realizing he would never see his son again. Young Solti was not so visionary, and instead, was abrupt with him, saying he would be back in ten days. He said in his autobiography *Memoirs* (1997) that this flip rejoinder haunted him for the rest of his life.

In the same volume, he describes a trip to Hungary in 1997. In February, after recording in Budapest Bartók's *Cantata Profana*—the folktale of seven sons who could not return home to their father because they had been turned into mythical stags—he made an excursion to Balantonfökajár, where his own father was born. He had come back to the country he said he was lucky to be born in, since it so lives and breathes music.

A surprise party was held in Solti's honor. Afterward, the mayor led him down a narrow country lane to an old Jewish graveyard where he saw for the first time the graves of his ancestors. He said that as he stood there in the afternoon sunshine, and later, as he stood on a hill overlooking Lake Balaton, he felt a sense of belonging for the first time in sixty years.

Just seven months later, in the south of France on September 5, 1997, Solti died unexpectedly of a heart attack. He was one month short of his eighty-fifth birthday. He had served as music director for orchestras in Munich, Frankfurt, London, and Chicago, had made more than 250 recordings, and had received more Grammy Awards than any other artist: thirty-one. He was wealthy, powerful, successful, famous, and he had notched a place for himself in music history—but coming back to his roots was, for him, the most meaningful experience of all.

MUSIC, POP

140. BENNETT, TONY

IN THE 1950S AND 1960S, TONY BENNETT WAS ONE of the top musical acts in the world. But after the invasion of the British rock bands and a seismic shift in popular musical taste, his popularity waned. Columbia Records suggested the best strategy for Bennett was to cover top-ten hits. He tried it, but some of the new songs were such an anathema that he literally threw up before the first recording session.

He moved to Hollywood in 1976, at fifty, and took up cocaine and marijuana. He had no record label, no manager, and was performing almost exclusively in Las Vegas. His big spending on everything but taxes landed him in serious trouble: the IRS began proceedings to take away his house. The death of his mother and marital woes compounded his misery. Finally, one night, high on drugs, Bennett passed out in the bathtub. His heart stopped, but his wife found him just in time. This near tragedy catalyzed a new attitude: he decided to change his life.

Bennett reached out to his sons, rock musicians Danny and Daegal, whom he considered savvy observers of the music business scene. First, after analyzing his expenses, Danny suggested that his father curb his spending. Bennett knew he had to cut back, but his wife wasn't onboard. After telling her of their new and necessary fiscal conservatism he was served with divorce papers, so Bennett moved out of his Beverly Hills mansion and into a one-bedroom apartment on New York's West Fifty-Seventh Street. That was a first step in his new life-to-be.

By now, Danny had taken the lead and become manager. He further advised his dad to get out of Las Vegas (right money, wrong image) and aim at building a younger audience; he suggested Bennett appear on *Late Night with David Letterman*, *SCTV*, *The Simpsons*, and *MTV Unplugged*. The message: Tony Bennett is hip. It worked—after an eleven-year recording hiatus, Tony got re-signed to Columbia Records in the mid-1980s. A new generation became fans. *Spin* magazine editor Bob Guccione Jr. epitomized the change in public attitude; when asked who the essence of rock and roll was in 1988, he cited James Brown and Bennett. They were the essence of cool, he said, and that's what it was all about. Millions more thought the same and bought Bennett's CDs.

Bennett and Danny reached the summit at the 1995 Grammy Awards when *Tony Bennett: MTV Unplugged* won album of the year. Bennett invited his son and manager onstage to share the glory—the culmination of a fifteen-year comeback and a near half-century career. He said it felt like he had been to the moon and back.

141. BERRY, CHUCK

CHUCK BERRY WAS IN AND OUT OF CONTROVERSY AND IN and out of prison for much of his career. But he kept pushing ahead, writing songs, recording, and touring his way into rock history.

His troubles started early. After two trials, Berry was found guilty of violating the Mann Act (transporting a minor across state lines). He maintained his innocence, but was sentenced to three years in jail and a $10,000 fine. On February 19, 1962, Berry, then thirty-six, entered prison. He swabbed the floors and cleaned the kitchen, but he also used his own time to study business management, law, and accounting.

All the while, out in the world, his tunes kept right on playing, covered by three of the greatest rock bands of all time. In March 1963, the Beach Boys released *Surfin' USA*, which closely resembled *Sweet Little Sixteen* (so closely, in fact, that Berry eventually received writing credit and royalties for the tune). The Rolling Stones released their first single, a version of *Come On*; not long after, they covered *Carol*, *You Can't Catch Me*, and *I'm Talkin' About You*. In 1963, the Beatles started their ascent to the top with covers of *Rock and Roll Music* and *Roll Over Beethoven*. With all that attention from the new generation, the marketplace was crying out for a comeback and Berry obliged, creating some of his most memorable tunes: *Nadine*, *No Particular Place To Go*, *You Never Can Tell*, and *Promised Land*—all composed in the Federal Medical Center in Springfield, Missouri.

The 1970s were a dry period for Berry and ended badly with a 1979 jail term for tax evasion. But another comeback would follow when Michael J. Fox lionized Berry in the $350 million box-office smash *Back to the Future* in 1985. In short order, Berry was inducted into the Rock and Roll Hall of Fame, his autobiography was published, and the documentary film *Hail! Hail! Rock 'n' Roll*, which captured a concert given by Berry on his sixtieth birthday, was released.

There would be more controversy surrounding the star in later years, and more lawsuits. By now it seemed he had been knocked down and had gotten back up more than any other star in rock history. But he did one thing: he kept coming back with the hits. Beatle John Lennon once said that if you tried to give rock and roll another name, you might consider calling it "Chuck Berry." Rolling Stone Bill Wyman recalled meeting Berry at the legendary Chess Records recording studio at 2120 S. Michigan Avenue (the address made famous by a Rolling Stones tune of the same name) in Chicago on June 10, 1964, where the master encouraged the young band with the irrepressible sentiment: "Swing on gentlemen. You are sounding most well, if I may say so."

142. CHER

AFTER SPENDING THE 1960S AND 1970S IN THE world of pop rock and on television, and the 1980s in film (*Silkwood*, *Mask*, *The Witches of Eastwick*, and *Moonstruck*), the 1990s were quiet, too quiet for Cher. In 1999 she went back to her music roots and climbed to the top of the pop charts with *Believe*. The song made her, at fifty-two, the oldest American woman ever to record a No. 1 hit. The comeback was a long time coming: it was the longest Billboard chart span between No. 1 songs (1965's *I Got You Babe* to 1999, thirty-four years) of any pop recording artist.

Believe sold eleven million copies and hit No. 1 in more than twenty-five countries. The tour sold out, with thousands of screaming fans paying to see the buff star in person. The next year, Cher's *Believe* overwhelmed her (much younger) Grammy competition, beating out hits by divas Jennifer Lopez, Gloria Estefan, and Donna Summer for best dance recording.

143. COLE, NAT KING

NBC FEATURED NAT KING COLE IN A PRIME-TIME television program in 1955, but despite good ratings, the jazzy, sophisticated program did not attract a sponsor and therefore was not renewed after its first year. (Sponsors perceived the potential audience as predominately black, which was not a sought-after demographic in those days.) Competing with new rock and old-style crooners, Cole's popularity slipped in the years following. A three-pack-a-day smoker, Cole died in 1965 at just forty-five years old from lung cancer.

Through the miracle of digital technology, he made a posthumous comeback when his daughter Natalie blended her voice with his on a new rendition of *Unforgettable* in 1991. It hit No. 1 on the pop charts. The *Complete Capitol Recordings of the Nat King Cole Trio* was released the same year, winning high critical praise. He left us with *A Christmas Song*, *Unforgettable*, and songs that will play on—smoother than silk—for generations to come.

144. Hooker, John Lee

"Do your work for six years; but in the seventh, go into solitude or among strangers, so that the memory of your friends does not hinder you from being what you have become."

In 1967, at fifty, bluesman John Lee Hooker packed his car with his clothes, two guitars, an amplifier, and $12,000 cash. He set out from Detroit to Oakland, California, to start a brand-new life. He knew no one there. He was leaving behind thirty years in Detroit, twenty-three years of troubled marriage, and six children. He had no way of knowing it, but his best thirty years, artistically, were straight ahead.

Out west, he was no longer just another working Detroit bluesman: he was a blues god. He came in contact with a large number of bluesmen who had relocated to the San Francisco Bay area such as Elvin Bishop, Michael Bloomfield, Charlie Musselwhite, and Luther Tucker. He was accorded royal status in the blues community, and plenty of ready backup musicians and companions. A special relationship arose with the blues band Canned Heat. The band had mastered Hooker's famous boogie down to the last lick. Eventually, together they recorded *Hooker 'n Heat* in 1970; it would be Hooker's best-selling album of the 1970s.

The rest of the 1970s and 1980s were slower than Hooker would have liked, despite his all-too-brief appearance in *The Blues Brothers* in 1980. But a major upsurge came in 1989: with the help of slide guitarist and producer Roy Rogers, Hooker laid down *The Healer*, with guests Carlos Santana, Bonnie Raitt, Robert Cray, Canned Heat, Los Lobos, and Charlie Musselwhite. The album won a Grammy and got Hooker's name in the Guinness Book of World Records as the oldest performer to ever reach the top five on the pop charts—with the sultry *I'm in the Mood* duet with Bonnie Raitt. Hooker was now hot property, a full-fledged pop icon—at age *seventy*—and six albums followed in the 1990s and 2000s.

Mr. Lucky followed in 1991 and featured cameos from Albert Collins, John Hammond, Van Morrison, and Keith Richards. Next came *Boom Boom* (1992) and the cool and somewhat jazzy *Chill Out* (1995). *Don't Look Back* (1997) was produced by old friend and one of the young musicians Hooker influenced in the early 1960s, Van Morrison. Hooker followed up with *Best of Friends* (1998) and *Face to Face* (2003).

In his second life, Hooker even found love, meeting his fourth wife, Millie Strom, while performing in Vancouver. She spent several years with Hooker, but the marriage ended. They separated as friends, and Hooker later said the happiest time of his life was with Strom.

He spent his last years in a relaxed and exalted state of semiretirement, indulging his passion for watching baseball, performing occasionally, and showing up in commercials from time to time.

A true American original, John Lee Hooker made a risky and radical life-changing move at age fifty and climbed to unimaginable heights, finding fame, fortune, and even love. He knew he would "never get out of these blues alive," so he made a run for it and succeeded. There's a quote from physicist Leo Szilard that accurately captures Hooker's brilliance and bravery: "Do your work for six years; but in the seventh, go into solitude or among strangers, so that the memory of your friends does not hinder you from being what you have become."

145. SANTANA, CARLOS

GUITAR VIRTUOSO CARLOS SANTANA BROKE ON TO the music scene in 1969 at Woodstock, and a string of albums made him a star in the early 1970s. Then, as his music began to lean more and more toward jazz, Santana's career withered. Between 1974 and June 1999, Santana had no successes to match his early acclaim, and by the 1990s, he could not even get a recording contract.

Some twenty-five years after falling out of the limelight, at age fifty-two, Santana made *Supernatural* in 1999. A recording phenomenon, it sold more than twenty-five million copies (approximately one million copies for every year he was out of the spotlight, making up all the lost ground all with one album). *Supernatural* dominated the Grammy Awards, winning eight categories: best record, best album, best pop duo/group with vocals, best pop collaboration with vocals, best pop instrumental performance, best rock duo/group with vocals, best rock instrumental performance, and best rock album. He had come full circle through his talent and persistence. Santana believes in the power of music, that "sound," as he puts it, "rearranges the molecular structure of the listener."

146. SINATRA, FRANK

THE BUZZ WAS THAT FRANK SINATRA, THIRTY-FOUR, was washed up. In 1949, he was fired from his radio show, his New York concerts were flops, his affair with Ava Gardner was a scandal, and he and his wife were divorcing. As a result, in 1950, Sinatra was released from his MGM film contract, and his agent, MCA, dropped him. Sinatra lost his voice due to a vocal cord hemorrhage (he had been doing as many as forty-five shows a week, singing one hundred songs a day, smoking and drinking too much and sleeping too little). His lifestyle put the spin on the rumor mill, and some said he even attempted suicide.

At this low point, Sinatra made a change: he turned to acting. Landing the role of Maggio in *From Here to Eternity* in 1953, Sinatra earned an Academy Award for best supporting actor. With this success, more roles became available, notably *The Man With the Golden Arm* (1955), *The Manchurian Candidate* (1962), and *The Detective* (1968). His recording career came back, too, and today he is regarded as, quite simply, the best of his era, maybe any era.

Pushed aside by the British rock bands, like all the other crooners, Sinatra said he was retiring in 1971 but made many comeback concert tours and recordings during the next two decades, and actually stayed on stage for the next twenty-three years. When his 1980 recording of "New York, New York" climbed to number thirty on the pop charts, he became the only singer to notch hits five decades in a row. Eight years later, Sinatra joined up with fellow Rat Packers Sammy Davis Jr. and Dean Martin and took the show on the road. He last performed in concert in 1994 at age seventy-eight. He died from a heart attack at age eighty-two on May 14, 1998.

Reports of the demise of this icon's career at thirty-four had been, paraphrasing the famous Mark Twainism, highly exaggerated.

147. TWAIN, SHANIA

In 1987, at age twenty-one, Shania Twain's world was shattered in one instant when both her parents were killed in a car crash. She came back home from her budding Toronto music career to be Mom and Dad to her three younger siblings. To generate cash, she sang and danced at the Deerhurst Resort in Muskoka, Ontario. This experience of combining music with theatrical perform-ance—from musical comedy to Andrew Lloyd Webber to Gershwin—helped her develop the showmanship that she would later use to catapult herself to the top of the pop world. Her pop-rock-country-contemporary crossover megahits included *You're Still the One* (1998), *From This Moment* (1998), and *Forever and for Always* (2003). Twain has said that all she ever tried to do was earn a living; every-thing she's achieved since then is above and beyond.

148. WILSON, BRIAN

The Beach Boys produced eight albums in their first three years together. Brian Wilson wrote sixty-three of the eighty-four songs on those albums, including *Surfin' USA*, *Surfer Girl*, *Little Deuce Coupe*, *Shut Down*, *All Summer Long*, and *Concert*. The stress was too much, however: Wilson suffered his first emotional collapse in December 1964, and decided he could no longer tour.

Depressed, paranoid, and hearing voices, he stayed home to smoke marijuana and take LSD. But he still wrote music and the hits kept coming: *Dance, Dance, Dance*; *Help Me, Rhonda*; *California Girls*; *Wouldn't It Be Nice*; and *Sloop John B* (from the *Pet Sounds* album (1966), which many consider the greatest American pop album of all time. Beatle Paul McCartney cited *Pet Sounds* as his favorite album, the transcendent *God Only Knows* his favorite song of all time.)

Wilson started work on what was to be his magnum opus, *Smile*, in 1973. It was to be "a teenage symphony to God." Then, Wilson faltered again, more seriously this time. He was unable to finish any work. In 1974, he suffered another nervous breakdown and, this time, stayed in bed for three years. Reports have it that he listened to the Phil Spector production of "Be My Baby" one hundred times a day or more. Soft drugs, hard drugs, LSD, diet pills, and prescription drugs—he consumed large, dangerous doses of each. His weight soared to 340 pounds.

He was fired by his own Beach Boys. In 1979, wife Marilyn divorced him and left with their daughters. Wilson was now in and out of mental institutions. Enter clinical psychologist Eugene Landy, who moved in with Wilson, became his executive producer, and made every decision in his professional and personal life. He determined what contact Wilson would have with the outside world, including the intimate relationship Wilson had developed with girlfriend Melinda Ledbetter. Landy's "twenty-four-hour therapy" helped pull Brian out of his destructive lifestyle and put him on the road to mental and physical health, but some accused him of stealing from Wilson and brainwashing him. Legal wrangling followed.

Still, the comeback was under way: Wilson released his first solo album, *Wilson*, in 1988. It reached number fifty on the sales chart. Wilson married Ledbetter in 1995; the birth of daughters Daria and Delanie followed, and the new family moved from California to rural Illinois. Wilson was working seriously again for the first time in ten years, contributing to other projects and finally recording his own album, *Imagination*, in 1998.

The biggest comeback yet was in the works: After thirty-seven years, Wilson returned to *Smile* in February 2004, when he and a ten-piece band performed the entire work at London's Royal Festival Hall for fans from around the world, including Paul McCartney. The prospect of performing live was daunting, and up to the last moment, Wilson was unsure if he could do it. So he meditated, backstage, alone. It worked—it was one of the most eagerly anticipated events in pop music history and fans and critics raved. A CD and documentary DVD followed. Wilson had triumphed against long odds, emerging from a debilitating depression to find and affirm love, life, and his very special music.

149. YOUNG, NEIL

SUFFERING FROM A MIGRAINE, NEIL YOUNG'S VISION went blurry, and he thought both would pass. But when symptoms persisted the next day, the rock star suspected something more. He was shaving and saw something in his eye that looked like a piece of broken glass. It kept getting bigger and bigger, and he knew he had to see his doctor right away. After his consulting with five specialists, by the next morning the verdict was in: Young had had a brain aneurysm, one that required very prompt attention. This was Thursday; surgery was scheduled for Monday.

Some individuals might have holed up in self-pity— Young chose to go to Nashville that very night to work on his album. The words and the music came fast, some songs in less than fifteen minutes. In this state of hypersensitivity and facing his own mortality, everything he saw inspired him. A phone message from a friend prompted the song *Falling off the Face of the Earth*. By the time he flew back to New York for surgery on March 28, 2005, Young had penned and recorded eight numbers in just four days.

The result of this whirlwind of activity in the face of a life-threatening situation was the album *Prairie Wind* (2005). The songs of reminiscence and mortality struck a nerve, generating positive reviews all over the rock landscape, not to mention sales; it debuted at No. 1 on Amazon, and six months later could still be found in the top twenty-five.

Young's health? He made a full recovery after the procedure.

PHYSICAL AND EMOTIONAL CHALLENGES

150. Brunstrom, Dr. Jan

At the tender age of one, Dr. Jan Brunstrom was diagnosed with cerebral palsy. She entered physical therapy and by age three was walking. But life was tough. She wore metal leg braces and classmates called her "Eiffel Tower." As a teen, boys were interested in her as long as she was sitting down; when she stood, would-be suitors were horrified. Still, life went on. The brainy girl graduated as her high school valedictorian at age sixteen and went on to Virginia Commonwealth University School of Medicine.

Though Brunstrom invested nearly ten years in general pediatric neurology, fellow doctors inveighed upon her to open a cerebral palsy clinic. She began with a staff of two and one hundred patients; today, her Pediatric Neurology Cerebral Palsy Center at St. Louis Children's Hospital has grown to ten doctors and six hundred patients. The goal is nothing less than maximum independence for each patient.

Brunstrom uses traditional therapies, like muscle relaxants to ease spasms, but she also thinks outside the box. An athlete herself, she prescribes aerobic exercise for all her patients—she says it gives the kids energy. She founded the first martial arts program for children with cerebral palsy, and some aspire to black belt status.

Brunstrom says this is what she was put on Earth to do. But the day scientists find a cure for cerebral palsy, she's said, she'll be happy to be out of a job.

151. CHOPRA, DR. DEEPAK

As A YOUNG PRACTICING PHYSICIAN IN THE BOSTON area, Deepak Chopra drank gallons of coffee, smoked a pack a day, and in the evening, anaesthetized himself with Scotch. When he took up Transcendental Meditation, his health habits changed. So, too, did his avocation.

Chopra began to write books to go along with the change in his personal life and his clinical practice. These were met with a mixed critical and popular reception. One reason was that they were controversial (a 1988 volume claimed that meditators could levitate). Undeterred, the doctor, who once envisioned a career in literature or journalism, responded by writing *more*.

On his *fifth* effort, in 1993, lightning struck. His

Ageless Body, Timeless Mind sold more than one million copies in hardcover alone, and 137,000 after an appearance on *Oprah*. Why? Many reasons, but the most salient might be timing: the world had caught up with him. The time was finally right for this holistic medical practitioner and his innovative approach to mind-body healing.

Since then, Chopra has become a virtual one-man mind-body industry. He's written more than twenty-five books that have been translated into thirty-five languages. He is also the star of more than one hundred audio- and videotape series, including five critically acclaimed programs on public television.

In 1999, *Time* magazine selected Chopra as one of the Top 100 Icons and Heroes of the Century. Venturing ever further from medicine into metaphysics, he published *How to Know God: The Soul's Journey Into the Mystery of Mysteries* (2001) and *The Book of Secrets: Unlocking the Hidden Dimensions of Your Life* (2004). He no longer practices medicine, but spends all his time writing, speaking, and leading seminars. All this success because he just kept thinking and writing while giving his ideas the time they needed to become accepted.

152. CHUNG, DR. WOOSIK

WHEN HE TOUCHED A WHIRLING ENGINE-FAN BLADE at age three, Woosik Chung's hands were severed. Unable to find a specialist because it was a Chinese national holiday, his father, Dr. John Chung, reattached his child's hands himself with a risky and rare nine-hour surgery that he had never before performed. He said he simply prayed to God and did his best. After the bandages came off, his grandfather, a tae kwon do master, gave young Chung martial arts instruction several hours a day—the only physical therapy he received. After two years, he had regained full use of his hands.

The scars faded, but still he was teased and called "Frankenstein," and he got into fights. But he was always happy just to have his hands. At fourteen, Chung and his family moved to the United States. He devoted himself to academics, earning a degree from Yale in molecular biophysics, and he excelled in martial arts. Ranked second in tae kwon do in the U.S. for his weight class, he would have competed for a berth on the 2002 Olympics team, but chose to pursue medicine instead.

Today, Chung is himself a medical doctor and surgeon in New York City. He plans to devote his life to orthopedic and microvascular surgery, passing his restorative gifts on to others as he received them from his own father, the man he calls "his personal hero." He received a gift, he says, and he wants only to repay it.

153. COUSINS, NORMAN

In 1964, AFTER A STRESSFUL TRIP TO COLD WAR Russia, *Saturday Review* editor Norman Cousins became almost completely paralyzed. He was diagnosed with the rare disease ankylosing spondylitis, which causes the breakdown of collagen, the fibrous tissue that binds together the body's cells. Given a few months to live, he was in great pain and unable to sleep. But he discovered that laughter gave him some relief. He checked himself out of the hospital and into a hotel room, where he could watch comedy films whenever he wanted to.

Away from the clinical environment, his condition started to improve. He was also lucky enough to win the support of his doctor, who, against conventional wisdom, prescribed megadoses of vitamin C. Tapping into the power of the body to heal itself through the combination of laughter and vitamin C, he slowly regained use of his limbs. As his condition steadily improved over the following months, Cousins resumed his busy life. He detailed his journey in *Anatomy of an Illness* (1979), a landmark in the holistic health movement. Cousins's experience made medical workers realize that we cannot treat disease in isolation; we are not simply collections of organs that go wrong and have to be treated with drugs in order to "fix" them. Each of us is a whole person, and our thoughts and feelings are just as important as the various physical processes going on inside us; in fact, these thoughts and feelings are physical processes, releasing biochemicals into our bloodstreams.

Then, comeback number two: some fifteen years later (December 1980), while teaching at the University of California medical school, Cousins was struck down with a near-fatal heart attack. As he was brought into the hospital on a stretcher, he sat up and managed to tell the doctors he wanted them to know that they were looking at the darnedest healing machine that was ever wheeled into their hospital. He was kick-starting his positive mental attitude from the very first moments of his setback.

Just like with his previous ailment, Cousins took charge. He refused morphine, dialed down on visitors and up on rest, and improved. He wrote about the experience in 1983's *The Healing Heart*. He was an advocate of laughter and hope, saying that one's best weapon in overcoming serious health problems is one's will to live. He also said education's greatest failure was that it did not prepare people to comprehend matters of human destiny.

Though slated by the physicians to die in 1964, he lived until 1990. He was 75 years old at his passing.

154. DRESCHER, FRAN

THERE IS AN UNCANNY CURSE THAT SOMETIMES seems to follow success: call it The Cover Curse. For instance, after a company makes the cover of *BusinessWeek*, strangely, its fortunes often turn down. Athletes often suffer a similar fate following a *Sports Illustrated* cover appearance. And so it was that, after publication of her autobiography *Enter Whining* in 1996, Fran Drescher's life went downhill fast. Her successful television series *The Nanny* slipped in the ratings, she separated from her husband, and—in the peculiar way life's troubles seem to gang up on you—her beloved dog Chester Drescher died.

But still, the worst was yet to come: mysterious bleeding, cramping, and pain. She went to a gynecologist, an internist, a hematologist, an oncologist/breast specialist, back to another gynecologist, and then to a vascular specialist, a neurologist, and finally a third gynecologist before discovering the cause: uterine cancer.

Becoming proactive, she underwent surgery but refused radiation, and recovered. She talks about the experience in 2002's *Cancer Schmancer*. Drescher, most famous for her loud, nasal voice, advises readers to open their mouths when dealing with their doctors: speak up, do your own research, don't delegate responsibility to others, and make your own decisions. There is no other way. Drescher also believes in securing support from close friends, family, and, in her case, her new love, a man sixteen years her junior. This event triggered the idea for a new television series for her in 2005, *Living with Fran*.

Life is precious, she says, and doesn't allow room for anger. Drescher says that since her illness and recovery, she has felt the presence of angels.

155. EUSTICE, CAROL

"But the loss of oneself is really just a rebirth, a chance to refocus, to begin anew and do things differently."

WHEN SMACKED DOWN BY A DISEASE, SOME FIGHT back by becoming doctors; others raise funds. Carol Eustice compiles and publishes information to help thousands. Eustice succumbed to rheumatoid arthritis at age nineteen. In subsequent years, she would suffer through a long list of various surgeries. Nevertheless, after earning a BS in biology from Cleveland State University and completing her medical technology training, Eustice worked in a hospital laboratory for sixteen years until her disability put a premature end to her career.

Then she turned her attention to helping others with the disease. She started small, moderating the weekly Rheumatoid Arthritis Chat Group on America Online.

She went on to become the arthritis guide at About.Com. There she assembled a vast compendium of information about the disease, including articles, links, newsletters, bulletin board forum, and a chat room. She has also written a book on the subject, *The Everything Health Guide to Arthritis*, for Adams Media (2007).

Today, her site links to more than one thousand web pages and is the most comprehensive arthritis resource on the Internet. Eustice helps countless numbers of people sort through the facts and fiction about this debilitating disease. Most important, she helps them learn to go on with courage and persistence, despite it all.

Eustice Quote:
- "The person I was before rheumatoid arthritis is a cherished memory, almost like a lost love or lost pet, always a part of you and yet gone. But the loss of oneself is really just a rebirth, a chance to refocus, to begin anew and do things differently."

156. FRANKL, VIKTOR

IN 1938, DR. VIKTOR FRANKL WAS ARRESTED BY the Nazis and placed in a concentration camp. When they took his wedding ring from him, a realization struck: there was one thing no one could ever take from him, his freedom to choose how to react to what happens to him. This would be the cornerstone for his 1946 work, *Man's Search for Meaning*. He spent time in four Nazi death camps and closely watched who did and did not survive, concluding that those who have a "why" to live for can withstand any "how."

Frankl returned to medicine and teaching after the war. He developed his ideas into the theory of meaning, which he called "logotherapy." He saw that hope is power—that people who had hope of being reunited with loved ones, projects they felt a need to complete, or great faith in God tended to have better chances of their wishes coming true than those who had lost hope. Another Viennese psychiatrist, Freud, postulated a will to *pleasure* as the root of all human motivation; his student, Alfred Adler, thought it a will to *power*. For Frankl, the root of human motivation was a will to *meaning*. He poured out his ideas into thirty-two books that were eventually translated into twenty-six languages.

Frankl said that man should not ask what the meaning of life is, but rather must understand that it is *he* who is asked. He also said one should live as if in a second life, as though you had acted wrongly the first time.

Still, for Frankl, there was something more than meaning, much more. His work took him beyond the meaning that he ascribed to his life to something he called "supra-meaning," that more fundamental *some-*

thing that is beyond our experiences, creativity, or attitudes. This is the idea that there is, in fact, *ultimate* meaning in life, not dependent on others, on our projects, or even on our dignity—it is meaning related to God, and God alone.

157. FUHRMAN, DR. JOEL

JOEL FUHRMAN, AT TWENTY YEARS OLD, WAS A world-class athlete and Olympic figure-skating hopeful. He ranked No. 2 in the nation in pairs skating in 1973 and 1976. In 1974, he suffered a severe injury to his foot in a skating accident. Any weight on his foot, even a bedsheet, caused excruciating pain, so he was on crutches. The U.S. Olympic Committee sent him to a top orthopedic surgeon. Endless tests ensued, all to no avail. A year passed with scant improvement—Fuhrman was still unable to walk without pain.

He eventually was hospitalized. One day out of the blue, a nurse gave him pills in preparation for a surgery the next morning. Having not even been consulted, Fuhrman was outraged. He refused to take the drug and demanded that his physician discuss the proposed surgery with him. Later that day, the doctor rudely informed Fuhrman that the procedure would expose the injured tissues and use the scalpel to cut a checkerboard pattern to stimulate healing. He said the surgery was required to promote the healing of his foot, but finally confessed it was experimental, and as such, he could not guarantee any outcome.

Not wanting to be a guinea pig, Fuhrman refused. The physician told him that without the surgery he would never walk again, but Fuhrman stuck by his guns and checked out of the hospital. At this low point, an idea hit him: he recalled that several years earlier, his father, suffering from arthritis, had recovered his health by fasting. He had read his father's books and articles and realized that this ancient technique might be his last and best hope. Determined to give it a go, he wanted expert supervision, so he traveled to the San Antonio offices of the renowned physician Dr. Herbert M. Shelton (who lived to be one hundred). The noted physician specialized in supervising fasts and advocated raw food diets. There, Fuhrman fasted for forty-six days. He was healed, able to walk again. One year later, he placed third in the World Professional Figure Skating Championships.

In San Antonio, Fuhrman's eyes were opened wide to the power of fasting. He saw asthmatics cured, breathing freely; he met colitis patients who recovered with no drugs or surgery. He saw cardiac patients who had suffered chronic chest pain now riding bicycles and jogging for the first time in years—without pain. In brief, Fuhrman saw firsthand how the body could heal itself when the causes of disease were removed. It was a revelation.

Fascinated now with the healing power of fasting, he contacted other practitioners who used it and natural diets to heal patients. Fuhrman decided to become a physician himself and specialize in sharing these techniques with patients. Now a board-certified family doctor who has helped thousands reverse and prevent disease through nutritional methods, Dr. Fuhrman has written several life-changing books on the power of fasting and high nutrient, plant-based diets. He has appeared on dozens of television and radio shows, including *Good Morning America*, CNN, *Good Day NY*, and the Food Network. Today he consults with patients around the world via drfuhrman.com

158. HAMILTON, BETHANY

ONE OF HAWAII'S TOP YOUNG SURFERS, DESTINED to become a professional, Bethany Hamilton, thirteen, was attacked by a shark on October 31, 2003. She lost an arm. Amazingly, fearless Bethany was back in the water less than thirty days later, on Thanksgiving Day in 2003. On January

10, 2004, she was back competing. Bethany placed fifth in her age group in the Open Women Division of a National Scholastic Surfing Association meet. "It was definitely a good start," she said. And, indeed, just a start: She continues surfing and competing, astonishing spectators and pro surfers alike.

159. Klein, Florence

In 1992, at age seventy, Florence Klein took a time-out to make a comeback. After a long career as a bookkeeper and dental supplies salesperson, she still had intellectual curiosity and a will to learn. Now she decided to satisfy those cravings. She enrolled in Kingsborough Community College in Brooklyn, New York, as part of the unique "My Turn" program for seniors sixty and older. The program allowed seniors to earn a degree tuition-free, only paying a $70 registration fee each semester. She found her way into mental health and human services, earning her associate degree in 1994. She turned next to the City University of New York and the New York City Technical Institute, a combined program where she earned her BS degree in behavioral science in 1997.

In her eighties, she developed her own practice with a specialty in grief therapy. She helped individuals and their family members all over the nation cope with chronic illnesses and death. Klein herself was a cancer survivor, so she knew what she was talking about. She earned her certification as a counselor and workshop facilitator from Exceptional Cancer Patients Inc. and became a certified hypnotherapist as well. For more than three years, Klein led the American Cancer Society's weekly Hoping and Coping Cancer Support Group in New York City. She believed counseling should *empower*, should stimulate the patient's own inner strength in order to foster healing and growth. She believed the patient should be an active partner in recovery and healing. Some things can't be delegated, Klein believed. Health is one of those.

160. Mullins, Aimee

Aimee Mullins was born missing the fibula leg bone in *both* legs. Doctors told her parents that, with amputation, Aimee could walk, but without she would be wheelchair bound. They chose to have the operation on her first birthday; more surgeries followed at ages three, five, and eight. A very tough kid with a large and supportive family, Mullins made the best of it.

As a Georgetown University student, she made history

as the first disabled athlete to compete on a NCAA Division I team. Mullins represented the United States at the 1996 Paralympic Games and set world records for leg amputees in the 100 m and 200 m dashes and the long jump.

In 1999, she made her mark in the fashion world. British designer and enfant terrible Alexander McQueen employed Mullins, then twenty-two, to front his London catwalk show. This ignited her modeling career, which in turn led to work in film. Mullins starred in *Cremaster 3* (2002), *Marvelous* (2006), and *Quid Pro Quo* (2007). For Mullins, acting was just another new adventure.

She told one interviewer that *confidence* is the sexiest thing a woman can have, much more so than any particular body part. She also defined beauty as radiating the fact that you like yourself.

161. PENNEBAKER, DR. JAMES

"When I was turned down for tenure at the University of Virginia, I was just beginning this research [on expressing emotions]," said Dr. James Pennebaker, professor of psychology at the University of Texas in Austin. "The experience initially left me

bitter and angry. However, writing about it helped me to appreciate the role I had played in all of it. Ironically, then, the writing I did in response to being turned down for tenure served as the basis of my research for the next twenty years."

That research determined that journaling, writing about important personal experiences, is good for not only your mental health but also your physical health. Author of *Opening Up: The Healing Power of Expressing Emotions*, Pennebaker has been called the guru of "confession research." His numerous studies since the 1980s have found that writing about upsetting personal experiences for just twenty minutes at a time, over three or four days, can result in a significant drop in blood pressure and a healthier immune system.

He further concludes that simple writing and/or talking exercises can reduce the need for a physician, medical costs, and alcohol use, while also increasing work performance. He's recently focused on the ways people use language in their daily lives. Many of the words people normally use on a daily basis, he says, can reveal hidden sides of their thoughts and emotions. Meanwhile, his prescription for better health is simple, cheap, and effective: write it down.

162. Pető, Dr. András

Sometimes an individual will take it upon him- or herself to facilitate the comeback of others less fortunate. So it was for Hungarian doctor András Pető. Just after World War II, he set about creating an environment and a method whereby brain-damaged children could learn to walk, care for themselves, and function in society. He believed their "forgotten" sensory, motor, and linguistic skills could be reestablished through hard training and perseverance.

Today some 1,500 children follow his regimen at the Pető Institute in Budapest, as well as many other children around the world. The young patients undergo an arduous, all-day conductive educational program, sometimes to the point of exhaustion, but they gain startling results. The institute states that if the program is started between the ages of six months and three to four years, 80 percent of the children will go to a normal elementary school. Those are odds that many parents can't turn down.

163. RIDKER, DR. PAUL

DR. PAUL RIDKER FIRST MADE THE PAGES OF THE prestigious *New England Journal of Medicine* at age nine, as a parasite victim. While visiting India, he contracted a rare immunological disease that allowed parasites to flourish. Surrounded by physicians and a hubbub of medical activity, his curiosity was aroused and his future cemented. Medicine was fascinating to him. In an unusual twist, he studied furniture design as an undergraduate and followed it with medical school.

Ridker began his research into heart attacks as a cardiology resident at Boston's Brigham and Women's Hospital. Doctors knew that cholesterol contributed to heart attacks, but since half the victims had normal cholesterol, there had to be more to the story. Ridker designed the first large study in an attempt to prove that inflammation has a connection to heart attacks, as well as to measure the effect of the inflammation on the arteries. Easy to say, hard to do. There were many who said it couldn't be done.

Selected from a series of blood chemical candidates, C-reactive protein (CRP) became the focus of Ridker and his team. Their tests showed that patients with low cholesterol and high CRP are as equally prone to heart attacks as patients with high cholesterol and low CRP. They also discovered that statin drugs lower CRP as they fight cholesterol. This research gave the medical world an entirely different way to look at heart health.

Inflammation and cholesterol work together, apparently, to create unstable plaque. When this plaque ruptures, its debris is strewn about in the arteries, where it clots and causes the heart attack itself.

Ridker moved on to the Harvard School of Public Health and conducted more groundbreaking research on the relationship of protein to heart disease, and all because a young boy visiting India was attacked by parasites. An amazing turn of events, and an amazing long-term comeback.

164. VINCENT, MARY

IN 1978, MARY VINCENT, FIFTEEN, RAN AWAY FROM her Las Vegas home. After three months, she was ready to go back and decided to hitchhike home. Lawrence Singleton, sixty, picked her up in his blue van. He raped her and then chopped off her forearms with an ax. He threw her down a hill and left her to die. Somehow Vincent survived and was found the next morning, wandering near a roadway and holding her arms in the air to prevent blood loss.

Singleton was captured and convicted, but he got only eight years for his crime. He repeatedly wrote Vincent's attorney, saying he would kill Vincent when he got out. She lived in hiding, paralyzed by the fear that he would make good on his threat. In 1997, Singleton was released from prison. Nine days later he murdered a prostitute in Florida.

Meanwhile, Vincent had recovered, married, and had two children. Then she was deserted by her husband. Poverty followed: Vincent, a thirty-four-year-old single mom, declared bankruptcy in 1995. She held one of her eighteen-year-old artificial limbs together with yarn. When a newspaper reporter tracked her down for a comment after Singleton murdered his Florida victim, Vincent and her children were homeless, living in an unheated gas station. Overcoming her trepidation, she traveled to Florida to testify against him and put him away for good. He died in prison in 2001.

She would later find some relief in an unlikely place: art. After a date (with the man who would later become her second husband, though they, too, would eventually divorce), she stayed up all night drawing a picture of herself for him. It was professional quality and he encouraged her to keep drawing. With the help of former ABC news anchor and friend Asha Blake, Vincent organized a showing of her artwork in 2002.

Having overcome an unspeakably brutal attack, homelessness, poverty, and despair, Vincent was now showing the mayor of Seattle and interested collectors her artwork. She can't erase all the bad memories, but she can make new ones now, she says, and amazing works of art as well.

165. WHITESTONE, HEATHER

WHEN SHE WAS JUST EIGHTEEN MONTHS OLD, Heather Whitestone contracted flu and meningitis and was rushed to the hospital. She was left deaf in one ear and had only 5 percent hearing in the other. Whitestone was taught by her schoolteacher mom to use what little hearing she had. She learned to speak and was mainstreamed with her regular class. The goal was to make Whitestone functional in the hearing world. In fourth grade she learned about Helen Keller, who would provide special inspiration. She spent time at a special school for the deaf, but returned to public school to graduate from high school with a 3.6 average.

A precocious child, Whitestone decided when she was very young that she wanted a chance at the Miss America title, refusing to allow her deafness, peer pressure, or anything else to stop her. She began competing in beauty pageants, spurred in part by the promise of scholarship money. She came in second for Miss Alabama twice. Thinking it wasn't meant to be, she was ready to give it up, but family and friends urged one more try (Whitestone knew something about persistence; it had taken her six years to correctly pronounce her last name).

After another year of hard work on all parts of her competition program, on her third try, she won Miss Alabama. Then, several months later, competing for the Miss America title in 1995, Whitestone wowed the audience with her ballet to Sandi Patti's *Via Dolorosa*. She moved gracefully across the stage in a flowing white chiffon dress. The only sign of her disability was her hearing aid. During finalist interviews, Whitestone told host Regis Philbin about her platforms, "Youth Motivation— Anything Is Possible," and S.T.A.R.S. (**S**uccess **T**hrough **A**ctions and **R**ealization of your dream**S**. Whitestone said she chose the power of positive thinking, explaining she could be a role model to demonstrate how self-esteem and hard work can overcome obstacles.

The judges agreed, and her dream came true; she couldn't hear the crowd roar, but she could see their reactions. Whitestone made history as the first woman with a disability to be crowned Miss America. Following her reign as America's beauty queen, Whitestone quietly left the public eye to spend full time being Heather Whitestone McCallum, wife of husband John, and mom to two sons. They operate Heather Whitestone Inc., and she is the author of several inspirational titles. She received a cochlear implant on August 7, 2002, and her hearing was greatly improved.

Summarizing her experiences, Whitestone said it was her attitude that helped her traverse the hard time. She said the best thing about being Miss America was that it gave her the opportunity to bring a positive awareness about the deaf community to the wider world. After all, she said, we are all people, whatever our abilities or limitations.

166. WILSON, CARNIE

FIRST CHILD OF ROCK-AND-ROLL LEGEND BRIAN Wilson of the Beach Boys, Carnie Wilson was overweight from age four. Her father fought personal demons for many years and was distant from his daughter. When her parents divorced, food became comfort. She became ever heavier, eventually unable to play sports in gym class. Six months after graduating from high school, Wilson joined her sister, Wendy, and their childhood friend Chynna Phillips to form the singing group Wilson Phillips. Deciding she had to be thin for the group, Wilson began her quest to lose weight on her twentieth birthday. Inspired by the prospect of an exciting career, she dropped ninety pounds.

Wilson Phillips was a hit—the group's debut album in 1990 sold more than ten million copies. Wilson was twenty-two. But old habits die hard, and two years later, she had regained every pound and more. She was hungry all the time. She wanted sugar, Hostess Cupcakes, Twinkies, cheesecake at 3 a.m. After Wilson Phillips's second album, the group fell apart.

A setback? Yes, but she didn't quit. Wilson and her sister formed a duo and produced another album in 1994, but their record company decided not to promote it. Wilson suspected her obesity as the reason. More setbacks followed. She retooled herself as a talk show host, but her show only made it one season. A workout video for the significantly overweight also flopped. With her career spiraling downward, Wilson's eating disorder went wild and her weight shot up. She hit and passed three hundred pounds. Her health declined rapidly; she suffered from hypertension, joint pain, shortness of breath, and high cholesterol. She spent much of her time in and out of doctor's offices. Insult added to injury—she was parodied by Chris Farley on *Saturday Night Live.*

Drastic situations call for drastic means. Distraught and carrying a death sentence on her own frame, Wilson turned to laparoscopic gastric bypass surgery. On August 10, 1999—one of the most important days of her life, she has said—she underwent the ninety-minute procedure at San Diego's Alvarado Hospital Medical Center. The surgery was broadcast live over the Internet and seen by some 250,000 people. Her stomach was sewn shut to accommodate only very small amounts of food. It worked not only physically—she lost more than 130 pounds—but also psychologically. She felt a tremendous relief mixed with hope.

Wilson married in June 2000. Some two hundred guests attended. She picked out her dress ahead of time and needed to have it altered two weeks before the ceremony because she was still losing weight. She even posed for *Playboy* in August 2003—something totally unthinkable several years earlier. Her advice for others struggling with weight is to pay attention to what you really want—you have the power to change your life.

167. WINFREY, OPRAH

OPRAH WINFREY HAS TRIUMPHED OVER A BROKEN family, childhood sexual abuse, poverty, and discrimination to become one of the richest and most famous individuals on the planet. Her name today conveys success, intelligence, and activism.

She had a rough start. Start with her name: an accidental misspelling of the biblical character Orpah. When she was a child, Winfrey spent time living with her grandmother in Mississippi, her mother in Milwaukee, and her father in Nashville. Milwaukee was the worst; it was there at age nine that she was sexually abused by a nineteen-year-old cousin. On her show, she said she took a lesson from it: abuse teaches you not to let people abuse you. This positive reworking of the pain helped her overcome the trauma. Nothing could better illustrate her mastery of the situation than that kind of matter-of-fact refusal to be a victim.

Winfrey's spirituality also helped get her through the dark days and is no doubt a major source of her widespread appeal. It is at the root of her mid-1990s turn from a tabloid television host to a show encompassing broader and more positive themes of psychology, spirit, and human potential. That's what made her, well, Oprah, instead of just another television talk host. Directed by a kind of supernaturally inspired sense, Winfrey says she makes time to read a scripture verse every morning. She is guided by a higher calling, she says, not an audible voice but an inner feeling, an instinct. If it doesn't "feel right," she says, she just doesn't do it.

168. WITTGENSTEIN, PAUL

PIANIST PAUL WITTGENSTEIN'S RIGHT ARM RECEIVED a bullet wound in World War I and had to be amputated.

Shaken, depressed, but eventually resolute, he decided to play the piano with his left hand alone. While a prisoner of Russia he practiced his fingerings from memory. After the war, he studied intensively and resumed his public career, playing from scores transcribed for one hand. Some of the new pieces were composed for him by his old teacher Josef Labor (who was himself blind).

Wittgenstein began once again to give concerts and became well-known and beloved by audiences. Emboldened, he approached more famous composers, asking them to write works for the left hand alone. Benjamin Britten, Paul Hindemith, and Richard Strauss obliged. So, too, did Maurice Ravel. Wittgenstein became particularly famous for Ravel's Piano Concerto for the Left Hand.

John Barchilon wrote the novel *The Crown Prince* (1984) based on Wittgenstein's doggedly determined life. Millions more learned of his amazing story through the episode "Morale Victory" of the television series *M.A.S.H.*, which featured a soldier—a concert pianist before the war—who lost the use of his right hand in combat. The character Major Winchester provides him with the sheet music for Ravel's *Concerto for the Left Hand* and tells him the story of Wittgenstein, encouraging him never to give up his music.

Another comeback story with a different ending: pianist Leon Fleischer was a real-life example of a former child prodigy and gifted artist who lost the use of his right hand at thirty-seven, through overuse or a nerve disease or both, and then specialized in piano literature for the left hand (1965 to 1995). He was able to resume playing with both hands. During his time of disability he said he realized that it wasn't the piano that was the most important thing in his life; it was music. Consequently, he began to teach and conduct as well. He says his playing now engenders a state of grace, a state of ecstasy.

169. YEAGER, CHARLES "CHUCK" E.

"You do what you can for as long as you can, and when you finally can't, you do the next best thing. You back up but you don't give up."

SHORTLY AFTER WORLD WAR II, THE U.S. AIR Force set out to break the sound barrier. The date of the mission was to be October 14, 1947. The pilot: World War II ace Chuck Yeager. Yeager was nothing short of a legend: on one occasion, he took on five German fighters and downed each in succession.

On the night of October 12, 1947, two days before he was due to pilot the plane that would break the sound barrier, Yeager went horseback riding and fell off. The next day his right side ached, but, afraid of being taken off the flight, he decided not to see an air force doctor. He drove to a local town and saw a private physician. The diagnosis: two broken ribs. Despite the excruciating pain, Yeager was not about to quit. He told no one about his injury. As he was unable to close the plane's right side door, he improvised: he took a broom handle with him into his test plane and used it to close the door with his *left* hand.

October 14 came, and early in the morning, still hurting, Yeager went up in the B-29 bomber that hauled the X-1 plane. At seven thousand feet, he strapped himself into the X-1 and locked himself in using his broomstick. At twenty-six thousand feet, the B-29 released the X-1. At .87 Mach the X-1 shook violently, but Yeager pushed it harder. The plane smoothed out at .96 Mach and then cruised past Mach 1. On the ground, the support crews heard the first sonic boom. Yeager pushed further, to Mach 1.05, and stayed in that zone for a full seven minutes. On the way down, he celebrated with a few victory rolls and wing-over-wing stunts.

A long and illustrious career followed. The most famous American pilot, Yeager was promoted to brigadier general in 1969. He held different and varied positions in the Air Force until retirement (1975). He was a featured character in Tom Wolfe's book *The Right Stuff* and the hit movie based on it that came out in 1983.

POLITICS AND PUBLIC SERVICE

170. BRADY, JAMES

I T'S THE DREAM OF MANY PUBLIC RELATIONS
practitioners to one day be White House press secretary.
James S. Brady achieved that dream in January 1981, when
he received his appointment from President Ronald
Reagan. But a mere two months later, John Hinckley Jr.
shot both Brady and the president, as well as two law
enforcement officers.

Although seriously wounded in the head, with speech
and movement greatly impaired, Brady gradually
regained functionality through multiple surgeries and
therapies, slowly, step by step. Brady took the hard road
and worked diligently to make a comeback—he remained
the White House press secretary until the end of the
Reagan administration. No one would have blamed him
for retiring from the public scene, but Brady had the guts
and determination to finish the job no matter what.

After leaving the White House, Brady lobbied with his wife, Sarah, via Handgun Control Inc., for stronger gun laws. It took twelve long years, but on November 30, 1993, President Clinton signed the Brady bill. It requires a national waiting period and background check on all handgun purchases. His story was told by Mollie Dickinson in 1987 in *Thumbs Up: The Life and Courageous Comeback of White House Press Secretary Jim Brady*. That comeback, made manifest by way of the Brady bill, would make us all a little safer.

Exactly twenty-five years after the shooting, Brady and his wife were interviewed on ABC news on March 30, 2006. They cited three things that helped him recover: his sense of humor, his support from his wife, and the desire to build new memories to replace the old ones.

171. CHENEY, RICHARD "DICK" B.

IN HIGH SCHOOL, DICK CHENEY HAD EVERYTHING going his way. Senior class president and football hero, he won a scholarship to Yale University. But he left during his second year because of poor grades and took two years off to work.

Returning to college, this time the University of Wyoming, he earned a bachelor's (1965) and master's degree (1966) in political science. He went on to earn a

PhD from the University of Wisconsin in 1968. From then on, it was pretty much straight up the ladder. His career included posts as White House deputy counsel, assistant director of the Cost of Living Council, vice president of an investment firm, White House deputy chief of staff, White House chief of staff (at the young age of thirty-four), U.S. congressman, minority whip, secretary of defense, presidential candidate, chief executive of Halliburton Company, and, finally, vice president. Not a bad résumé for someone who failed out of Yale.

172. CLELAND, MAX

"Without pain there is no pleasure, without valleys there are no mountain tops, and without struggle there is no sense of achievement."

IN APRIL 1968, U.S. ARMY CAPTAIN MAX Cleland had one month left on his tour of duty in Vietnam. Jumping out of a helicopter, he stooped to pick up a grenade he thought had fallen off his belt. It exploded. The blast jammed his eyeballs back into his skull, blinding him. The story is told in his 2000 book *Strong at the Broken Places*. When he could see again, he realized his right hand was gone. So, too, his right leg and knee. He would have screamed but couldn't—

a piece of shrapnel had cut his esophagus. After five hours of battlefield surgery and forty-one pints of blood, he survived. Months later at the Walter Reed Army Hospital, he wished he hadn't.

He descended into despair. He drank heavily, favoring Wild Turkey and daiquiris. Hospitalized for the flu, he hit rock bottom on Easter in 1969. He sank into a very deep depression, sobbing uncontrollably, bitter over the past, and afraid of the future. The present seemed unbearable. He had to choose, live or die, and right at that moment he chose life.

He decided to fight back and make it back through his rehab. How? Inspiration. Celebration. Challenge. He says he was inspired by the tenacity of George Washington, Winston Churchill, FDR, and Jesus. His favorite (paraphrased) quote from Churchill: "Never give in Never. Never. Never." He also celebrated each victory, no matter how small. He pushed to have his doctors outfit him with artificial limbs and eventually he walked.

Then he pushed himself in new ways. He ran for a seat in the Georgia legislature in 1970 and won. He was appointed head of the Veterans Administration in 1976 and elected to the U.S. Senate in 1996. He had been to hell and come all the way back again.

Cleland Quote:

• "We think adversity itself is darkness, but the reality

of the darkness is that it can serve to illuminate the light. Without pain there is no pleasure, without valleys there are no mountain tops, and without struggle there is no sense of achievement."

173. CLINTON, WILLIAM JEFFERSON

UNDER FIERCE ATTACK DURING THE 1992 PRESIDENTIAL primary campaign for lack of character, marital infidelity, and avoiding the draft, Bill Clinton responded in a speech in Dover, New Hampshire: "I'll tell you what the real character issue is: who really cares about you." The voters responded to that kind of straight talk: He came in second in the New Hampshire primary. News outlets dubbed him the "Comeback Kid," and he went on to win the White House and stay for eight years. During that time, he would have many chances to prove his comeback ability in crises like Cattlegate, Travelgate, Whitewater, Monica Lewinsky, Paula Jones, Gennifer Flowers, Kathleen Willey, Chinagate, and, of course, impeachment. How was he able to do it?

- Stamina. He simply would not quit—the basic building block of any comeback story. Though many called for his resignation, he would not resign his post.

- Charisma and charm. He had his partisans, his support network. Many journalists and people in general have commented on Clinton's seductive blend of height, charm, and intelligence. He made people like him.

- Ability. Even though Republicans traditionally represent business and finance, this Democratic former Oxford University scholar had a sure grasp of international economics and a sound rapport with the Federal Reserve Bank. Though no president by himself makes gross domestic product go up or down, his years in office were boom years, generating budget surpluses of $122.7 billion for fiscal year 1999 and $230 billion for 2000.

- Attitude and optimism. Former Clinton aide Betsey Wright once said that Bill Clinton had a unique ability to wake up each day as if it were a brand-new world, and then view the world with rose-colored glasses.

174. CLINTON, HILLARY RODHAM

SHE SAID SHE WASN'T JUST SITTING THERE, LIKE SOME little woman, standing by her man like Tammy Wynette in the old country ballad. In 1992, Hillary Rodham Clinton,

Wellesley graduate, attorney, and activist, made a pair of notorious gaffes that branded her a "radical feminist." That statement was the first. News outlets all over the country replayed it for weeks. The other was her comment that she "could have stayed home and baked cookies and had teas" instead of pursuing a career. Just thirteen minutes later the comments were on the AP newswire. The media positioned both comments as an affront to homemakers and soccer moms.

Hillary didn't fare much better in operational politics. President Clinton asked her to chair the Task Force on National Health Care Reform in 1993; the project was not a success, and under public pressure, she backed off. She was also implicated in scandals relating to cattle futures trading and a real estate venture known as Whitewater. Clinton became the only first lady called to grand jury testimony.

Subsequently, she turned her attention to somewhat lower-profile and surely less controversial activities. One new enterprise was writing a weekly newspaper column entitled Talking It Over, a collection of observations on her life as a first lady, as well as the impressions of women, children, and families she had encountered around the globe. This led to the book *It Takes a Village and Other Lessons Children Teach Us* in 1996. It became a bestseller, and her recording of it won a Grammy. Most significant, during her spouse's impeachment proceedings, Clinton kept her poise, composure, and her own counsel, walking away from a difficult situation with her dignity firmly intact.

Slowly but surely she was regaining public acceptance. When Hillary Clinton was elected to the U.S. Senate representing New York (November 7, 2000), she became the first sitting first lady to win elective office. She was almost immediately considered a presidential contender. Like her husband, she had made a remarkable comeback.

175. GIULIANI, RUDOLPH

PROSTATE CANCER, DIVORCE, AND SCANDAL CAUSED Rudy Giuliani to give up his U.S. Senate run in May 2000. It was a low point for the mayor, who had previously cleaned up and rebuilt New York. His miscues became fodder for the late-night talk show hosts. Yet he was only sixteen months from his greatest hour, when all the world came calling to draw on his personal courage and calm in the face of catastrophe. On September 11, 2001, the day terrorists attacked the World Trade Center and the Pentagon, Giuliani's leadership earned him the admiration and respect of the entire world, and especially of the grief-stricken residents of New York City.

Unlike President Bush, who was out of sight that day

due to security protocols, Giuliani headed straight for the trouble; he arrived at the World Trade Center just after the second plane hit. When the south tower collapsed, he was nearly trapped inside his nearby firehouse command center. After making a bevy of rapid-fire decisions on security, rescue, police, and fire operations, Giuliani quickly got on the air to let people know someone was in charge and responding. Then he toured hospitals, comforting families of the missing. He went to Ground Zero repeatedly.

Words have power, and taking a position has power too. Giuliani told *Time* magazine that when he said the spirit of the city would survive the blow, he had no way to be sure of that. He just hoped it. He said there are parts of you that say, "Maybe we're not going to get through this." He had been studying Churchill in the weeks before 9/11, and realized that Churchill couldn't have known Britain would survive Hitler, but he said it anyway. Since he couldn't decide if it was rashness or madness or courage until after the fact, he decided to take the most positive, most courageous posture possible. At least one thing is sure: in doing so, he inspired others—a whole country, much of the world, and one very battered but very tough city.

Sometimes, how we respond in a crisis affords us the opportunity to recoup a lot of lost authority, confidence, and usefulness. When catastrophe hit New York,

Giuliani responded with courage, calm, and ability, becoming the face and voice of America, leading New York to inspire the nation and the world.

176. GORE, AL

RUNNING AGAINST GEORGE W. BUSH FOR U.S. president in 2000, Al Gore won the popular vote but lost the November 7 election, after more than a month of hanging chads, anxiety, acrimony, and finally, a Supreme Court decision (December 12) that brought the matter to a conclusion.

It was a devastating blow to the former Vice President Gore. After time for healing, he turned his attention to a single issue that had captured his imagination since his Harvard days: the environment. He turned from politics to issue advocacy, creating a multimedia presentation documenting the alarming rise of global warming. He took it on the road to venues around the world, making more than one thousand talks. Additionally, he advocated urgent action by the U.S. to match resolutions undertaken by some 160 other nation signatories to the Kyoto Treaty (1997), and by individuals as well (e.g., get a hybrid car, ride bikes, walk, use solar power, recycle, and "if you believe in prayer, pray, but move your feet" as per an old African proverb).

Gore's presentation became the centerpiece of his documentary, *An Inconvenient Truth* (2006), reaching a still wider audience.

Through his passion, precision, and self-deprecating humor, he rehabilitated his fallen political image into that of a thoughtful international visionary. In some quarters, he was mentioned again as a possible presidential candidate—unthinkable after his bitter defeat six years earlier. Gore was suggested by some as *Time* magazine's Man of the Year and was featured in its year-in-review issue (*Time* chose "you" for 2006 instead). Nevertheless, a CNN commentator called his comeback a "magnificent transformation."

177. HUCKABEE, MIKE

TIPPING THE SCALES AT 280 POUNDS, GOVERNOR Mike Huckabee of Arkansas was diagnosed with type 2 diabetes in 2003. He was also experiencing chest pains, made all the more disconcerting because a close friend had just died of a heart attack. With his doctor predicting dire consequences if he didn't do something, Huckabee took action. He changed his diet, eliminating the fried Southern specialties he loved so well, and took up running. A year later, in an amazing turnaround, there was 105 pounds less of him. Two years later, he was winning athletic awards. After he completed the Little Rock marathon in four and one-half hours, USA Track & Field named him Athlete of the Week. Registration for the marathon increased 30 percent, an increase credited to the governor's promotional efforts and personal story.

Huckabee wrote a book about his experiences, *Quit Digging Your Grave with a Knife and Fork: A 12-Stop Program to End Bad Habits and Begin a Healthy Lifestyle*. He launched the Healthy Arkansas Initiative to promote healthy living habits. He has espoused converting sick days to vacation days for healthy workers, exercise breaks rather than smoking breaks, and the publication of caloric and fat content by restaurants. With obesity a national epidemic and health-care costs spiraling out of control, Huckabee believes the solution is change at the individual level. He hopes to save taxpayers billions in health-care costs and insurance by promoting healthy lifestyles. This new outlook has also proved a boon for his own career, catapulting the governor to national prominence; some have mentioned him as a prospective presidential candidate. An amazing comeback for an individual who, two years earlier, was in failing health with a negative prognosis for his obesity-related ailments.

178. KENNEDY, JOHN F.

"Change is the law of life. And those who look only to the past or the present are certain to miss the future."

JOHN F. KENNEDY LOST THE ELECTION FOR FRESHMAN class president at Harvard in 1936. After graduation, he enrolled in graduate school at Stanford but left to volunteer for naval service in 1941. During World War II, he applied for hazardous combat duty. One night, a Japanese destroyer attacked and sliced his PT boat in two. Though suffering severe back injuries that plagued him the rest of his life, Kennedy rescued his entire crew, including a badly burned man he dragged to safety by pulling him by a strap in his teeth through the icy water. The crew hid from the enemy on a tiny island until they were able to summon help.

While recuperating from a subsequent back surgery in 1956, Kennedy occupied his time writing *Profiles in Courage*, a study of courageous political acts by eight U.S. senators. He was flat on his back in a Palm Beach hospital, writing in longhand on yellow legal pads. The book won a Pulitzer Prize in 1957. *Profiles in Courage* gave Kennedy an image of intellectuality and high-mindedness that his workaday political rivals lacked. Four years later, he was elected president. (He "wrote" his own chapter in *Profiles in Courage* when he faced down the Russians during the Cuban missile crisis in 1962.) Writing a book proved a very powerful tool for his comeback and generated benefits far beyond the royalties.

179. LINCOLN, ABRAHAM

"THE THOUGHT OF THE SNOW AND RAIN ON HER grave fills me with indescribable grief. My heart is buried there." Lincoln never got over the death of his fiancée Ann Rutledge, who passed away at age twenty-two on August 25, 1835. It was one of many heartbreaks and setbacks he suffered in his life. Shortly after Ann passed away, Lincoln seemed to be teetering on the brink of madness, walking alone by the river, through the woods, muttering to himself. To foster a recovery, he eventually moved in with friends William and Nancy Green of New Salem, Illinois. The grief would stay with him his whole lifetime, however Later in his life, when Lincoln's sorrow had become a memory, he told a friend: "I really and truly loved the girl and think often of her now. And I have loved the name Rutledge to this day."

Lincoln had already suffered some setbacks by the time his sweetheart died. He lost his job as a store clerk in 1832 and wound up in the local militia fighting Native Americans. He failed as a storekeeper in 1834 and went to work for the post office. Then a positive development: he was elected to the Illinois state legislature. He ran for speaker of the House of Representatives in 1838 but was defeated. He was elected to Congress in 1846, but two years later, he lost his renomination. He was subsequently rejected for land officer and defeated for the U.S. Senate. He was defeated for nomination for vice president in 1856, and then again in his bid for the U.S. Senate in 1858. But in 1860, he was elected president, and became one of the handful of our very greatest—a remarkable comeback from a daunting string of setbacks and tragedy.

180. REAGAN, RONALD

RONALD REAGAN APPEARED IN SOME FIFTY-THREE films, his most famous role being that of George Gipp in *Knute Rockne—All American* in 1940, but his film career declined over time. However, General Electric (GE) chose him to host its weekly television series in 1954 for a $150,000 salary. The job included public relations duties, so Reagan traveled to GE plants across the country on employee relations missions. Speaking, then hosting question-and-answer sessions was a powerful learning experience. His conservatism grew with each interaction: he became more and more incensed with high taxes and resented the way excessive government regulation impeded corporate progress.

After a successful eight-year run, GE terminated Reagan's contract in 1962. He was out of a job, yes, but his public-speaking skills had grown so much he was now in demand as a political speaker. He cochaired the Barry Goldwater California campaign and eloquently endorsed him at the 1964 Republican Party convention. By this time he himself was a rising star on the political scene. Reagan was elected governor of California in 1966. But then his upward progress stalled. He made a run for president in 1968, but was not nominated. He challenged President Ford for the Republican nomination in 1976 but did not receive it.

However, 1980 would be his comeback year. He won the presidential nomination and took the White House in a landslide. In the years following, the Great Communicator led a nation out of despondency suffered from the Iran hostage and energy crises. After his landslide reelection, Reagan engaged new Soviet leader Mikhail Gorbachev in serious arms-reduction talks. Aided by the escalating decline of the Soviet Union, Reagan helped engineer the end of the Cold War, and he is remembered for his June 1987 speech near the Berlin Wall, with the now immortal line, "Mr. Gorbachev, tear down this wall!" Two years later, the wall indeed came down. Reagan's ability to come back from setbacks and influence others with his confident, easy humor carried him to the highest office in the land, and the world, a very long way towards peace.

Reagan Quotes:
- "All great change in America begins at the dinner table."
- "Entrepreneurs and their small enterprises are responsible for almost all the economic growth in the United States."
- "There are no great limits to growth because there are no limits of human intelligence, imagination, and wonder."

181. ROOSEVELT, FRANKLIN D.

FRANKLIN DELANO ROOSEVELT CONTRACTED POLIO at age thirty-nine in 1921—a humiliating "child's disease," he called it. Paralyzed from the waist down, at the outset he required constant care from wife Eleanor, from whom he had been estranged for some four years. Biographer Richard T. Goldberg wrote that FDR put on a mask of cheerfulness, but it covered profound clinical depression. FDR wondered why more was not being done for him and was highly unrealistic about his prognosis. But alongside the depression, and fear, and the unrealistic expectations for recovery, there was courage, too.

By the time the disease struck, Roosevelt had been active in politics for some eleven years, including posts as New York state senator, assistant secretary of the navy, and 1920 Democratic nominee for vice president. His mother urged retirement, but encouraged by wife Eleanor and by advisers, Roosevelt regained his aspiration for public office and simply would not allow the polio to stop him. Intensive therapy, including swimming, brought about a partial physical recovery, but he never again walked without leg braces, crutches, or canes and the support of his son or an aide.

Work was what saved him. At the 1924 Democratic National Convention, Roosevelt signaled his comeback with his Happy Warrior speech that placed Governor Alfred E. Smith of New York in nomination for the presidency. In 1928, FDR won the governorship of New York; in 1932, he won the presidency itself in an overwhelming victory. In the years that would follow, he would tackle and manage an unprecedented string of challenges: the collapse of the banking system, the Great Depression, the attack on Pearl Harbor, and World War II—all from a wheelchair. Some writers attribute his compassion and steely determination to the character he built up in his fight to conquer polio, but whatever the genesis for his abil-

POLITICS AND PUBLIC SERVICE

ity, the Roosevelt presidency proved one of the most eventful in U.S. history.

Roosevelt Quote:

- "The only thing we have to fear is fear itself."

182. SZÉCHENYI, COUNT ISTVÁN

"Again and again, incessantly."

IT'S CHALLENGING ENOUGH TO MAKE A PERSONAL comeback; what about leading an entire nation to a comeback? That's the job István Széchenyi set for himself—and Hungary—in the nineteenth century.

In 1791, Johann Gottfried Herder, a German writer, prophesied the disappearance of Hungary. It was then a rural and declining outpost of the Austro-Hungarian empire, stuck in a feudal past where a few were very, very rich, and most were very, very poor. This idea haunted Széchenyi, even though he was one of the very rich. He loved his nation, backward though it was, and could see great things for it in his mind's eye. Influenced by his studies in England, he championed the preservation and modernization of Hungarian economic, social, and intellectual life. The key was to make change gradually, he believed. He believed modest beginnings can produce significant results.

301

First Széchenyi contributed a year's income from his aristocratic estate toward founding an institute to preserve the Hungarian language. Next, he formed the National Casino—not a betting parlor, but rather a club (Italian for club is "casino") where leaders could gather to dine and read and discuss newspapers, as well as economic, scientific, and artistic periodicals. Everyone was welcome regardless of birth, class, or party affiliation—a radical idea in the class-minded society of the day. Then, he wrote voluminously, economic and political essays to stimulate the development of liberal thought: *On Credit* (1828), *Light* (1831), *Stadium* (1833), *Hunnia* (1834), *A Few Words on Horse-racing* (1839). These pieces were "peculiar minglings of moral, educational, political, and economic topics," as George Barany said in his biography of Széchenyi.

As Hungary was under the rule of the Austro-Hungarian Empire at the time, his works were considered radical and often censored, but he would not relent. Széchenyi was as much a practical man as well as a radical thinker: one of his many visions was the opening up of the Danube for trade from Buda to the Black Sea. He personally conducted a naval expedition from Pest to Constantinople to prove it was possible. Government officials were persuaded, the traffic soon flowed, and he became minister of transportation.

Later, opposing the revolutionary war cries of the

preeminent Hungarian of the day, lawyer and politician Lajos Kossuth, Széchenyi wrote to him: "Trample on me without ceremony, but for God's sake don't use the nimbus of your popularity to plunge Hungary into chaos." Széchenyi's view was the minority. The majority wanted the revolution and it came in 1848. The setbacks of war, death, destruction, and a rupture with the dynasty were more than Széchenyi could bear, and he was removed to an asylum where he lived another twelve years.

But his visionary work was not forgotten: Kossuth would later call Széchenyi "the greatest of the Magyars." Indeed it was his vision and creative and relentless political activism that preserved and promoted Hungary as a nation, and averted the realization of Herder's prophecy.

Széchenyi Quotes:
- "The smallest perfection gives satisfaction because it brings us closer to the possibility of serving the land which begot us and of serving the people we love."
- "A spiritually and physically active life alone can carry us to the highest level of human happiness."
- "I work diligently and with self-reliance. If my wings are clipped, I shall walk on foot. If my feet are cut off, I shall move along on my hands. Should they be torn out too, I shall crawl on my belly."
- "Metternich's system ceases with his life. Mine will begin only after my death."
- His motto: "Again and again, incessantly."

183. TRUMAN, HARRY S.

AFTER SERVING IN WORLD WAR I AS AN ARTILLERY CAPTAIN in France, Harry S. Truman returned home and joined a friend in opening a haberdashery. It went bankrupt, so he turned to politics. He was more successful there. Truman was elected county judge in 1922, presiding judge in 1926, and Missouri senator in 1934 and again in 1940. When FDR was nominated for his fourth term in 1944, he tapped Truman for vice president. Truman had served eighty-two days as vice president when FDR died suddenly of a massive cerebral hemorrhage on April 12, 1945. As president, it would be Truman's daunting task to authorize the dropping of the atomic bomb on Hiroshima on August 6, 1945, bringing World War II to an end.

Entering the 1948 election as incumbent president, Truman covered 22,000 miles and made 271 speeches. Nevertheless, the entry of two new parties into the battle made the outcome doubtful. He went to bed on election night as the *Chicago Tribune* published an "extra" with the headline: "Dewey Defeats Truman!" The next morning, President Truman learned that he had not only carried the country with a plurality of two million votes (24,105,812 for Truman; 21,970,065 for Dewey), but had also won a Democratic Congress.

The failed men's clothier was now the newly *elected* U.S. president.

Truman Quote:

- "I always remember an epitaph which is in the cemetery at Tombstone, Arizona. It says: 'Here lies Jack Williams. He done his damnedest.' I think that is the greatest epitaph a man can have—when he gives everything that is in him to do the job he has before him. That is all you can ask of him and that is what I have tried to do."

- His motto: "The buck stops here!"

POVERTY

184. MURRAY, LIZ

LIZ MURRAY'S PARENTS LOVED HER, BUT THEY WERE so racked by problems that her life was a horror. Her father was addicted to cocaine, and her mother was infected with HIV. Her childhood homes in the Bronx were dirty apartments and public shelters. While still a child, Murray bagged groceries and pumped gas to earn food money. At fifteen, she left home, choosing a life on the mean streets.

Following the death of her mother, Murray was no longer willing to let her depressing circumstances define her. Determined to change, she decided to make something of herself. Liz realized education was the key. Begging her way back into Humanities Preparatory School in Greenwich Village, she became a superb student despite the fact that, being homeless, she camped out in New York City parks during the day and rode the subway all night. At nineteen, with funding from a scholarship and a part-time job with the New York Public Interest Group, Murray enrolled at Harvard University.

Her story was told in the 2003 Lifetime film *Homeless to Harvard*. Murray coproduced and played a cameo role as a social worker.

Subsequently, Murray was accepted into Columbia University as a film student. She speaks to audiences across the country about going from hopelessness to empowerment, and she enjoys the positive feedback she has received from people who saw Lifetime's rendition of her story. One twenty-two-year-old Bostonian wrote, expressing her regrets at not being able to see the film. So Murray, then twenty-one, invited her to her New York apartment for a personal screening. Murray's memoir, *Breaking Night*, came out in 2005.

185. POLAK, PAUL

FOR DENIZENS OF THE UNDERDEVELOPED WORLD, making a comeback means something altogether different than for those of us whose every need is consistently met: just earning enough cash to eat is a major accomplishment. Some 1.1 billion people subsist on less than $1 per day; 75 percent of them live in rural areas. Some Westerners think big and espouse giving billions in aid to foreign governments. But Paul Polak thinks small and focuses on the individual.

Polak spent the first twenty-three years of his career as a psychiatrist. He saw links between mental illness and poverty and resolved to do something about it. He believes if you can marginally increase a farm worker's income, then broader economic development—schools, clinics, roads, and so on—will follow. Through successful investments in real estate and oil, he was able to create an organization to attack the problem.

His small Denver-based nonprofit, International Development Enterprises (IDE), designs and markets low-cost, low-tech devices such as foot-operated pumps, ceramic water filters, and drip irrigation systems. IDE operates on $10 million in revenues from the U.S. Agency for International Development (USAID), the Swiss government, and individual donors.

These $2 to $200 kits are sold to small farmers in developing nations around the world. Typically, a farmer can make back the cost in just one season, which makes all the difference. IDE has sold some two hundred thousand kits because they are *affordable*.

Is IDE making a difference? Consider the story of Manek Raut, of western India, who farms three and a half acres. He borrowed $125 from friends and invested it in an IDE irrigation kit. As a result, he earned more than $300 the first year in cotton *alone* and added egg-plants, okra, and beans as well. Without the irrigation system, the land would have yielded nothing, Raut says.

Suresh Adhetrao farms in Maharashtra, India. He started with a $50 drip system and expanded from there. He recently made $4,600 in a year. He bought a new house, a twenty-one-inch color television, and a VCR.

Polak believes that development efforts must be informed by the people who need the help—after all, who knows what they really need more than they do? He believes in innovation and entrepreneurship for individuals, not just handouts from government to government.

The moral: think small to solve big problems.

Postscripts: In 2005 eBay founder and billionaire Pierre Omidyar announced plans to donate $100 million to Tufts University—but with the stipulation that it can only be invested in micro-finance ($600 on average) loans to entrepreneurs in the developing world. The next year, 2006, the Nobel Peace Prize was awarded to micro-finance banker and economist Muhammad Yunus of Bangladesh.

186. Vanzant, Iyanla

Trouble surrounded Iyanla Vanzant from the day she was born in the backseat of a taxi. Her mother died when she was two, and she was given to her grandmother. She was abused, sought solace in food, and became obese. She had her first child by sixteen, three by twenty-one. Her husbands were abusive, and she found herself on welfare.

Education would be her way of escape, and first came the education of her soul. Vanzant turned to God. *Practicing the Presence* by Joel Goldsmith was a special catalyst that tied together ideas from other Christian texts she was reading: Fillmore, Holmes, Ponder, the Bible.

Vanzant sought formal education, too, earning a BS from Medgar Evers College, then a law degree from Queens College Law School. Her first job was as a public defender in Philadelphia.

Vanzant was working with women on public assistance when she felt led to write *Tapping the Power within: A Path to Empowerment for Black Women*, a collection of spiritual principals, self-affirmations, and personal rituals. Published by Harlem Readers & Writers in 1992, it became a bestseller. She was on her way to a new career as an author.

Four of her twelve books—*In the Meantime, One Day*

My Soul Just Opened Up, *Yesterday I Cried*, and *Until Today*—were national bestsellers, ranking for weeks on the *New York Times*, *USA Today*, and *Wall Street Journal* lists. She has said that God told her to do four things: tell her story, teach his law, write books, and make people laugh.

She took her message to television, with her own show in 2001 and the program *Starting Over*. Vanzant says she is just an ordinary person committed to doing extraordinary things.

187. YEBOAH, EMMANUEL OFOSU

BORN INTO POVERTY AND WITH A DEFORMED RIGHT leg, soon abandoned by his father, Emmanuel barely made it over his first big hurdle—he stayed alive. In Ghana, his native country, disabled individuals are regarded as cursed and evil. Many are "seen off," as they say—put to death by poisoning or abandonment in the wilderness. That's what some suggested to Yeboah's mother, Comfort. Instead, she raised him herself in a home with a dirt floor, no electricity, and no plumbing. She also withstood local prejudice and enrolled him in the village school alongside 239 able-bodied children. When he was very young she had to carry him there, two miles each way. When he got older he made the journey himself, hopping on his one good leg.

As he turned thirteen, his mother became ill and Yeboah dropped out of school—against her wishes—to support her. He moved to Accra, the capital, and found employment shining some thirty-five pairs of shoes each day for a total of $2.

As his mother died on Christmas Eve in 1997, she left him with an admonition: "Don't let anybody put you down because of your disability." He said her words to him were a gift and motivated him to show everyone that physically challenged people can do anything they put their mind to.

Yeboah decided to ride a bicycle the 370 miles across Ghana to draw attention to his *ability* rather than disability, and begin to change his country's perceptions about the disabled. He would pedal with only his left leg. All he needed was the bike. He had heard of the Challenged Athletes Foundation (CAF) in California. Writing the first letter he had ever composed in his life, he asked, not for money, but for a bike to undertake his self-created challenge.

CAF founder Bob Babbitt received the letter and provided the bike, plus shorts, socks, gloves, and a helmet. Yeboah hit the road in quest of his dream. He completed the ride in the spring 2001 and became a celebrity in Ghana. Babbitt invited him to compete in

CAF's San Diego triathlon in fall 2002, all expenses paid. Yeboah accepted and rode the fifty-six miles on one leg. Media-savvy, Babbitt also contacted documentary maker Lookalike Productions, which produced *Emmanuel's Gift*, narrated by Oprah Winfrey.

Yeboah was introduced to doctors who eventually partially amputated his right leg and fitted him for a prosthetic leg in April 2003. It helped him cut his time in the bike portion of his next CAF triathlon from seven to four hours. Not long after, Yeboah, a devout Christian, put on two shoes and long pants for the first time in his life and walked into his church in a tan suit.

Gaining more attention from the likes of U.S. President George Bush, countryman Kofi Annan, Ghana's King Osagyefuo, and the media, Yeboah received $25,000 in grants from Nike, which CAF matched. He used the the $50,000 to send disabled Ghanaian children to school and provided some eight hundred simple wheelchairs (lawn chairs with wheels) for disabled Ghanaians, the first time they have experienced mobility after a lifetime of crawling. He promoted a bill in the Ghanaian parliament to provide the disabled greater access and is leading a movement to create a Ghanaian Paralympic team for the 2008 Beijing Olympics.

Just 5 feet 3 inches tall and weighing a mere 115 pounds, Emmanuel came back against disability, the loss of his parents, and social ostracism to become a giant who galvanized the disabled individuals of his country and the world. He advises not listening to the naysayers and doing one's best.

SCIENCE

188. ATKINS, DR. ROBERT

DR. ROBERT ATKINS, A COLUMBUS, OHIO, PHYSICIAN, published his *Dr. Atkins Diet Revolution* back in 1972. It recommended a low-carbohydrate, high-protein, high-fat diet to lose weight and keep it off. For the next quarter century, experts largely dismissed his ideas. But after twenty-five million patients lost weight on the diet, the scientific community had to take a second look. New studies were undertaken and the results were positive. In a Duke study, Atkins dieters lost thirty-one pounds; low-fat dieters, twenty pounds. In a Cincinnati study, Atkins dieters lost eighteen and a half pounds to other dieters' eight and a half pounds. Many other studies showed the same results, even while maintaining normal cholesterol levels.

Why? To melt fat, the Atkins method targets insulin, the hormone that regulates blood sugar levels. The bodies of most overweight people are so good at releasing insulin to convert carbohydrates to fat that there's almost always too much of it in the bloodstream. Scientists call this "hyperinsulism." This makes the body want to store fat continuously. Atkins's diet is extremely low in carbohydrates, which helps decrease circulating insulin. Less insulin results in less fat storage and fewer food cravings. Also, if you cut carbs and keep your protein intake the same or slightly higher, you ingest fewer calories.

Weight loss and health is an extremely complex subject. Most experts agree that lower weight is healthier, but how to get there is a debatable issue. While high-carbohydrate, low-fat advocates like Dr. Dean Ornish retain their partisans, the playing field between the protein crowd and the carb crowd seems to have been leveled after twenty-five years of tilting hard to the pasta side. The debate will surely go on.

Atkins's personal story ended on an extremely sad note. He died in April 2003, one week after suffering a fall and head injury—just as his diet was gaining new attention from the scientific community.

189. CARLSON, CHESTER

AS A YOUNG PATENT ANALYZER FOR AN ELECTRICAL component maker, Chester Carlson, who suffered from arthritis, would spend painful hours redrawing documents by hand. He thought there had to be a better way. He began researching and came across the ideas of Hungarian physicist Paul Selenyi, who demonstrated how charged particles attach themselves to an oppositely charged surface.

After much experimentation, Carlson made the theory work. He patented the dry-copying process in 1937. In 1938, he took the idea to the biggest companies: IBM, GE, and RCA.

All said no.

But Carlson stayed with it, building a wooden prototype machine and refining it over the next five years. In 1944, he got Battelle Memorial Institute to invest $3,000 in research and development. Battelle teamed with the Haloid Company when it ran out of funds. Haloid bought a license from Carlson to develop the process and put its first copy machine on the market, the XeroX Model A, tagged the "ox box" because it took fourteen different manual operations to make a copy. It was a failure.

Eventually, Haloid introduced the Xerox 914 copier, cumbersome at six hundred pounds but able to use ordinary paper. This made all the difference. Haloid changed its name to Xerox in 1961, and vaulted to the forefront of corporate America.

Carlson had been living in poverty and had gotten divorced in 1945 as a result of spending too much time on his invention, but now he was immensely wealthy. He would eventually donate $100 million to various charities. Elapsed time from process to commercial success: twenty-three years! And the $3,000 Battelle invested? Over time, it would return the research organization more than $350 million.

190. CURIE, MARIE

AT THE PEAK OF HIS SCIENTIFIC POWERS, SCIENTIST Pierre Curie died in a Paris street accident in 1906. His wife and research partner, Marie, was devastated. To blot out her grief she immersed herself all the more in their scientific work. Accepting her husband's physics professorship, Curie became the Sorbonne's first female faculty member. She successfully isolated pure polonium and pure radium, winning a second Nobel Prize in 1911 (her first, in 1903, was for discovering radioactivity with Pierre).

Next she devoted herself to the development and use of X-radiography for medical purposes during World War I. After the war, Curie campaigned to raise funds for a hospital and laboratory devoted to radiology. This investigation into uranium also gave birth to atomic physics.

Despite her overwhelming loss, and at great personal cost, Curie found the strength to come back to her work. As a result, the worlds of science and medicine were catapulted forward. Albert Einstein said of her, "Marie Curie is, of all celebrated beings, the only one whom fame has not corrupted."

191. EINSTEIN, ALBERT

"Do not worry about your difficulties in Mathematics. I can assure you mine are still greater."

As AN INFANT, ALBERT EINSTEIN'S HEAD WAS SO large his mother feared he suffered from some kind of brain malady (he did not). As a child, he was considered a slow learner. The German-born Einstein failed his first entrance examination to the Swiss Federal Institute of Technology in Zurich in 1895. After remedial work, he gained admittance the next year and graduated in 1900.

When Einstein was unable to find a job, a friend, mathematician Marcel Grossmann, got his father to recommend Einstein to the director of the patent office in Bern, Switzerland. Einstein was appointed as a technical expert third class and worked in the patent office from 1902 to 1909.

In his spare time, without facilities or colleagues, Einstein earned a doctorate from the University of Zurich in 1905 for his thesis, "On a New Determination of Molecular Dimensions." Einstein's second paper proposed what is today called the special theory of relativity.

In 1906 he was promoted to technical expert second class. Much greater acclaim lay ahead. For his theory of relativity (including the equivalency of mass and energy expressed in the incredibly succinct and immortal: $E=mc^2$), this former "slow learner" would eventually be regarded as the foremost scientist of the twentieth century and one of the greatest physicists of all time.

192. FULLER, BUCKMINSTER

IT WAS 1927 AND BUCKMINSTER FULLER WAS unemployed, a failure in his father-in-law's mortarless-brick building system. His first child, Alexandra, had just died. In utter despair, Fuller, on the banks of Lake Michigan, considered drowning himself. He thought he would swim out until he was exhausted, and then just give in, sink, and die. Wrestling with the decision for several hours, eventually, he said, a voice told him: "From now on you need never await temporal attestation to your thought. You think the truth."

Instead of suicide, Fuller decided to commit "egocide" instead and devote the rest of his days to determining what kind of positive difference an individual could make. It turned out to be a large one. Over his lifetime, Fuller:

- was awarded twenty-five U.S. patents
- authored twenty-eight books
- received forty-seven honorary doctorates in the arts, science, engineering, and the humanities
- and received dozens of major architectural and design awards.

The coiner of the term *spaceship earth*, Fuller is best known for the invention of the geodesic dome—the lightest, strongest, and most cost-effective building structure ever devised. Today there are more than five hundred thousand such domes around the world.

Energy was another of his interests, and Fuller was one of the earliest proponents of renewable energy sources. His research demonstrated that humanity could satisfy all of its energy needs while phasing out fossil fuels and atomic energy. One example: he calculated that a wind generator put on top of every high-voltage transmission tower in the United States would generate 350 percent of the country's total recent power output. He said there was no "energy crisis" per se, but a crisis of ignorance.

Fuller's can-do attitude motivated thousands of creative individuals to think their way out of the problems that face us all—starting with despair, and moving onward and upward from there.

193. HAWKING, STEPHEN

STEPHEN HAWKING HAD A NORMAL, IF NERDY, childhood. The disease ALS struck him in 1963, just as he was completing his college studies. Incurable, ALS attacks nerve cells and the body wastes away slowly. The mind is not affected at all, and there is no physical pain, but the despair of seeing one's body wasting away can break the strongest will. Once diagnosed, Hawking, twenty-one, was not expected to live long enough to complete his doctorate. But he did. Sixteen years later, in 1979, he was appointed to the post of Lucasian Professor of Mathematics—the same one held by Isaac Newton in 1669. His subsequent work on the nature of the universe earned him a reputation as one of the top theoretical physicists in the world.

His bestseller *A Brief History of Time* (1998) sold an astonishing ten million copies. The tough read is liberally illustrated with photos and drawings, as well as a few thoughtful quotes from the likes of Shakespeare. He followed this with *The Universe in a Nutshell* (2001)—another bestseller.

Hawking has an obsession to remain in control, and it is perhaps this need that drives him to conduct cosmic research. He once said that if you understand how the universe operates you control it, in a way. He also said that while his body was stuck in a chair, with the Internet, his mind could go to the ends of the universe—even though his interaction with his computer is controlled by an infrared beam that is, in turn, governed by the twitch of his cheek.

194. NASH, JOHN

BY AGE THIRTY, MATHEMATICIAN JOHN NASH WAS suffering from paranoid schizophrenia and finally had to be hospitalized. He received insulin shock treatment to erase parts of his memory. This was a gruesome and dangerous therapy (later discontinued) that induced coma and provided only temporary relief.

Nash had spent his twenties in better circumstances, in graduate school at Princeton, associating with Albert Einstein, John von Neumann, and other mathematic greats. Nash was too pompous, dismissive, and antisocial to be popular, yet his outstanding abilities attracted a few friends who put up with his behavior for the sake of his genius. After he suffered his breakdown at thirty, Nash would spend the next thirty or so years in and out of mental hospitals.

In the early 1970s, he mysteriously reappeared on campus, where he became known as the "Phantom of Fine Hall" for his utterly bizarre behavior, like leaving cryptic formulas on classroom blackboards, wandering the campus, spooking the students. At this time, his wife, whom he had abandoned, took him back in. Something of a recovery ensued.

Then, out of the blue, Nash, sixty-six, won the 1994 Nobel Prize in Economics for his work on game theory at age twenty-one. It provided further positive impetus for his recovery.

Since fewer than 8 percent of schizophrenics recover, and since Nash became well enough to teach at Princeton, his most significant comeback may be his conquering of mental illness. He attributes this unlikely feat to the help of his wife, for allowing him to be in the company of friends and family and not institutionalized and laboring under shock treatment and drugs (a story chronicled in the book and movie *A Beautiful Mind*).

Most significantly, Nash believes that schizophrenia can be overcome by willpower, that it's only a matter of

the rational mind taking control of that part of the mind
that is irrational and delusional.

195. SZENT-GYORGYI, ALBERT

IN 1926, ALBERT SZENT-GYORGYI WAS READY TO
end it, to commit suicide after an embarrassing career setback. The scientist, thirty-two, had written a paper and
handed it into his boss for approval to publish. His boss
tossed it in the trash. Crushed, humiliated, concluding
(very wrongly) his life was a failure, the young researcher
quit. Unable to support his wife and child, he sent them
home to her parents. His final wish was to attend one last
scientific meeting, to be among scientists, to have one last
good time. So he went to the 1926 International
Physiological Society Triennial Congress in Sweden.

Sitting in the audience, lost in self-pity, Szent-
Gyorgyi listened to the president of the society, Sir
Frederick Gowland Hopkins, refer to the fine work of
an obscure researcher: Szent-Gyorgyi! After the speech,
gearing up his courage, he introduced himself to
Hopkins. The great man invited the young scientist to
Cambridge to do further work.

Szent-Gyorgyi's life went from desolation to elation
with that one encounter. He proceeded to discover the

oxidation-preventing action of vitamin C, in Hungarian paprika. He won the Nobel Prize in Physiology and Medicine for his biological combustion discoveries in 1937 and the Lasker Award for his research on heart-muscle contraction. He also discovered the controversial vitamin P, plant pigments that reduce capillary fragility and protect against radiation damage. He accounted for his success by saying that discovery is seeing what everyone else has seen but thinking what nobody else has thought. One might say that, similarly, the first step in making a comeback is seeing it in the mind's eye, when no one else can.

SPIRITUALITY

196. DALAI LAMA, THE

"If you want others to be happy, practice compassion. If you want to be happy, practice compassion."

BUDDHISM STARTED IN THE FIFTH CENTURY BCE, a quiet and contemplative religion of awakening, enlightenment, poetry, and meditation. It teaches that suffering is in the mind, caused by attachment to things of this world, and that through nonattachment one might attain freedom. Buddhism made its way east from its beginnings in India and established itself throughout Asia century by century. Today it is the world's fifth-largest religion, with some two hundred to seven hundred million adherents.

In Mongolia, Buddhist monastic life established itself in the 1500s, took root, and grew steadily for the next four hundred years. But after the establishment of Soviet communism there, Buddhism was regarded as an enemy of the state. Some seven thousand lamas (religious teachers) were executed and Buddhism was nearly wiped out.

Mongolia freed itself of Soviet rule in 1991 and the door reopened for religious freedom. To help pry the door open even further, the Dalai Lama, spiritual leader of Buddhism, has visited Mongolia some five times since then. In his peaceful way, he is helping Buddhism make a comeback in Mongolia. Most recently, in August 2006, he visited Mongolia's Gandantegchinlin Monastery, the nation's largest.

The Dalai Lama's visit raised hackles in neighboring China; officials there criticized Mongolia for hosting the Dalai Lama, who many regard as the rightful head of the state of Tibet, and who reigned there from 1950 to 1959. (He now lives in Dharamsala, India, where he heads the Central Tibetan Administration, a government in exile.) As a longtime champion of Tibetan freedom, the Dalai Lama naturally comes into conflict with China. "The Chinese government strongly opposes . . . any country providing the Dalai Lama with a venue for his separatist activities," the Foreign Ministry said in a statement carried by state media. "The Dalai Lama is not a simple or pure religious figure. He is a political exile who undertakes secessionist activities abroad and damages the unity of nationalities."

Mongolia responded by saying the visit was sponsored by the monastery, not the government. The office of the president of Mongolia did allow that a meeting between President Nambaryn Enkhbayar and the Dalai Lama was possible. In any case, thousands of Mongolians traveled to the capital, Ulan Bator, to welcome the Nobel Peace Prize–winning Tibetan leader-in-exile to Mongolia, his mere presence a strong invitation to take up and engage the ancient faith of their ancestors.

The Dalai Lama—his name means "Ocean of Wisdom"—travels and speaks around the world. He is a prolific writer; his titles include *Healing Anger: The Power of Patience from a Buddhist Perspective* (1997), *The Art of Happiness: A Handbook for Living* (1998), and *An Open Heart: Practicing Compassion in Everyday Life* (2001). Throughout many trials the Dalai Lama has persevered and done his best to promote his faith's tenets of peace and enlightenment.

197. KUSHNER, RABBI HAROLD

IF YOU HAVE YOUR HEALTH, CONSIDER YOURSELF A multimillionaire—anyone suffering from a chronic condition would gladly pay millions, billions to be rid of it, if it were only that simple. If it is your child whose health is at stake, you would gladly pay many times that. One of the cruelest experiences in life is to watch your child suffer and be unable to help. Such was the experience of Rabbi Harold Kushner. As a young theology student he had read the Book of Job and puzzled over it, like every other student. He even counseled others through pain and grief. But when he was told that his three-year-old son Aaron would die in his teens of progeria, a hideous disease that induces premature aging, Kushner experienced the nature of tragedy on the most profound level.

Like every other victim of random and seemingly meaningless injustice, Kushner wondered where he could find the resources necessary to cope. He found them, in part, in writing a book about God, suffering, evil, and injustice: *When Bad Things Happen to Good People* (1981). He said he wrote it out of a need to put into words some of the most important things he knew and believed. He wrote it to help others.

Kushner's book became a classic, a bestseller that transcended Judaism and helped millions of every faith. It was followed by many other titles: *Living a Life That Matters* (2001), *The Lord Is My Shepherd* (2003), *Overcoming Life's Disappointments* (2006), among others. Kushner was cited by the Christophers, a Roman Catholic organization, as one of the fifty individuals who have most made the world a better place in the last fifty years; he was named clergyman of the year by Religion in America in 1999. He overcame his personal tragedy and used the knowledge he gained to help millions more in need, making his comeback all the greater.

198. MAI, MUKHTAR

"Education is power. People can be trampled on if they are not educated. But if they are educated they can fight back."

THERE IS THAT PERVERSE BUT OFTEN TRUE SAYING that "no good deed goes unpunished." In the case of Mukhtar Mai, of Pakistan, that punishment was multiplied to the power of one hundred.

Following the customs of rural Pakistan, Mai, age thirty, decided to make a good-faith effort to settle a complex criminal and familial dispute with the neighboring Mastois tribe in 2002. She took her case to a *panchiat* court, a tribal council court that decides matters ranging from animal theft to murder. These councils have no official legal status—just tradition. The justice that comes out of *panchiat* court is often brutal.

The elders heard Mai's plea and determined that to restore the honor of the accusing Mastois party, Mai would be subjected to *karo kari*, beating and rape. Four volunteers and some ten accomplices carried out the sentence as a mob of two hundred onlookers cheered. Afterward Mai was thrown into the street and forced to walk home half naked through a village of staring eyes. She and her family were now utterly disgraced, and, according to tribal law, justice was done.

According to local custom, the only way for Mai to erase such disgrace was to commit suicide, but she refused to take her life. Her family nursed her back to health and her friends stood by her, helping her bring her "dead soul" back to life.

Karo kari aims to steal one's dignity and future, one's entire life. But Mai, educated as a teacher of Islam and the Koran, understood her rights and received important support from her religious community. The local Islamic cleric called for Mai's condemners and attackers to be brought to trial before a civil court and encouraged her to file a police complaint. When her complaint was ignored, Mai turned to the international news media, telling one interviewer that she holds on to the indescribable pain and puts herself in the public eye no matter what anyone says—all for the cause of justice.

The post-9/11 world somewhat changed the climate in Pakistan. Mai pressed charges again, and fourteen men were arrested. Six were found guilty and one sentenced to death. At the behest of President Pervez Musharraf, the government awarded Mai $8,000, about twenty times the average national salary, and offered her a home in Islamabad, where she could live a life of relative luxury and no one would know what had happened to her.

She turned the home down, but accepted the funds and used them to build two local schools. "Education is power. People can be trampled on if they are not educated. But if they are educated they can fight back," she said.

Then came a setback. The convicted men appealed, and the provincial court set them free. Mai's life was at risk again, but she would not relent. The Pakistan supreme court reviewed the case and ruled in Mai's favor. All fourteen rapists and accomplices were put back in prison, some sentenced to death.

Mukhtar Mai emerged from the ordeal as an internationally recognized and celebrated spokesperson for human rights. She not only recaptured and restored her dignity, but inspired millions around the world.

199. PHAN THI, KIM PHUC

CLOTHES SEARED FROM HER BODY BY A NAPALM BOMB, the little girl runs, naked, in agony, screaming. For many, this famous, tragic, Pulitzer Prize–winning photograph summarized the Vietnam War. Suspected of harboring Viet Cong guerrillas, the village of Trang Bang was bombed on

June 8, 1972. Many were killed. Some, like Kim Phuc, were set on fire. Photographer Nick Ut captured the image, then rushed her to Cu Chi hospital. It would take seventeen operations and numerous trips abroad for plastic surgery before Kim could assume a "normal" life.

As a young adult, Kim studied medicine. Eventually, however, Vietnamese authorities required her to serve as a propaganda tool, speaking to foreign journalists about her childhood war experiences. It took a huge emotional toll. Kim searched for meaning in her life, praying to God. After a family member took her to his church, Kim discovered that God could actually heal her emotional pain. She became a Christian in 1982.

After a successful appeal to the head of the Vietnamese government, she was allowed to go to Cuba to continue her education. She married, then honeymooned in Moscow. On the October 1992 return flight to Cuba, she snuck off the plane while it was refueling in Newfoundland and sought political refuge. She applied for and received Canadian citizenship. When her new countrymen found out that the little girl from the 1972 photo was now a Canadian citizen, they raised $30,000 to help her settle there.

Free at last, Kim became a very public peace advocate. In 1996, she traveled to the United States to meet Nick Ut and the doctors who had operated on her in Saigon (also called Ho Chi Minh City). On Veteran's Day that same year, Kim spoke at the Vietnam Veteran's Memorial in Washington, D.C., on the need for healing and reconciliation for everyone involved in the war.

In 1997, she founded the Kim Foundation in Chicago (http://www.kimfoundation.com/en/) to help innocent victims of war. That same year, the United Nations Educational, Scientific, and Cultural Organization (UNESCO) named her a Goodwill Ambassador.

During a December 2003 church presentation in the United States, Kim demonstrated the power to forgive and the healing power in forgiveness—a video showed Kim publicly meeting and forgiving the pilot responsible for bombing her village. The man said he felt like the entire world was lifted from his shoulders.

Though she never did go back to finish her medical studies, Kim said she has found an even greater purpose in life: to share the importance of having a relationship with Jesus Christ and the healing power of forgiveness and freedom. She said the fire from the bombs burned her body and the doctors mended her skin, but it took God to heal her heart. She spends her life spreading this message to others.

200. TADA, JONI EARECKSON

A NORMAL, ACTIVE TEEN, JONI (PRONOUNCED "Johnny") Eareckson dove into a shallow lake in July 1967, fractured her spinal cord, and was pulled out of the water a quadriplegic. She plunged into despair and routinely begged friends to help her commit suicide. Fortunately, they didn't.

A friend encouraged Eareckson to put her faith in God to help her through the tough times. Additionally, her church supported her and her family through the crisis. As a result, she resolved to devote her life to ministering to others and be a model of patience, endurance, and the hope of heaven.

Powered by this resolve, she has inspired millions around the world. Today, Tada is involved in many different spiritual endeavors·

- Writing: In addition to her autobiography, the best-selling *Joni*, and some thirty-five other books (including *When God Weeps: Why Our Sufferings Matter to the Almighty*), Tada writes for *Christianity Today*, *Today's Christian Woman*, *The War Cry*, and numerous other periodicals.
- Radio: Tada has a daily five-minute radio program, *Joni and Friends*, which won Radio Program of the Year from the National Religious Broadcasters in 2002.
- Ministry: She and husband Ken Tada travel to and

minister at spiritual conferences around the world.

- Charity: Through the Wheels for the World program, more than thirty-five thousand wheelchairs have been collected, rebuilt by inmates at seventeen correctional facilities, and distributed to needy individuals in some seventy developing countries.
- Government service: Tada has expanded her work beyond the church and has been appointed to national councils on disability, including those sponsored by the State Department and the National Council on Disability.

Tada is also an accomplished artist, having learned to paint with the brush held between her teeth. Collectors seek out her highly detailed paintings and prints. She is also a talented singer and has produced several CDs.

Everyone experiences setbacks and heartbreaks, but supremely courageous and faith-filled individuals like Joni show us that yes, even the worst of these can be overcome, through the power of God and the power of resolve.

201. JESUS CHRIST

"This same Jesus, which is taken up from you into heaven, shall so come in like manner as you have seen him go into heaven." Acts 1.11

New Testament Quote
"And if I go and prepare a place for you, I will come again." John 14.3

Old Testament Quote
"For I know that my redeemer lives, and that he shall stand at the last day upon the earth." Job 19.25

202. YOUR COMEBACK

Start writing your own personal comeback story here.

_____

_____

_____

_____

_____

_____

_____

_____

_____

_____

_____

_____

_____

_____

_____

_____

_____

_____

_____

_____

_____

_____

_____

_____

_____

_____

Then, if you wish, please post your story as a comment to thecomebackblog.blogspot.com, or email it to comebacks@sarkett.com. Same for your favorite comeback story.

Here's wishing you a great comeback. —*J.S.*

EPILOGUE:
Four Paradoxes to Light Your Way

And so, with the weight of all this evidence, we must conclude that, even though you have been knocked down *hard* (which is only to say you're human), you can make a comeback. You have these 201 cases in your hand that prove it, and innumerable others. So, before you go off to begin (or continue) yours, here are four paradoxical quotes to consider.

Growing up in Russia, soccer star Mike Lashoff was the youngest ever to play for the Russian World Cup team. Later, he emigrated to the United States and became a youth soccer coach in Glenview, Illinois, a suburb of Chicago. During a tournament before his team was to play a citywide all-star squad, I heard him tell his players: "Yes, you can go out there and lose."

This is strikingly different from the typical pep talk. I had never heard anything like it. Was he courting defeat? Clearly not. He was liberating his players. He was giving each of them permission to go out and *try their very best*—no matter what, the outcome would not be held against them. This is something of a radical thought in the highly accountable, scoreboard-minded sports world. In one pithy statement, Lashoff captured the reality that we can't always determine the final outcome, but we should always try; in other words, the journey *really is* more important than the destination.

A quote from Dag Hammarskjöld raises the paradoxical ante: "Never let success hide its emptiness from you, achievement its nothingness, toil its desolation. And so...keep alive the incentive to push on further, that pain in the soul which drives us beyond ourselves. Do not look back. And do not dream about the future either. It will neither give you back the past, nor satisfy your other daydreams. Your duty, your reward—your destiny—are here and now."

The outcome of your comeback effort matters, of course. But even more important is that simply in trying, you regain your now, your spirit, your life, and your being. Quoting Hammarskjöld again: "The only kind of dignity which is genuine is that which is not diminished by the indifference of others."

You will come to a place in the road where you realize that what you think about yourself—down very deep in the crevices of your being—means the most to your soul, your spirit. It means more than money, fame, or accomplishment—more than what others think. And that in starting your comeback, you regain the thing you *really* want back the most: your spirit. You dislodge the wedge driven through your heart by loss. You heal. You make your comeback—*irrespective of any kind of further results.*

As Senator Max Cleland, Vietnam War hero and triple amputee, put it: "We think adversity itself is darkness, but the reality of the darkness is that it can serve to illuminate the light. Without pain there is no pleasure, without valleys there are no mountaintops, and without struggle there is no sense of achievement."

You are a survivor, a conqueror of all that has come against you—and you are better for having gone through it.

You have become that symphony that only you can become, the culmination of all your unique experiences. As T. S. Eliot once said: "You are the music while the music lasts."

Music, spirit, darkness, light, gain, loss, your comeback, you—there is no way to separate them. Nor do you want to. They are one. They are you, transcendent.

BIBLIOGRAPHY

Andersen, Christopher P. American *Evita: Hillary Clinton's Path to Power*. New York: Morrow, 2004.

Armstrong, Lance. *Every Second Counts*. New York: Putnam, 2003.

———. *It's Not About the Bike: My Journey Back to Life*. New York: Putnam, 2000.

Ash, Mary Kay. *Mary Kay, You Can Have It All: Lifetime Wisdom from America's Foremost Woman Entrepreneur*. Rocklin, California: Prima Publishing, 1995.

Auletta, Ken. *Media Man: Ted Turner's Improbable Empire*. New York: Norton, 2004.

Barany, George. *Stephen Széchenyi and the Awakening of Hungarian Nationalism, 1791–1841*. Princeton: Princeton University Press, 1968.

Barrett, Wayne. *Trump: The Deals and the Downfall*. New York: HarperCollins Publishers, 1992.

Bennett, Tony. *The Good Life*. New York: Atria, 1998.

Bingham, Howard L. *Muhammad Ali: A Thirty-Year*

Journey. New York: Simon & Schuster, 1993.

Bradshaw, Terry. *Keep It Simple*. New York: Atria, 2002.

Brady, Kathleen. *Lucille: The Life of Lucille Ball*. New York: Hyperion, 1994.

Brockovich, Erin. *Take It from Me: Life's a Struggle but You Can Win*. New York: McGraw-Hill, 2002.

Buchwald, Art. *Leaving Home—A Memoir*. New York: Putnam, 1993.

Burns, George. George Burns: In His Own Words. New York: Carroll & Graf Publishers, 1996.

———. *Living It Up: Or, They Still Love Me in Altoona*. New York: Putnam, 1976.

———. *100 Years, 100 Stories*. New York: G.P. Putnam's Son, 1996.

Burns, James MacGregor. *The Three Roosevelts: Patrician Leaders Who Transformed America*. Boston: Atlantic Monthly Press, 2001.

Cannon, Lou. *President Reagan: The Role of a Lifetime*. New York: Simon & Schuster, 1991.

Carnegie, Dale. *How to Stop Worrying and Start Living*. New York: Pocket Books, 1944.

Carreras, José. *Singing from the Soul: An Autobiography*. Los Angeles: Y.C.P. Publications, 1989.

Carter, Betsy. *Nothing to Fall Back On: The Life and Times of a Perpetual Optimist*. New York: Hyperion, 2002.

Chodes, John. *Bruce Jenner*. New York: Grosset, 1977.

Chong, Denise. *The Girl in the Picture: The Story of Kim*

Phuc, the Photograph, and the Vietnam War. New York: Viking, 2000.

Chopra, Deepak. *Ageless Body, Timeless Mind.* New York: Harmony, 1993.

———. *The Book of Secrets: Unlocking the Hidden Dimensions of Your Life.* New York: Harmony, 2004.

———. *How to Know God: The Soul's Journey into the Mystery of Mysteries.* New York: Harmony, 2000.

———. *Return of the Rishi.* New York: Houghton Mifflin, 1988.

Clarke, Donald. *All or Nothing at All: A Life of Frank Sinatra.* New York: Fromm International, 1997.

Cleland, Max. *Strong at the Broken Places.* New York: Berkley Pub Group, 1985.

Clinton, Hillary Rodham. *Living History.* New York: Simon & Schuster, 2003.

Coe, Jonathan. *Jimmy Stewart: A Wonderful Life.* New York: Arcade, 1994.

Colford, Paul. *The Rush Limbaugh Story.* New York: St. Martin's Press, 1993.

Collis, John. *Chuck Berry: The Biography.* London: Aurum Press, 2002.

Cousins, Norman, *Anatomy of an Illness as Perceived by the Patient: Reflections on Healing and Regeneration.* New York: Norton, 1979.

———. *The Healing Heart: Antidotes to Panic and Helplessness.* New York: Norton, 1979.

Crawford, Roger. *Playing from the Heart*. New York: Prima, 1998.

Davis, Clive. *Clive: Inside the Record Business*. New York: Morrow, 1975.

Demény, János. *Béla Bartók Letters*. New York: St. Martin's Press, 1971.

Dickenson, Mollie. *Thumbs Up, the Life and Courageous Comeback of White House Press Secretary Jim Brady*. New York: Morrow, 1987.

Dodson, James. *Ben Hogan: An American Life*. New York: Random House, 2004.

Drescher, Fran. *Cancer Schmancer*. New York: Warner Books, 2002.

Drohojowska-Philp, Hunter. *Full Bloom: The Art and Life of Georgia O'Keeffe*. New York: W. W. Norton & Company, 2004.

Drucker, Joel. *Jimmy Connors Saved My Life*. Wilmington, DE: Sport Classic Books, 2004.

Epstein, Daniel Mark. *Nat King Cole*. Thorndike, Me.: G.K. Hall, 1999.

Farnam, Alan. *Forbes Great Success Stories: Twelve Tales of Victory Wrested from Defeat*. New Jersey: Wiley, 2000.

Flaherty, Tina Santi. *What Jackie Taught Us: Lessons from the Remarkable Life of Jacqueline Kennedy Onassis*. New York: Perigee, 2004.

Flatow, Ira. *They All Laughed. From Light Bulbs to Lasers: The Fascinating Stories Behind the Great Inventions That Have*

Changed Our Lives. New York: Harper, 1993.

Flutie, Douglas, and Perry Lefko. *Flutie.* Toronto: Warwick, 1998.

Foreman, George. *George Foreman's Guide to Life: How to Get Up off the Canvas When Life Knocks You Down.* New York: Simon & Schuster, 2002.

Fox, William Price. *Satchel Paige's America.* Tuscaloosa: University of Alabama Press, 2005.

Frankl, Viktor. *Man's Search for Meaning.* New York: Insight, 1997.

Fuhrman, Joel. *Eat to Live: The Revolutionary Formula for Fast and Sustained Weight Loss.* Boston: Little, Brown, 2003.
———. *Fasting and Eating for Health.* New York: St. Martin's Press, 1995.

Gill, Brendan. *Late Bloomers.* New York: Artisan, 1996.

Giuliani, Rudolph. *Leadership.* New York: Miramax, 2002.

Gladwell, Malcolm. *Blink: The Power of Thinking without Thinking.* New York: Little, Brown, 2005.

Goldberg, Richard T. *The Making of Franklin D. Roosevelt: Triumph over Disability.* Cambridge, MA: Abt Books, 1981.

Graham, Katharine. *Personal History.* New York: Vintage Books, 1997.

Greene, Katherine, and Richard Greene. *The Man behind the Magic: The Story of Walt Disney.* New York: Viking Penguin, 1991.

Hamilton, Scott, and Lorenzo Benet. *Landing It: My Life*

On and Off the Ice. New York: Kensington Books, 1999.

Hawk, Tony, and Sean Mortimer. *Hawk: Occupation: Skateboarder*. New York: Regan Books, 2001.

Henderson, Bruce B. *True North: Peary, Cook, and the Race to the Pole*. New York: W. W. Norton & Company, 2005.

Higham, Charles. *Lucy: the Life of Lucille Ball*. New York: St. Martin's Press, 1986.

Hillary, Sir Edmund. *View from the Summit*. New York: Pocket Books, 1999.

Holtz, Lou. *Winning Every Day: The Game Plan for Success*. New York: Collins, 1999.

Holzer, Harold. *Abraham Lincoln, The Writer. A Treasury of His Greatest Speeches and Letters*. Honesdale, Pa: Boyds Mill Press, 2000.

Huckabee, Mike. *Quit Digging Your Grave with a Knife and Fork: A 12-Stop Program to End Bad Habits and Begin a Healthy Lifestyle*. New York: Center Street, 2005.

Hurt, Harry. *Lost Tycoon: The Many Lives of Donald J. Trump*. New York: HarperCollins Publishers, 1992.

Hybels, Bill and Lynne Hybels. *Rediscovering Church: The Story and Vision of Willow Creek Community Church*. Grand Rapids: Zondervan, 1995.

Iacocca, Lee A. *Iacocca: An Autobiography*. New York: Bantam Books, 1984.

Irvan, Ernie, and Peter Golenbock. *No Fear: Ernie Irvan: The NASCAR Driver's Story of Tragedy and Triumph*. New York: Hyperion, 1999.

Jacobs, Timothy. *100 Athletes Who Shaped Sports History*. San Francisco: Bluewood Books, 2004.

Jenner, Bruce. *Decathlon Challenge: Bruce Jenner's Story*. Englewood Cliffs, N.J.: Prentice-Hall, 1977.

Jenner, Bruce. *Finding the Champion Within: A Step-by-Step Plan for Reaching Your Full Potential*. New York: Simon & Schuster, 1996.

Jones, Quincy. *Q: The Autobiography of Quincy Jones*. New York: Doubleday, 2001.

Kanfer, Stefan. *Ball of Fire: The Tumultuous Life and Comic Art of Lucille Ball*. New York: Alfred A. Knopf, 2003.

Karnazes, Dean. *Ultra Marathon Man: Confessions of an All-Night Runner*. New York: Penguin, 2005.

Kaufman, Michael T. *Soros: The Life and Times of a Messianic Billionaire*. New York: Knopf, 2003.

King, Larry. *Larry King by Larry King*. New York: Simon & Schuster, 1982.

King, Stephen. *On Writing*. New York: Scribner, 2000.

Kinney, Jack. *Walt Disney and Assorted Other Characters: An Unauthorized Account of the Early Years at Disney's*. New York: Harmony Books, 1988.

Kinni, Theodore B. *No Substitute for Victory: Lessons in Strategy and Leadership from General Douglas MacArthur*. Upper Saddle River, NJ: FT/Prentice Hall, 2005.

Knight, Bob and Hammel, Bob. *Knight: My Story*. Waterville, ME: Thorndike Press, 2002.

Kroc, Ray. *Grinding It Out: The Making of McDonald's*.

Chicago: Regnery, 1977.

Lamparski, Richard. *Whatever Became of—? All New Eleventh Series: 100 Profiles of the Most-Asked-About Movie, TV, and Media Personalities. Hundreds of Never-Before-Published Facts, Dates, etc. on Celebrities. 227 Then-and-Now Photographs.* New York: Crown, 1989.

Levin, Doron P. *Behind the Wheel at Chrysler.* New York: Harcourt Brace & Company, 1995.

Lewis, Michael. *The New New Thing.* New York: Norton, 2000.

Lincoln, Abraham. *An Autobiography of Abraham Lincoln: Consisting of the Personal Portions of His Letters, Speeches, and Conversations.* New York: The Bobbs-Merrill Company, 1926.

Manchester, William. *American Caesar, Douglas MacArthur 1880–1964.* Boston: Little, Brown. 1978.

———. *The Last Lion: Winston Spencer Churchill, Alone 1932–1940.* New York: Little, Brown, 1988.

Mayer, S. L. (Sydney L.). *The Biography of General of the Army, Douglas MacArthur.* New York: Gallery Books, 1982.

McCartney, Heather Mills. *A Single Step.* New York: Warner Books, 2002.

Miller, Arthur. *Timebends: A Life.* New York, Grove Press. 1987.

Morgan, Ted. *FDR: A Biography.* New York: Simon and

Schuster, 1985.

Morris, Jim, and Joel Engle. *The Rookie.* New York: Warner Books, 2002.

Mosley, Leonard. *Disney's World: A Biography.* New York: Stein and Day, 1985.

Moss, Ralph W. *Free Radical Albert Szent-Györgyi and the Battle over Vitamin C.* New York: Paragon, 1988.

Murray, Charles S. *Boogie Man: The Adventures of John Lee Hooker in the American Twentieth Century.* New York: St. Martin's Press, 2000.

Muzikowski, Bob. *Safe at Home.* Grand Rapids: Zondervan, 2001.

Nasar, Sylvia. *A Beautiful Mind: A Biography of John Forbes Nash, Jr., Winner of the Nobel Prize in Economics, 1994.* New York: A Touchstone Book, 1998.

Noonan, Peggy. *When Character Was King: A Story of Ronald Reagan.* New York: Random House, 2001.

Norris, Geoffrey. *The Master Musicians: Rachmaninoff.* Oxford: Oxford University Press, 1976.

O'Donnell, John R. *Trumped! The Inside Story of the Real Donald Trump—His Cunning Rise and Spectacular Fall.* New York: Simon and Schuster, 1991.

Paige, Satchel. *Maybe I'll Pitch Forever: A Great Baseball Player Tells the Hilarious Story behind the Legend.* Lincoln: University of Nebraska Press, 1993.

———. *Pitchin' Man: Satchel Paige's Own Story.* Westport, Conn.: Meckler, 1992.

Pegg, Bruce. *Brown Eyed Handsome Man: The Life and Hard Times of Chuck Berry.* New York: Routledge, 2002.

Pennebaker, James. *Opening Up: The Healing Power of Expressing Emotions.* New York: Guilford, 1997.

Perret, Geoffrey. *Old Soldiers Never Die: The Life of Douglas MacArthur.* New York: Random House, 1996.

Piersall, Jimmy. *Fear Strikes Out.* New York: Little Brown, 1955.

Reeve, Christopher. *Nothing Is Impossible: Reflections on a New Life.* New York: Gardner, 2002.

Resnick, Judy. *I've Been Rich, I've Been Poor, Rich Is Better.* New York: St. Martin's Griffin, 1998.

Reynolds, Burt. *My Life.* New York: Hyperion, 1994.

Rivers, Joan. *Bouncing Back: I've Survived Everything—and I Mean Everything—and You Can Too!* New York: Harper Collins Publishers, 1997.

———. *Don't Count the Candles: Just Keep the Fire Lit.* New York: HarperCollins Publishers, 1999.

Robinson, Edward G., and Leonard Spigelgass. *All My Yesterdays.* New York: Hawthorne, 1973.

Robinson, Jane. *Edward G. Robinson's World of Art.* New York, Harper & Row, 1971.

Sampson, Anthony. *Mandela, the Authorized Biography.* New York: Random House, 1999.

Sanders, Coyne Steven, and Tom Gilbert. *Desilu: The Story of Lucille Ball and Desi Arnaz.* New York: William

Morrow and Company, 1993.

Sanders, Harland. *Life as I Have Known It Has Been Finger Lickin' Good*. Carol Stream, IL: Creation House, 1974.

Sanello, Frank. *Jimmy Stewart: A Wonderful Life*. New York: Kensington, 1997.

Schonberg, Harold C. *Horowitz: His Life and Music*. New York: Simon & Schuster, 1992.

———. *The Lives of the Great Composers*. New York: Norton. 1970.

Schuller, Robert. *Turns Hurts into Halos*. Nashville: Nelson, 1999.

Schwager, Jack. *Stock Market Wizards: Interviews with America's Top Stock Traders*. New York: HarperCollins, 2003.

Seroff, Victor Ilyitch. *Rachmaninoff*. New York: Simon and Schuster, 1950.

Shatner, William. *Get a Life!* New York: Atria, 1999.

Sieden, Lloyd S. *Buckminster Fuller's Universe: His Life and Work*. New York: Plenum, 1989.

Siegel, Frederick F. *The Prince of the City: Giuliani, New York and the Genius of American Life*. New York: Encounter Books, 2005.

Smith, Starr. *Jimmy Stewart: Bomber Pilot*. St. Paul, MN: Zenith Press, 2005.

Solti, Sir Georg, *Memoirs*. New York: Knopf, 1997.

Starr, Michael Seth. *Art Carney: A Biography*. New York: Fromm International Publishing, 1997.

Stewart, Mark. *Mario Lemieux: Own the Ice.* Brookfield, CT: Millbrook Press, 2002.

Stryk, Lucien, *The Awakened Self.* New York: Kodansha America, 1995.

Sullivan, Russell. *Rocky Marciano: The Rock of His Times.* Urbana: University of Illinois Press, 2002.

Takahashi, Shinkichi. *Triumph of the Sparrow.* New York: Grove Press, 1986.

Tarbell, Ida. *Life of Lincoln.* New York: McClure, Phillips & Co. 1895.

Terkel, Studs. *Hope Dies Last: Keeping the Faith in Difficult Times.* New York: The New Press, 2003.

Tresniowski, Alex. *When Life Gives You Lemons: Remarkable Stories of People Overcoming Adversity.* New York: McGraw-Hill, 2000.

Trump, Donald J., and Kate Bohner. *Trump: The Art of the Comeback.* New York. Random House, 1997.

Tyrrell, R. Emmett. *Madame Hillary: The Dark Road to the White House.* Washington, D.C.: Regnery, 2004.

Ujfalussy, József. *Béla Bartók.* Boston: Crescendo Publishing, 1972.

Wedemeyer, Charlie. *Charlie's Victory.* Grand Rapids: Zondervan, 1993.

Weihenmeyer, Erik. *Touch the Top of the World: A Blind Man's Journey to Climb Farther Than the Eye Can See.* New York: Plume, 2002.

White, Michael. *Stephen Hawking: A Life in Science.*

Washington D.C.: Joseph Henry Press, 2002.

Zamperini, Louis. *Devil at My Heels*. New York: Morrow, 2003.

INDEX

American Diabetes Association, 194

American Dreams: Lost and Found (Terkel), 175

American Film Institute, 129

American Football League (AFL), 67

American Paralysis Association, 134

American Poetry & Literacy Project, 156

American Skandia, 112

American Society of Composers and Performers (ASCAP), 220, 221

Amos, Wally "Famous," 87–89

Amsterdam Admirals, 80

Anatomy of a Murder (movie), 147

Anatomy of an Illness (Cousins), 257

Andreessen, Marc, 93–94

Andrews, Dame Julie, 11–12

And to Think That I Saw It on Mulberry Street (Seuss), 172

Angelou, Maya, 103

Annan, Kofi, 314

Any Given Sunday (movie), 133

Apple, 106, 107–8

Arena Football League, 80

Arista Records, 96, 97

Armstrong, Lance, 25–26

Arnaz, Desi, 121–22

Art critics, 17

Art in America (magazine), 18

Art of Happiness, The (Dalai Lama), 331

Art of the Comeback (Trump), 119

Arts
  Andrews, Dame Julie, 11–12
  Moses, "Grandma" Anna Mary Robertson, 13–15
  O'Keeffe, Georgia, 12–13
  Picasso, Pablo, 15–16
  Rockwell, Norman, 17–18
  Vincent, Mary, 273–74
  Ash, Mary Kay, 89–90
  Ashikaga, Shizan, 173

Athletics
  Agassi, Andre, 22–23
  Ali, Muhammad, 24
  Armstrong, Lance, 25–26
  Azinger, Paul, 26–28
  Beane, Billy, 29–31
  Boston Red Sox (2004), 21–22
  Braddock, James "Jimmy" J., 32–33
  Capriati, Jennifer, 34

B

EFM Media Management, 196
Egg Beaters, 194
Einstein, Albert, 321–22, 325
Eleven on Top (Evanovich), 158
Eliot, T. S., 345
Emerson, Ralph Waldo, 178–79
Emmanuel's Gift (documentary),
    314
Emotional challenges. *See*
    Physical and emotional
        challenges
Empowerment, 267
Energy, 323–24
Enkhbayar, Nambaryn, 331
Entrepreneurs. *See* Business
Equestrian dressage, 44
Erno Fodor School of Music,
    234
Esquire (magazine), 195
Estefan, Gloria, 242
Eustice, Carol, 260–61
Evanovich, Janet, 158
Evening Shade (sitcom), 135
Everest, 5–6, 10
Every Day with Rachel Ray
    (magazine), 206
Everything Health Guide to
    Arthritis, The (Eustice), 261
Exceptional Cancer Patients
    Inc., 267

Expeditions
    Everest, 5–6, 10
    North Pole, 7–9

F

Fables for Our Times
    (Thurber), 176
Fabulous Wallendas, 149
Face to Face (album), 244
Falling Off the Face of the
    Earth (song), 251
Faludi, Susan, 146
Famous Amos, 88
Farley, Chris, 277
Farr, Tommy, 33
Fashion industry, 268
Fasting, 264–65
Fazio, George, 48
Fear Strikes Out (movie), 70
Fear Strikes Out (Piersall), 70
Federal Reserve Bank, 288
Few Words on Horse-racing, A
    (Széchenyi), 302
Fila, 74
Film. *See* Show business
Financial markets
    Cook, Mark D., 95–96
    Gardner, Chris, 101–3
    Kudlow, Larry, 111
    Resnick, Judy, 113–15

O

ABOUT THE AUTHOR

A VORACIOUS READER OF BOOKS AND PERIODICALS, John A. Sarkett would often photocopy or tear out notable features and then file them away. While these ranged the gamut of subjects, the collection included a significant number of "comeback" stories—stories about individuals who had met with a setback but refused to accept it, found a way to overcome it, and sometimes even achieved undreamed-of success.

Ambling through a large bookstore one day, Sarkett searched for a title on comeback stories. To his surprise, he couldn't find one. He searched the Internet booksellers as well: same result. He determined then to write *Extraordinary Comebacks*, drawing on his cache of features, and researching new stories. (Since that time, there have been two other titles on the subject, both published while the research and writing of this volume was underway; one featured twenty-seven stories, the other thirty.)

Sarkett has worked in the marketing, public relations, television production and syndication, software, and financial industries. He holds BS and MS degrees from the Ohio State University. He believes that the human spirit—which no one has ever actually seen or put under a microscope—just might be the toughest material on the planet. Read a few of these stories; see if you agree.